MW01045975

THE ILLEGAL JOURNEYS

To Mr. Sergio Grillone

Merry Christmas

Ali Akbari

THE ILLEGAL JOURNEYS

FROM EAST TO WEST

Ali Akbari

Copyright © 2011 by Ali Akbari.

Library of Congress Control Number: 2011911722
ISBN: Hardcover   978-1-4628-9664-6
               Softcover   978-1-4628-9663-9
               Ebook   978-1-4628-9665-3

All rights reserved. No part of this book may be reproduced or transmitted in any
form or by any means, electronic or mechanical, including photocopying, recording,
or by any information storage and retrieval system, without permission in writing
from the copyright owner.

This book was printed in the United States of America.

To order additional copies of this book, contact:
Xlibris Corporation
1-888-795-4274
www.Xlibris.com
Orders@Xlibris.com
99930

CONTENTS

BOOK 3

BOOK 4

This book is dedicated to Mr. Jeff McDonald,
for always being there for me.

ACKNOWLEDMENTS

I want to thank my teachers and classmates at City Adult Learning Centre, who read my stories and encouraged me to write this book. Their names are too numerous to mention individually.

My thanks go out to Chandy, Paul, and the staff of the Crescent Town Club (community services Toronto) for their help and encouragement.

I want to express my special thanks to my faithful friends at the gym, Mr. Adil Hossioni, Mr. Sobir, Mr. Hassan, Mr. Attnan Khan, Mr. Jeo Yusuf, Mr. Oven, Mr. Afshin Rabbani, who all read my story. Their feedback and comments were very useful and encouraging.

Lastly, I don't know how to thank my unique, special, loyal friend, *Mr. Jeff McDonald,* for his kindness, support, assistance, and useful advice, reading, re-reading, and helping me edit every single page of this novel—for your understanding and the time you spent on this novel, I am indebted to you a thousand times. I don't know what I would have done without you.

Ali in Tehran, Iran at the age of 13 working as a construction worker.

INTRODUCTION

Now, standing on that big gray boulder, high up on the side of that very high mountain, above our village, I looked for the last time at the land below.

Right in front of me, grazing and bleating, were our sheep, slowly wandering. Stupid animals, sheep, everyone knows that. The fresh cold wind raced up the frosted winding valley, tearing at the grass and trees, whisking away the fragile new blossoms from the fruit trees below. Up it blew around me, snatching at my clothes and my straggling hair. Father said it came from China, across the Himalayas and the high passes of North Pakistan and on over our land, looking for Iran or the sea, but he said a lot of things, because he thought he knew everything.

It was spring, and everything, every twig and creature, was renewing itself toward the promise of the coming summer. The sun had risen, sharp and strong, over the many distant peaks on the other side of the valley. On our high mountains, any rain that fell overnight would turn to ice along with the dew. The sun, as it rose high in the clear air of that ice blue sky, would steam it away instantly, then burn down severely on everything and everyone for the rest of the day, making work all the harder. I had brought the sheep up there, as I was told to do, but it was going to be the last time I would be doing what I was told to do, by him, my father, that is. I took a long last look all around and jumped down. Then I ran away.

I was about thirteen or fourteen. I'd had enough. I ran easily down the slope, even faster than our donkey. Sometimes she would run away. Father could not catch her. He would send me after her. She could run faster than me, but she was a stupid donkey, I could easily do a trick and catch her. I was not only running away from my father and that bleak farm, I was running from so many other things that were not right. Just too many. I had loved him once, really loved him. That was when I was a child and he was a younger man. But I had begun to hate him, and Mom and I had never really got on. We had all grown older, but both he and my mom had aged much more than their years.

A lot of things, memories, came into my head. It was a big thing for me to run away, I remembered when I had loved him. It was when I was little. When I first started school.

BOOK 1

Ali in Ghazni, Afghanistan, standing on the rock
looking down on his village for last time.

CHAPTER 1

AT THE BEGINNING

I remembered, sometimes my father took me to school, other times Mom took me. That was when we lived in Qalay-e-Vazer in Kabul City, in Afghanistan. Father made me memorize our address when I was very young, in case I got lost.

My mom usually woke me each morning at seven and took me into the yard where we had our wells, to wash my face and brush my teeth. I preferred it when I went to school with my father, but he was not always at home because he was a businessman and had to go away for several days at a time. The name of the school was Spein Kaley. I started there when I was about six years old. I say "about six years old" because in Afghanistan no one has a birth certificate, so the exact date of someone's birth is not written down.

All children had to go to school, boys and girls, but we were taught in different classes. School was about five hundred meters away from our house. If you stood by our front door, you could see it. It looked like a ruin. Some of the classrooms had been destroyed during the fighting, and chairs, tables, boards, window, and walls were badly damaged. There was not enough room for everyone to sit in the classroom, especially for younger kids. They had to sit down on the ground outside of the room, in the schoolyard. The ground was not even concrete. Our class had no chairs or tables. We had to find a flat stone, a brick, or a glazed tile to sit on. Sometimes, we used our schoolbags for chairs. My father did not like the school, but he could not complain, because hundreds of other Afghan children were in the same school, and we all had the same problems. It was just better than being illiterate. The teachers were absent sometimes, due to illness or vacation. Many teachers were not paid for long periods, and that caused lots of problems. My classmates and I were happy when our teachers were absent. We were only little boys and wanted to play. We mixed water with the soil and made some round balls with mud, which dried rock hard in the hot sun. The very small balls we used to play games of *Toshla bazy* (in the West this is called a game of marbles. A game played with small glass balls.) The larger balls, we used as cricket balls. We also had the most amazing fun when we divided in two groups and had long wrestling matches. We got so dusty and dirty and hurt our knees and elbows. Every day I went to school very clean and neat, and I came back home very dirty and hungry, and sometimes my clothes were ripped, because there were some violent kids in that school. Still, my parents encouraged me to go, because it was better than nothing or staying home.

Occasionally we received some notebooks, pencils, and rubbers from our school board. We ripped the paper off the pads and made airplanes, ships, guns, and rockets and played with them. If the teachers caught us, they caned us or told us to stand on one foot for fifteen minutes in the corner. There were many problems in the city, because the stupid *shorawee* (Russian) fighters had made my country like a broken glass, which never could be put back as it was. The city had been badly shelled during the shorawee (Russian) occupation. Their tanks, personnel carriers, and heavy equipment had badly damaged the streets, and the burned-out wreckage of them was strewn everywhere. There were craters from mines and shelling in every road, and damaged buildings, houses, cinemas, hotels, restaurants, and bathhouses all bore the scars of the wars. The shorawee fighters had planted many land mines. Our teacher showed us pictures and images of mines and told us never ever to touch them, if ever we came across them. They had injured four of my classmates. Three boys had only one hand each, and another had had his leg blown off. There were many other kids in that school who had lost a part of their body because of mines.

We grew up among all this evidence of war but did not really notice it. The devastated land had reverted to nature. Weeds and grass and even small trees grew on the bombsites, wherever the thin soil would support them. Children made little dens in the middle of the chaos with mud bricks from the damaged houses, and *we* played there and on the burned-out Russian tanks and troop carriers, despite warnings about the danger of mines and unexploded shells. We had never known anything different, we never knew if the rubble we played on had once been a beautiful building a few years before. We accepted what we saw. It was natural to us. We thought nothing of the fact that guns and ammunition were sold at the corner shops, at very cheap prices to anyone of any age.

We had a small house with a big yard, which was about one hundred meters long by forty meters wide, with a high wall all around it, made of reddish brown mud bricks. All the other houses were the same; high mud brick walls surrounded each house and yard. This made many narrow passageways. The walls looked dull from the outside, but within there often were cool colorful tree-shaded gardens. For water, we had two wells, one was for the water pump, and the other was used when there was no electricity to drive the pump. Power cuts happened every day without warning. Each well was twenty meters deep and about one and a half meters square at the top. I did not know how the water got into the wells; I only knew it was always there. Sometimes I had to help to pull up the water for Mom's small vegetable garden, when Father was away. In her patch, she grew a small amount of salad vegetables, spring onions, cooking onions, garlic, carrots, cucumbers, tomatoes, green watermelons, and spicy hot yellow peppers. It was a patch full of color. We had two apple trees about two meters tall and an old zardolo tree. In the spring, its blossoms were white and smelled nice. Small green nuts followed the blossom. They changed color throughout the summer, from green they changed to yellow and then to bright orange. In late summer, they fell off the tree, and we cracked the shells and ate them. They were sweet and delicious, but most of the nuts we put on sheets of plastic on the flat roof of the house to dry in the hot sunshine for five or ten days. We also kept hens and chickens for eggs. We had two cockerels. They crowed loudly, early every morning, but I was so used to them that they did not wake me. Cockfighting happened often. They seemed to like to fight. I liked to watch their fights.

My parents' marriage was an arranged one. While my father had been away on a business trip, his father engaged him to a girl he had never met. I heard from my father that he met my mom for the first time on the day of their marriage. He was then very handsome, six foot three, with broad shoulders, brown skin, and black hair, which he always kept cut short. My mom was five foot five, chubby, and very beautiful. She was married to my father at the age of fourteen.

I remember once Father and I went to Ghazni City for his friend's wedding party. When people got married, the Afghan tradition was that on the marriage night, a lot of the bridegroom's family, relatives, and friends fired guns and let off fireworks and made a lot of noise to celebrate the wedding. Father didn't take Mom with us to the wedding party, because he was in love with another woman, I think. I asked myself why my father did not divorce my mom if he was in love with another woman. Was he staying with Mom because of me? Or was he afraid of my grandfather, my mom's father, would kill him? My grandfather was a powerful man in the government. Also it was very bad for Mom's family if they got divorced. People would say bad things, like what was wrong with her, and so on.

When my father was not home, I had problems with my mom. The problem was that she did not give me what I was expecting from her. What I wanted was *qand* (sugar cane/confectionery or candy) or money instead of sweets so that I could buy them in school for my break time. (When I say "sweets," I mean the Eastern sweets. They cannot be made of chocolate or fats because it would melt away. They are made from almonds and honey and other nuts and dried fruit. They taste wonderful and are very good for you.)

My mother gave me boring food to take with me, like bolony or samosas or sandwiches. She did not want to give me qand or money. I knew if I complained enough, she would give me just a little qand or maybe a little money. My mother knew that I would be trouble without them. I didn't understand why she gave me a hard time about it, because I knew that my father had left enough qand or money for me, while he was away. Mom kept the money for herself, so if I did not get what I needed for school, I would argue and cause trouble and refuse to go. I suppose I was a bad boy at that time. Mom tried to force me. I got slapped and shouted at and so on. I wanted qand because all the other children in my class brought their favorite foods for their lunch break. All we really cared about was qand. I suppose it was because we were only little children.

Afterward, when my father came home, I told tales about what my mother had done to me. She had threatened that if I told him about it, she would hit me again when he was not home. She often slapped me for no reason. My father was so nice to me, the opposite of my mother. I think that he encouraged me to spy on Mom. My uncles Nassir and Mahmood, my mother's brothers, often came to visit us. They told me not to argue with Mom they hit me sometimes when I refused to take any notice of them. They were always on my mom's side. One day I told my father that my uncles had been hitting me for no reason. Father was very mad about it, and he said he did not like them either. He had a big row with Mom and lost his temper and hit her and told her to tell her brothers not to lay a finger on me or he would put them in hospital. Later in the day, I was very sorry for Mom and for myself. I did not like my mom crying, because that made me cry too. Mom pulled me to her side and pampered me.

One day my father announced, in front of all our relations, that if I got a good mark at school, he would buy me a bicycle. That day I decided that I would not fight with my mother, and I would go to school every day. At the end of the course, I got good marks, and my father bought me a bicycle. I did not know how to ride it, but he soon taught me, so I then cycled to my school and made all my classmates jealous.[1]

---

1. Looking back now, I realized that many women in the Middle East are abused. They have no one to complain to. Nobody hears their voices. They have no rights; they are not allowed to be employed outside the home. A husband can treat his wife anyway he wants. He is a "second God" for his wife.

   Hitting a child or women is not unusual in Afghanistan. Mom told me that everybody does it. We heard our neighbor hitting his wife often. Mom went there sometime to intervene. The police were not helpful. There was no punishment for abusing children or women, no equality for women with men, no choice in marriage, no jobs for women, no shelter for abused women or children, and no good health care. Many women died when giving birth. Most of them were not happy with their lives. They could not go out by themselves. They have no one to complain to, nowhere to go, no freedom. When they are single, their father has total control over them. When they get married, their husband has control.

   Women are the housekeepers, good at everything domestic. An Afghan wife does the cooking, cleaning, washing (by hand), and everything else. They wake very early in the morning before their husbands, make breakfast, and then wake everybody up. They work very hard all day long. Some of the stupid men do not appreciate them. Being born a female in Afghanistan and living there can be as bad as hell. They have to deal with their problems by themselves.

   Because of the constant fighting during the civil war and the Russian occupation, many thousands of men were killed, leaving behind many widows and little children. There was a great shortage of men. There was no support from anywhere for the widows left behind. They had to try to marry old men or live as a dependent on the head of the family. If there was no head of family left alive, they had to resort to begging or any other way to support themselves and their children. Sometimes the last option was prostitution, for which there was the severe penalty of being stoned to death for the women and hanging for the men who used them. There were lots of other problems in the country that the government could not sort out.

CHAPTER 2

TROUBLE

After two weeks, I could ride my bicycle perfectly. After school I went to play Toshla bazy (marbles) and *Charmagh bazy* (the same game played with walnuts); I really loved playing marbles. There were about four or six boys playing together. First, we needed to find some flat land and chalk or a piece wood or glass to make a circle mark on the ground. Then we started to play. Our neighbors' son was called Jawad. He and I played together in our yard most of the time. My mom and his mom were happy about this, because they could see what we were doing and see we were safe. I had heard a lot of awful stories about *Jad* (kidnappers). At that time children went missing. Nobody knew where they had gone. Some people in our street said that Jad stole children and took them to another city where they took their blood for transfusions for wounded fighters, or they killed them for organ transplants. Their organs, such as kidneys, heart, eyes, were sold to rich people who paid high prices for them. Jad were infamous in Kabul after the Russian occupation.

In the past, before I was born, there had been the violence of the Russians and the resistance to them, but there was also fighting between two fanatical religious groups, Shia Muslim and Sunni Muslim. They were long-standing enemies and were always vying for power.

Looking back now, I realized that as a child, I did not have a great amount of fun. First of all, Jawed did not show up sometimes. I was restricted to our house a lot of the time, and I could not go out because of violence on the streets and the Jad. My mother did not like me to be out of her sight.

One afternoon I was playing with Jawed in our yard when I heard someone crying. It was my mom; I did not take too much notice because we were enjoying our games and I was feeling happy. At five o'clock, Jawed left our yard. I was hungry, so I went into our house. I heard a man's voice. I wonder who it was, so I stopped and waited behind the door and listened carefully. I heard the man say that he had been working with my father in Harat City. They had become separated. My father had left Harat and was on the way to Kabul. There had been an explosion on the road, and my father may have been killed on his journey. The man in our house was Mr. Nazir, my mom's cousin. From my place behind the door, I heard every single word he said. When he stopped talking, I opened the door. I called to my mom. She told me to shake Nazir's hand and say "*Salaam*" to him, which I did. Mom said "good boy." That was the first time I had ever had a compliment from her.

"What is going on?" I asked. My mom didn't answer the question.

"Nazir is here just visiting us." That was all she said. I did not ask any more questions. I went to my room. My mother was very worried about what had happened to my father. She prayed all night. Next morning, she was very different than usual. I asked her, "What is going on?"

"Allah knows what will happen to us. Your father didn't come home last night. We can't do anything about it just *Doaa* (pray)," she said. She was very upset.

Two days later, my father came home about four in the afternoon. He did not bring anything with him. Usually whenever he came back, he brought little presents like candy or fruits. This time father was different. He was in a hurry. I could not work out what was going on. I just noticed he went to a room with Mom. After five minutes, he came back and told me to pack whatever I loved in the house because we were leaving. I went to the yard and took my bicycle. I heard shooting outside in the street and shelling. My father shouted at me to come back in and told me not to go out without him. He did not tell me what was going on. Very early that night, he told me to go in my room and said, "Try to go to sleep, my son." I tried to do what he told me because he was the only person I loved. He asked me to sleep, but I couldn't because there was too much noise going on. There was gunfire and explosions. I did not ask any more questions because I knew that I wouldn't get a sensible answer.

The next morning, my father said, "The place we are living in and the whole surrounding area had been taken over by the *Pashton* (Sunni Muslims). If they find Shia Muslim here, they will kill them and take over all their belongings."

We left right away, leaving everything behind except our clothing. We got into father's Mercedes Benz and went to his friend's house, which was in another part of Kabul. It was Sunday. We arrived there before noon. Mr. Basher was one of father's business friends. He was about five foot ten, and aged about thirty-five. I remember he had a big moustache, which covered his upper lip, his head was bald, and he was a little overweight. He welcomed us, but I was shy with him. He had three children. We stayed there for a week. The house had only two rooms, one on the ground floor and the other upstairs on the first floor. It was decided that nobody should go to the first-floor room because the shelling and gunfire made it unsafe. So there was only the one room on the ground floor for fourteen people. My father and his friend divided the room into two with a sheet just to give some privacy between men and women. The eight women and children stayed together.

I remember one moment precisely. It was about 8:00 p.m.; everything had quieted down except for some gunfire on the streets. I was sitting next to my mom reading the Koran, when there was a whining noise that grew louder and louder. When the shell hit the upstairs room, it made a terrific noise the whole building shook. It was right above our heads, and large lumps of plaster and dust showered down on us. We thought we all were to going die. The children were screaming, everyone was coughing, we could not see at all. There was no light. The room was very hot, and there was a strong chemical smell. We could not breathe properly. Everybody was calling out *"Khoda ya janemara najad bata* (God save us)."* Fortunately the shell had stopped at first floor and destroyed only that room, nothing else. A short while later, the men were deciding to go upstairs, but the women did not want them to, but they had to check the damage in case of fire. I wanted to go with father. Mom hung on to me.

That night, in the darkness among the dust and debris, we huddled together. We could hear the whining noise of flying shell followed by explosions. There was not enough food for everyone, no mention of candy, just some bread and water. Our parents said it was only for the children. My mom got me a glass of water and small a piece bread. While I was eating it, Mom said, "Son, my love, pray for us. God will accept your prayers, because you are innocent."

After my little funny dinner, I fell asleep. Mom woke me at about five thirty in the morning. All the children had slept, but the adults had spent the night praying.

Father was shouting at Mom, "Get ready, get ready, we are going to leave here."

Nobody had washed his or her face because there was no water left, even for breakfast.

I was so scared because my father's face was red, and he looked so worried. I asked him, "What's going on? Why is there so much noise and shooting outside?"

He told me, "Nothing, my son, just somebody getting married, that's all."

I thought that morning there was going to be a big party. After hearing my father say "the gunfire is all about a wedding party," I was happy and started telling Mom about the party Father had taken me to in Ghazni City.

Father asked his friend to come with us, but he was reluctant to leave his property to an enemy. They decided to go their different ways. My father thanked him and said, "It is no longer safe in Kabul for us. We are going to Mazar-i-Sharif."

CHAPTER 3

MAZAR-I-SHARIF

That day, the weather was cloudy, and a little windy. From my place on the car's backseat, next to Mom, behind father, I was looking out the window. We got onto the main road to Mazar-i-Sharif. At first, it was a good road, and we were able to drive fast. Then it became rough when we were clear of the suburbs of Kabul and out into the open country. We drove through wide valleys with many very high mountains rising at a distance on either side. The road conditions became terrible. The car was bumping up and down. We passed the wreckage of many rusting, burned-out Russian tanks, and other armored vehicles. My head hit the roof several times because I had not put on my safety belt and was standing on my seat. I had the window half down and was looking out and enjoying the view. When we passed another car, or one passed us, I was shouting at them, saying hello and singing. Father was driving, and he told me to watch my head. I liked him driving. He played some very old Afghani and Iranian music on the cassette player. I was excited, but my parents were very quiet. I thought they must have had another row. They seemed sad and worried. I did not know it was because of the fighting, or that we were homeless, going to another province to save our lives and leaving everything behind. They kept the facts of what was happening from me. I was only a little boy, I thought we were going to a big wedding party. I was happy and liked our trip, telling my father to "drive faster, drive faster." He said, "OK, my son, OK." Mom disagreed and said that I was in a different world. I did not know what she meant, but I did not bother. I was enjoying the ride as mountains, trees, houses, and farms flashed by. I was excited and made lots of noise. The journey was a long one. I kept asking "When will we be there?" and got the same answer every time, "Soon." The road rose into a mountainous area, and it began to get colder. I kept falling asleep and waking, a lot of the time, because we hadn't slept a lot the night before. Sometimes there seemed to be snow and ice outside, and the windows steamed up.

There were many cars on the highway leaving Kabul. Father pulled over several times for the call of nature, for food, and for prayers. We stopped near a bazaar for gas, and I thought Father would buy some qand for me, so I got out and went to see if there was a qand store. But he was in hurry, and he bought me some other kind of sweets. We got back in the car very quickly, and he drove off very fast. I was busy eating my sweets, they weren't qand, but they were better than nothing. The weather grew foggy, but still we drove on. We seemed to come down out of the mountains, and everything got warmer. Every so often, there seemed to be flattened ruins of villages and blasted trees. Father said that the villages had been destroyed because they were near the main road, and the Mujahadin attacked the Russian convoys with rockets from them. So the Russians flattened all villages and any other buildings within firing range of the road.

We were on the road for many hours. By evening, we were approaching Mazar-i-Sharif. From a distance, in a heat haze, or a sort of mist, we saw the city. Above everything rose the great pale blue dome of the mosque. Buildings sprawled around it and out toward the surrounding countryside. The mosque is famous throughout Afghanistan and the Islamic world. It is the shrine of Hazrat Imam Ali, who is said to be buried there. It is a holy site not only for Shia Muslims but also for Sunnis. Many people go there on *Zeyarat* (pilgrimage). It is known for miraculous cures. Families and loved ones bring the sick, the infirm, and the maimed to the shrine in fervent hope of healing.

We went first through the urban outskirts and on into the busy bustling suburbs, Father asking directions. Again we went to the home of another of his friends. It was dark when we arrived. I was very disappointed; there was no sign of a wedding or a party. It was only a small house. They had only one living room and a basement. Mom told me we were going to stay there for a few days, if Father's friend would let us. The room was too small for two families, but they made us as welcome as they could because we were guests and the Afghan tradition is that guests must be honored, and treated in the best way possible. Next day, my father's friend and family left their house for us and went to his brother's house. He had called my father "brother" and said, "Treat our house like your own, and enjoy it while you are here. I am glad you got out of Kabul safely."

After they left, my father and I went to find some shops. We drove around the suburbs to see what the city looked like. It was smaller than Kabul. It was very nice and clean. The streets were concrete in many places, and there were lots of trees, beautiful flowers, and nice gardens. Everything was green and smelled good. It seemed the Russian had not damaged Mazar-i-Sharif in the way they had done Kabul. It had been one of the main Soviet bases in Afghanistan, and they used the airport to bring in their supplies and to send out many planes to bomb the Mujahadin and any other areas of resistance in the region. Overall it was much better than Kabul, and safer. The ruler of the city was a general called Dostrum. He was an Uzbek and had his own army.

After a week, Father sold his car, and he told me that the general's face was on the money. We all went to the *Sakhijan* (mosque) to give thanks to Allah for arriving safely. It is located in the heart of Mazar-i-Sharif. It is surrounded by a green park and has four main entrances, north, south, west, and east. Each door was designed with many different beautiful flowers and trees in the gardens. The pathway was about four meters wide and a hundreds meters long leading to the entrance to the mosque. A lot of beggars were sitting by each door, asking for money. The ground was covered with beautiful glazed tiles. It was kept very clean and nice all the time. Nobody was allowed to walk there while wearing their shoes. If you did not remove them, you were not allowed to go in. The whole building was very colorful mostly in many shades of blue, white, pink, etc. It smelled very nice and always fresh. Hundreds of workers and lots of other volunteers tended the Sakhijan.

In Afghanistan, Shia Muslim and Sunni Muslim built their own separate mosques, but the Sakhijan in Mazar-i-Sharif is a very special place for everyone, Shia and Sunni Muslims. It is built over the site of the grave of Hazrat Imam Ali, who was the Prophet Mohammed's son-in-law. He was a very good, well-respected holy man. My family loved Imam Ali. I think that's why my father named me Ali. The Sakhijan was the only place that both religious groups revered. Everyone loved it. A lot of people made donations every day, from both sides, Shia Muslim and Sunni Muslim. People from all the different province of Afghanistan and beyond came to Sakhijan. This was the only building that has never been damaged with all the fighting in the history of Afghanistan.

Father rented a house, and we moved there. We had just two mattresses, one pillow, two blankets, a spoon, and a bowl, and nothing else. I was not very happy with our new surrounding and missed my home in Kabul. I wanted to go back to our house and my bicycle and my classmates. I did not like this house at all. I complained to my parents. My father said I should thank Allah that we had survived. He did not like the house either, but he promised me he would make my room as beautiful as my old room in Kabul, once he found a job.

Next day, we went to buy some basic furniture for the home. He headed for the *Mandayee* (the market). It was in the North of Mazar-i-Sharif. It covered a large area and was full of life. It was a confusion of noise color and dozens of different smells.

There were streets with shops on the one side, with stalls in front of them, while across the road were lines of handcarts and barrows. All the traders seemed to be shouting at people to buy what they were selling. The butchers were making the most noise, holding up hacked off parts of dead animals, and there were all sorts of other noises going on at the same time. You could buy anything at that market. Clothes stalls stocked everything from wedding outfits to swimsuits. Vegetable barrows were piled high with melons of all kinds and zambocha, apples and pears and plums, grapes, mulberries, and figs. There were several barrows selling guns, guns from the Russians, guns for hunting, and even very old rifles, and ammunition. And there were hardware shops stocked with pans and cups, tin openers, and pestles and mortars, while a large array of radios and TVs and all sorts of electrical goods were displayed in the open, standing on their own boxes, which were standing on the ground. There were mystic men offering miracle cures for every kind of illness, and even a dentist's caravan, where it was claimed, he would pull out offending teeth painlessly. (He had a man standing outside the van with a big drum, which he banged loudly every time a tooth sufferer went in, so that you couldn't hear the screams). And there were stalls selling soap and medicines, hundreds of rolls of cloth, bicycles, naan bread, carpets, lino, and plastic bins. Men were cooking lamb kebabs on charcoal, you could smell a mile away, and there were samosas and poppadoms and mounds of cooked rice, and to my delight, a shop window full of all kinds of qand, all in different shapes and colors. Pink and white coconut squares, green almond diamond shapes with pecan nuts on the top, creamy marzipan cherry blocks, dried apricots, raisin and honey mixes, and fruit jellyrolls cut into thick slices and dusted with sugar, and all sorts fancy boxes to put them in, with cellophane and ribbons. I wanted to stop there, but I had to keep a tight hold of my father because of the crush. Boys, not much older than me, were working and trying to shout as loud as the traders. Other kids were dodging about, in and out and under the barrows.

It turned out that the secondhand furniture and things like cookers and fridges were in an area of their own, at the furthest north end of the streets. They were easy to find because most of the roads in Mazar-i-Sharif were laid out on a grid pattern. At last we got there. Father got out his list and went around quickly picking out what he wanted. He didn't take any time. He decided what he wanted, then he gave the stallholder a hard time over the prices. It was a good lesson for me. I was proud of him, so I tried to pick up every one of his tricks. After a lot of bargaining, prices were agreed. He paid some of the money and said he would settle up the bill when he collected all the furniture with his friend the next day. Then he said, "Let's go and have kebabs." So we did.

Later he hurried me past the sweet shop three times. He did this to tease me. Then we went inside, and we picked out my favorites. They were put into a neat cardboard box, which the man handed to me. I wanted to start on them right away, but I had to wait until we got home. Somehow the house seemed a lot better.

About two weeks later, my father took me to school, which was a long way from where we were living. He took me each day until I was able to go by myself. In school, there was a shortage of chairs and tables. At break time, all my classmates and I went stealing chairs from other classrooms. We always chose the girls' classrooms because we knew they are weaker than boys. Older student were stealing our chairs, and we were stealing younger students' chairs. That was our fun at school. We all enjoyed it. After school, I went home for lunch. I had only one hour and half to go home and eat, and go to *massjet* (local mosque). There were about fifty students including me. We were learning how to read the Koran and to say prayers and how to ask Allah for help and so on. The Molla told us one day, if we had problems in our life or needed help, to ask Allah, "He is always with us, anywhere anytime." I was a very quick learner. I learned to read the Koran and many other religion books. In time, I became one of the Molla's assistants. I was very helpful to him, and I learned a lot myself.

One of my father's friends came to our home. He asked if my father would let me go to a boxing class with his son. My father said it was up to me. I said, "OK."

The first week was very difficult because I was not very fit, but I improved quickly. Now I became very busy. I had to go to school and had homework to do, Islamic school (mosque), and boxing twice a week. I complained to Mom, but she said nothing.

I began to get to know Mazar-i-Sharif, and Father wanted me to go with him to a Buzkashi game because he said Mazar-i-Sharif was famous throughout the country for the contest. Buzkashi (goat grabbing) was the national sport, and Mazar-i-Sharif was the main center where this wild and ancient game was played.

One day, Father and his friend took me to the contest held on a ground in the city suburbs. There was a huge crowd because when the Buzkashi was played, the city came to standstill. Everyone went to see the game, and I held Father's hand very tightly, in case I got lost. The game was very exciting. The horses were covered with heavy cloth for protection, and the riders wore long leather coats with fur lining and hats made of fur. The horsemen had to capture the carcass of a dead goat. As soon as one of them had hold of the carcass, his horse galloped to the goal area with terrific speed. The horseman had to ride with it around a flag and come back to drop it in a circle. Then he had scored. The other players had to try to stop him. They got very excited, hitting and baulking each other. Most of them continued playing with bad injuries such as broken ribs or arms. Father said it is a badge of courage if the players finish the game covered in blood. It was all very violent, but it was exciting. I heard from Father that the huge horses were specially trained for the Buzkashi game. They were massive in size, but they enjoyed the game as much as the Afghanis. I did not understand what the rules were, and Father got too excited to explain. After that day, I made him take me as often as he could. Mom didn't like me going. She said I was too small to be taken into such a rough crowd. She said it was "bad company" because there were a lot of men betting huge amounts of money, and they often got very nasty if their bets lost, and they swore a lot.

So we began to settle to our new life, and Father tried hard to get a new job. He had been a businessman when we lived in Kabul, and with his work, he had always travelled all around Afghanistan, but now he couldn't; there was too much violence everywhere. He got a job in a store at Mandayee (market), which sold many different kinds of goods. It belonged to a trader who had three or four stalls in different parts of the market, and so he had a manager to oversee things. Father was not happy in his new job. He had always had his own business and made good money and been able to afford a good standard of living. He had lost all that when we fled Kabul. He had been his own boss, now he had to accept being ordered about. The work was manual, the wages were poor, and his manager was not very intelligent (he was an Uzbek and had a bad attitude). But Father knew the situation he was in; he put his pride in his pocket and got on with the job.

We had settled into a routine way of living in Mazar-i-Sharif for a long while, when my father decided to go back Kabul to see what had happened to our house. We went to buy a coach ticket for him. The night before he left, he said to me, "*Mardee khana bia inja* (You are now the man of our house). You must never miss your school and always listen to your mom. I will come back soon, in about a month, *inshallah* (God willing)." I was about nine or ten years old.

After Father went away, Mom become very friendly, and she changed a little bit. She started to be very kind like other moms.

Life became very difficult without him. He had not got in touch with us since he left. If there had ever been any telephone and postal systems between Kabul and Mazar-i-Sharif (and anywhere else in the country), they had long been destroyed or become so neglected that they no longer worked. Large business companies had had to establish their own methods of communicating. Some had their own motorbike couriers, who made regular trips along dangerous war-wrecked roads, risking their lives. They could only be encouraged to do the work by offers of large amounts of money. Many were killed on the roads, shot, blown up by mines, or victims of accidents due to the dreadful road conditions. Ordinary people wanting to get in touch with friends or family in other areas could only do it by sending messages with anyone who might be travelling between the various places. Travelling anywhere could mean moving across the front line of opposing forces into the territory of an enemy.

One afternoon, three months after my father had left, I came back from my boxing class and found Mom crying and praying for Father to come back. She told me to sit down beside her. She looked at me, "Your father has not come back. I hope he is all right. We have almost finished the money, and all our provisions are running out. The flour, oil, tea, sugar, rice, and wood are almost all gone. If he doesn't come back in another two weeks, we will have to do something about it."

Father didn't come back. Mom decided to stop me going to school. "I am sorry," she said, "but you know that it is unacceptable for me to go out to work. You will need to go and work until your father comes back; otherwise we are going to starve."

Next week, Mom and I went to *mandayee* to where Father used to work. We asked the manager if they would hire me. First, he said I was too young for the work. Second, he didn't need any extra help. We went back home very disappointed.

Mom became more worried, so she decided to take me somewhere else. No one would hire me because I was too young. We went again to where Father used to work. Mom pleaded with the owner this time, telling him that we were desperate and near starvation. He said he would consider hiring me because my father was a good businessman and he had been a very good worker. "Come Saturday at 8:00 a.m.," he said, "and I'll give you a trial. I think the work will be too much for you. If you can't do the job, then that will be that."

I was aged about ten or eleven. I was tall for my age, slim, with narrow shoulders. I got through the trial period, and he gave me a job. I did not like the work, but I had no alternative. The job was very hard physically, and I had to remember the prices. At that time, I did not even know my right hand from my left. It was very hard to be responsible, to worry, and to think about money problems, at that young age. Like my father, I found the work very hard at first. Like him, I thought I should have been doing better things because the money I had been promised was very little, and like him, I thought the manager was stupid, although the owner was OK.

The store had an old warehouse next to it. When customers wanted something, if we did not have it in store, my manager would tell me to bring it from the warehouse. When I went there, everything was in boxes. They all looked the same. Sometimes the labels were not in Dari or Farsi, but in Chinese or English. I found it hard to lift one box over another and had trouble finding anything. The first few days, I was taking the wrong stuff over to the store because I mixed up their names, but I learned them very quickly. Still I had problems carrying some of heavier boxes over. If I took too long, sometimes the manager would come and twist my ear very hard and hit me on my back or slap my face, and then he would do the job himself. Every day I went home angry, and there were marks left on my body. I complained to my mom. She cried a lot and felt very sorry about it. Since that time, she never touched me again. So that is how, at that age, I started to work to support my mom and myself. Now I was in charge of my home, and my family. Qand was forgotten. "You're a man. Allah made all men for work. You'll be a very good worker and a famous businessman like your father," Mom said.

I decided that, in the future, I would not to tell her about the problems I was having with the manager. Her tears made me cry inside myself. I learned to deal with everything myself.

At the end of the first month, my boss gave me some money. It was very little. It wasn't enough for all we needed, but it was just enough to keep us alive. Mom began to love me now because I was the only person supporting her.

After working for a while, I found many friends at my workplace. There were lots of boys younger than me doing *mojeekiry* (shoeshine) and selling cigarettes, matches, and gums. They had little boxes made of wood and a thick string around their neck and were going around shouting, asking people if their shoes needed shining or if they needed cigarettes. Sometimes they came to our store and asked if our shoes needed shining. When we were not busy, the supervisor gave his shoes to be shined, and I sat beside the *mojeekiry* and watched how they did their job. They were very fast and got the money before they started working. If the supervisor gave him a little more money, he would clean properly and nice; otherwise, they never did more than they were paid for. The owner of the next store had a son who had mental problems. Most of the time he was normal, but his mind was only that of a child. His name was Tamim. He was about twenty-four years old. He ambled around most of the time, getting in everyone's way, but he was harmless. My supervisor never referred to him by his own name but called him *dewana* (crazy) and didn't want him around our store. He always asked me to ask Tamim to keep away. Tamim was very funny and made me laugh a lot, and I enjoyed talking to him and never called him dewana.

Every afternoon, just about sunset, there would be huge crowds in the mandayee. That was the rush hour. I had to stand up on a table and shout about our goods, to sell them faster and try to get people's attention and get them to come over and buy from our store. Many other marketmen and workers did the same thing. The louder you shouted, the more customers you would get. At the beginning of this job, I was shy, and I could not shout properly because my voice was high pitched and childish. In a very short time, after losing my voice completely, and it coming back again much hoarser, it became much easier, and it sounded very funny. There were some boys who were my rivals. We were trying to shout above each other and trying to mimic each other's style of shouting. We cupped our hands around our mouths and tried to make funny noises. We were all thinking how we could outdo each other, but none of them could do what I did. I was very happy when I was doing this, although I sometimes felt tired.

On one particular day, toward evening when the crowds were beginning to get bigger, a well-dressed trader or businessman came to the store and spoke to the supervisor. After a minute or two, I saw him pointing at me.

What have I done now? I thought. They came over, and the supervisor said, "This gentleman is asking for your father. Will you tell him what you know?" The man smiled, and the supervisor started to move away. "Salaam," the man said. "Salaam," I replied, and we shook hands.

"Your father was working here this time last year, so I thought he would be here today, but your boss says he's left. When will he be back?"

I was so surprised by his question that I could not speak. My mouth opened, but nothing came out. Then with a rush, I said, "I don't know where he is. He hasn't come back. He said he would be a month, and he's been . . . I don't know what has happened to him."

He calmed me down because my head was whirling, what did he want? Who was he? Had he any news? Eventually he managed to get our story from me, and he asked more questions, but I could not answer. Then he said, "I am sorry to upset you. I am a friend of your father, more of a working friend. I travel about a bit, like he used to. I met up with him again when he was working here about a year ago. So I call in here when I'm in town, just to have a chat."

"He went to Kabul months ago, and we don't know when he will be back. Do you know where he is?" I asked desperately.

"The last time I met him, it was here. He asked me to take some messages to his uncle in a village outside Ghazni City. I wasn't going straight there. I had business in Bala Morghab and Harat City, in the other direction, but he said the messages weren't important, any time would do. I got to Ghazni about two months ago. So his letter got there in the end," the man said.

"We don't know when he's coming back," I repeated. "Are you going to Kabul?"

"No. Not if I can help it. We had a business there, but we closed it two years ago."

The store was getting busy, and the supervisor was motioning to me with a jerk of his head to go to him. "I've got to go. Sorry, *agha*. My boss . . ." I started to say.

"Yes, right, just tell him, when you see him, that everyone is OK in Ghazni, and his grandfather sends his love. That's about it," he said, moving away. "Oh, just tell him Ahmad Husainni called in."

"Yes, agha, Thank you, I'll do that," I said, moving toward a customer who was picking up some of the stock.

"That's my name, 'Ahmad Husainni,'" he shouted as he went. "Don't forget."

Then he merged with the crowd in the aisles and had gone. In an hour or so, I had forgotten all about him.

The time passed so quickly at the mandayee. I worked there for about eight months. I remember every moment from the day I started, and how I developed my talent. By the age of eleven, I had learned a lot of things, dealing with problem, and resolving them quickly. I was working hard, and I learned many amazing new words (Mom said they were all bad), and the other boys told me a lot of things about sex that I did not believe. I was encouraged to keep up at my job and received compliments and even tips from many of our customers.

Everything seemed to be going OK until one afternoon. The store was not busy, and I was chatting with Tamim. There were many people wandering about, but no one was buying anything. He was asking for a gum from another boy and struggling to count his money and bargaining over the price. Suddenly my supervisor came out and shouted to me, asking why the people were not congregating in front of our store.

He said, "How many times shall I tell you to ask the Dewana to leave? He puts the customers off."

He was afraid to tell Tamim to go away himself or to hit him because his father was near at hand, and he would complain to our boss. He came toward me and was lifting his hand to slap my face. I was shocked. I grabbed his hand as it came down and shouted, "Why are you hitting me all the time! Go and hit him if he's the problem. If you have the balls." As I said that, it stopped him for a moment, and people began to look at us. He started to hit me about the head. I was shouting for him to stop, but he didn't take any notice. People began to gather around. Tamim shouted at me to hit him back. He was hitting me and asking stupid questions repeatedly. I lost my temper and hit him with all my power with an uppercut to his chin and another three quick punches to his belly, as I had been taught. I weighed only about one hundred pounds, but I put it behind my punches, and I found I had knocked him down. He was on the ground. I had winded him. He was desperately gasping for breath. People were laughing at him and saying, "Good job," "He deserved it," and "Go it, lad." I stood there for a few seconds, as surprised as everyone else. Tamim rushed over to where the supervisor was doubled up on the ground, trying to get his breath, and he comically started counting for him to get up, like in a real boxing match. He was saying, "1, 2, 5, 8, 20, 3, 14, 40, 47." Still he had not got up. Tamim shouted "out" and spun around and grabbed my left hand and shot it up in the air and said, "Winner! Winner of mandayee."

People clapped for me and laughed. Then I realized what I had done. Without waiting for anything, I ran into the store for my bag, and then I jumped into the street and began to run away from the store.

When I cooled down a bit, I realized I had made my way generally in the direction of home. I stopped and hung about for a little while, thinking about what I should do. I waited for it to get late. I was hungry and tired and very worried. I argued with myself, "What are we going to do if I've lost my job? I'll get another one in the market. Will anyone want me after what I've done? He deserved it. Oh Allah, what a stupid thing to do," I was talking to myself all the way home. "How do I tell Mom? There'll be a row. What do I do now? I went over what I thought she would say and what I would say and what she would answer, and so I reached home.

There was nothing for it, I would go straight in and get on with it. I used my key and opened the door. It felt different than usual. I thought the door at the other end of the room into the passageway was just closing, but the living room was empty. Funny, Mom was always there when I got home, always waiting for me. "Mom," I shouted. "Mom!" I threw my bag down and went for the other door, but it opened and a man was there and he said, "How is lovely my son?"

He opened his arms wide, and I jumped into them. When I ran into Father's arms, he held me off a little, saying, "Hold on, my son, not so rough, not so rough." I was dancing with happiness.

When father came into the room, there was laughter and tears as you would expect, and we were all delighted. Mom followed him into the room, leading a young boy by the hand. He was about ten years old, very skinny, with thick black hair. He kept his head down, so I could not see his face.

"This is Qader, Ali. Come and say hello."

"You remember Qader," Father said, "Qader, your cousin."

I was too surprised to want to say hello to anyone. I wanted to climb all over Father, but he held me off.

"Ali Jan say Salam to Qader. He has come to live with us. Make him welcome."

"Salam alaikum, Qader," I said, although I didn't want to, and I went to shake his hand.

He mumbled, "Alaikum a Salam," and lifted his head to look at me. I had expected a smile. I got a surprise because his face was a picture of utter misery. He shook my hand, but did not let go of it. I did not recognize him. I had several cousins who I knew well, but I did not know this boy.

His eyes searched my face as he tried to remember anything familiar about my features, and I suppose I was doing the same thing.

Father was reminding me about where I had last met Qader, and I eventually caught a glimpse of how he used to look, but he had changed a lot. Qader was my cousin from my father's side. If this was the Qader I had known, then something must have happened to him. He must have been ill or something, because the Qader I knew would be thirteen of fourteen by now and he had been of average build, but this boy looked about ten or eleven, and was skin and bone. He looked very tired. Although I had begun to recognize him, he did not seem to know me. He still held my hand. I looked to Father. "Come on, you two, let's settle down to talk and to eat. Ali, take Qader into the yard and go and wash your hands." I made for the door, and he followed me. It was strange because although I tried to talk to him, he seemed distant.

Mom had laid a beautiful food cloth on the floor in the center of the room. She had been hiding it away, keeping it for a special occasion. The food was frugal but filling. It was what we had got used to, while Father was away. Then especially for me, he produced a box of qand. And we had them with *chai*.

Father began to tell us where he had been for the last year. He spoke in a straightforward matter-of-fact way.

"We have lost everything. All that I worked for the last twenty-three years has gone. I went to see our house in Kabul, there was not much left of it. They even took the window frames and doors. They burned them instead of firewood."

"Do know you who did it?" I asked.

"I guess our neighbor. I don't know really who did it. I saw some of our stuff at a neighbor's home, but I did not mention it."

He went again to find out who had stolen our property. There was still fighting between Ahmad Shamakhsood (Sunni Muslim) and Mazar-e-Azbiwahdad (Shia Muslim) and others going on. Father was shot in his shoulder twice. That was why he had held me away, when I wanted to jump all over him. He believed he had been shot by the Sunni fighters. He bled badly. He managed to get himself to a doctor. When the doctor released him, he went to my uncle's house. When he got there, he found that the house had been destroyed by the shelling.

Father said, "I tried to find my sister's house, and I searched for all our other relatives. They were all gone. Allah knows where to. It was very dangerous. Thousands of people were found dead all over Kabul. I found some of our relatives dead in their own house. I buried them in their own yard, but I had a lot of trouble digging the land because my shoulder hurt a lot. I wanted to search for my sisters and brothers, but I was afraid of being killed myself by either side, Shia or Sunni. On the way coming back here, I found Qader in the hotel where he was working as a cleaner. Qader called out, "*Kaka Jan! Kaka Jan!* (Honey Uncle) I am Qader, I am your nephew."

"What are you doing here?" I asked, hugging him.

Qader started crying and said, "Father was killed, my mother my sister and my lovely brother were killed as well."

My mom started crying, and my father had tears running down his face. He reached over to Qader who was sitting next to him. He hugged Qader close to him and said, "I'll take care of you. Bad things are happening to everyone these days. It was very close thing for me too, I was nearly killed myself."

Qader had started listening to what Father was saying. It was as if he had suddenly woken up. He began to talk, and there was pain in his voice as he said, "My father told me to go and get some water from the well in the corner of the yard for the family for the morning. As I got to the well, the bomb dropped."

CHAPTER 4

QADER'S STORY

Qader said, "I was knocked over by the blast, and *my head* was cut, I got up, crying and shouting for help! Nobody heard me, nobody came to help. I was crying. I did not know what to do or where to go. The house had fallen in on top of everyone. There was a cloud of smoke and dust. I could hardly see. I could not move any of the bricks with my hands. I was shouting to Mom and Baba, but there were no answers. My mind wouldn't work. My head pained badly. I don't know how long I was there or what I was doing.

I found myself walking. I kept walking in the streets until I got very tired and very hungry. I understood that I had become an orphan. There was a bridge; I slept under that bridge for a short time. When I woke up and looked around myself, I saw there was money around me. I wondered where it had come from. Two minutes later, someone passed by and dropped a little money and said "pray for me" and walked away. I thought for a moment. A lot of homeless people nearby were begging for money, people must have thought I was a beggar too. I took the money, it was enough for some bread. I was very hungry and went looking for a bakery.

"For five days I was walking around, down, and up (south and north). I was getting very weak, finally I found a restaurant where my father and I used to go sometime for lunch or chai (tea).

"As I enter the restaurant, the boss recognized who I was. His name was Najib. Najib asked me where my father was. I started to cry and explained to him how my family had been killed. I said I've been sleeping for a week under the bridge. Najib put his hand to my shoulder, and I saw tears on his face. He began to swear about the people who have killed my family and other innocent people. 'Allah will punish them one day, Allah surely will,' he said. 'What can I do for you, Qader Jan? Do you want some food for free?'

"'No,' I said, 'Just let me stay here until I find my way.'

"'I opened this restaurant for customers. You can stay here as long as you want, if you have money,' he said.

"I said, 'My father is dead. Who can I get money from?'

"Najib said, 'I can't keep people with no money. How can I run a business? Go back the same way you came from.'

"I thought for a moment, I had nowhere to go. I couldn't go back and sleep under bridge or beg people to give me some food. I screamed and looked up to the ceiling, I said, 'Oh, Allah, why did you take my father? Why did you not take me? What do I do now?'

"I looked at Najib and pleaded and took hold of his leg. 'Just let me stay here.'

"Eventually he said, "OK. I'll let you stay if you do some work for me, such as washing dishes, sweeping the ground, and cleaning the bathroom.'

"I said, 'OK, Kaka Najib.'

"He said, "First, you need to change your clothes and take a bath and then you can start work.'

"The first night I slept by the back door. He didn't let me get a mattress because I was so dirty and had no money. Early next morning, he woke me. He said, "Go to the back of the restaurant, I have left you some water and some soap, do not use too much soap because it was very expensive.'

"There was a bowl of cold water and half bottle of shampoo. I had to wear Najib's son's clothes for one or two days until mine were washed and clean. I did not know how to work as a cleaner. I started doing it. Najib sometimes hit me or twisted my ear badly when he found me sitting on my break. He expected me to work like a machine, all day long without taking any breaks. The second day of work I was cleaning the kitchen. He said, "*Yadem bacha* (orphan boy)," took my ear and twisted it a little bit, and said, "your salary is only half bread for breakfast and a glass of tea. For lunch, one whole bread. For dinner, you will eat whatever has been left at the end of the night. If there is nothing left, you will have to eat secondhand food.'

"'Secondhand food' is when the customers finished their food and some of it was left on their plates, the waiter took the remaining food and put it on to a separate dish, instead of putting it in the garbage can. Sometimes they resold it. It depended on the manager. If he were a nice person, he would give it to very poor people. I did not like the way Najib

treated me, but I had no choice. Working at the restaurant, I heard a lot
of stories about what was happening to people. Some of them were worse
than my own. I saw people with no hand or no leg. Some people had died
from starvation. Hearing these awful stories and seeing terrible things I
had never seen before, I began to understand that there were thousands of
people like me, with problems."

"Apart from the injured, people who were alive had problems. Many
lost their jobs and couldn't find other work, and so had no money. Other
people were stuck in their homes and did not dare to go out because there
was too much violence on the streets. Different religious groups and clans
were fighting each other.

"Rich people had left the city. They had become refugees. If they hadn't
left Afghanistan already, they have lost any chance of leaving. Clan of Shia
fought clan Sunni, Sunni fought Shia. If they found each other in the
wrong street, they beat them up and broke their hands, head, or legs. They
did this to teach them a lesson so they that never came again.

"Every day, one or two people attempted to get food, for their families
by going into a different street or area. Often those people never came back.
Allah knows what happen to them. Some of them came back with no food
and badly injured. Some of the people, the lucky ones, brought food. It
also depended what kind of people they came across. There are really some
good people who are sharing their happiness and sadness with each other.
Some educated people love humans and keep the peace, helping others
respectfully. That was all about what civilians were doing to each other.

"Let me tell you about armed people. What they did!

"The next part of the story is unsuitable for younger people. There
was a crisis between Shia Muslims and Sunni Muslims. They committed
the worst crimes in the history of Afghanistan. I can say, even in the whole
world, things like this never happen anywhere, such as taking the eyes out,
cutting off hands, ears, penis, testicles, teeth, nails, legs, finger, heads, nose.
Sometimes they took the liver and made it in kebabs to eat. Even I heard
they eat blood. They did these things to each prisoner, one at a time in front
of other prisoners. Some of those forced to watch died of shock because of
what they witnessed. Some of the fighters became was very seriously mad.
They develop mental problem to get revenge for their comrades. Biting like
dogs. Burning people in the oven, instead of firewood. Taking the heart out
one by one. Stubbing cigarettes out in their eyes, their faces, and all over
the body. That was what happened to men. Let me tell you about women
and children if they had taken a kilometer of enemy territory. First, I want

to say about babies. They took the baby away from their parent. One man holding the right leg, another man the left. By counting 1-2-3, they pulled the baby's legs in opposite directions, attempting to tear the child apart. They then threw the remains in the parent's face. They killed all men first and raped the women. Sometimes they even cut off the breasts."

CHAPTER 5

THE BOXING CLUB

With all the fighting in Afghanistan, many people were very badly injured. All sides attacked their enemy as ferociously as they could.

My father said, "When I found Qader, I wanted to go to pay my respects for his father's death, but I was worried about my family too. If we went to pay our respects, we knew that we were going to be killed. I said to Qader, 'I am already missing my family. I haven't heard about them since I left home. I don't know if they're dead or alive.'"

"I eventually found a driver who was prepared to make the dangerous journey to Mazar-i-Sharif. Qader and I left Kabul. We were halfway here, when the driver suddenly pulled over and ordered everybody to get out. There were five armed men, their faces covered. None of the passengers recognized what clan or what religion the men were. They told everybody to put their valuables, watches, coats, shoes, and jackets on the ground. The people knew that armed men always got what they wanted. There was no arguing. One of the gunmen hit our driver with his *Kalanashnikov* rifle (Russian's gun), demanding money. He started to scream and said, 'I swear to Allah, I don't have any money.' At the same time we noticed another car coming from Kabul .The armed men took what they wanted and ran away. The car pulled over. They asked what was going on. We told them what had happened. The man said, 'There is a little village thirty minutes from here that was local people. They are just robbers. They don't harm anyone.' Our driver, with the other car following, drove all the way to Mazar-i-Sharif City."

It was very dark in our room when Father and Qader stopped talking. The time was about one o'clock on Friday morning. There was no electricity, so we had been sitting, talking, and listening by the light of a little candle with a small glass shade on it.

Father said, "Let's go to bed, it's very late."

It was still Friday morning when Mom woke me and sent me to the bakery to get four naan (bread). There was a queue. I waited for about half an hour. At last, there were only five people before me. Just then, a boy, who was a little older than me, pushed to the front of the line. It meant that I was now after six people. "I can't take it," I told myself. I went behind him and put my hand on his shoulder and said, "Look, we have all been waiting for thirty-five minutes, and you have just arrived. That's not fair."

"Shut up before someone else notices." he said cockily.

"Get off my face now, and go to the end of line," I said angrily.

He pushed me and said, "Get lost."

I pushed him back. He slapped my face. I defended myself. He started swearing at my family and called me *Soya afriqee* (black boy). "Let me take some bread and go," he said.

I repeated what I had said very firmly. I knew I could put him down easily. He was only skinny. I moved one foot forward. He punched me. This made me lose my temper.

People were looking at me. Some of them knew I was a good boxer. So I hit him with an uppercut under his chin. He fell down instantly. I saw his front teeth had broken. He was also bleeding. I threw my money to the cashier. He asked me, "How many naan do you want?"

"Four," I said.

He handed me the bread, and then I ran all the way home. My shirt was ripped because of the fight. My mom was waiting by the door. She said, "What happened to you? Why are you late? Why is your shirt ripped?"

I stood there and explained everything as it had happened. She didn't like me fighting. My father was nearby. He heard our conversation and said, "Good boy, you're my hero. You were right. You have to stand up for yourself. You are *mard* (a man)."

Later in the day, we went the Sakhijan (the blue mosque) to give thanks for Father's return. Father and Mom were walking a little ahead. Qader and I behind them, he was holding my hand.

"Do you remember the last time I saw you?" I asked.

"No," Qader said.

I believed that when Qader's family passed away, and he was lonely for a while, he lost his memory a little bit. I noticed that when I asked him several questions, he could not remember anything. He only remembered what had happened after he became an orphan. Mom said, "A lot of people lost their memory after they had had an accident."

Two weeks before we had left Kabul, Qader and his father were invited for lunch in our house. Qader and I, after lunch, went to play in our yard. I remembered it very well because I won all Qader's walnuts. He was so nervous, and I was laughing and happy because I was the winner. I reminded him about our game now we were in Mazar-i-Sharif, but Qader could not remember any things about it. I was very sorry for him, remembering in the old days, how wonderful he was, how proud he was. It was very hard to believe that he was the same person whose walnuts I had won. I remembered his happiness, his smile, his father, and his little brother, who always took his side when we had a little dispute. I was crying inside myself each time I looked at him.

I heard father call out, "Are you guys all right?"

"Yes, Father," I said.

Qader was very quiet all the time. I had tried my best to cheer him up, which Mom had told me to do, but I couldn't because he could only remembered the exact moment when his father told him go and get some water.

He wished he had been killed with his family. He had had a very bad time since his family passed away. So we walked all around the Sakhijan, prayed for him, and then we went home.

I did not go to work because I did not know what would happen about my fight with the supervisor, and besides, I wanted to remain with my father. My mom explained how we had carried on our lives while he had been away.

After lunch, Father said that Qader and I must go school. He said, "I will take care of everything. Thank you, my son, for helping your mom. Tomorrow, take Qader with you and go back to school and your boxing class too."

From then on, our lives settled into a comfortable pattern. Father got work in the market again but with another store, and Qader and I went to school, and in the afternoon we went and helped Father.

Four months later, Father bought bicycles for both of us. We liked school, but Qader did not like boxing.

One day, my coach said, "We are going to have a competition with another local boxing club. I have chosen twelve of you." That included me. We had five days to get ready for the competition. I told father about it. He said, "Let's get ready then."

On the day of the match, Father, Qader, and I went to the stadium. The stadium was really only a very large room. There were only a few chairs for the coaches and doctors. The audience had to sit on the floor, or they could stand. There was a big crowd. The place was full. A lot of people were hanging about, outside, pushing each other to get in. Some of the people were sitting on the window ledges. Mine was to be the third match of the competition. I went to the changing room with my other boxing friends and got ready.

We could here all the sounds of the matches, the bell ringing, the shouting, and cheering. I was excited. My heart was beating fast, and my head was whirling. The coach came up and talked to me and gave me some last instructions, and that settled my nerves. Out in the main room, they called out my name and that of another fighter. Then everything seemed to happen very quickly. We went out into the clamor and got into the ring. A bell rang. We had started. After the first five minutes, we were equal.

There were lots of noisy people shouting for each club. "Hit him, hit him," they said it repeatedly. I could hardly hear my father's voice. The room was too hot. There was no ventilation. I was very nervous, and the lights were too strong. In the second five minutes, my father was on his feet, yelling at me, "Hit him, my son. Hit him!"

Eventually I won the competition. The ref raised my arm in the air, and a cheer went up. I was elated and very happy. It was over so quickly.

Later, on the way home, Father said excitedly, "You will be the best boxer in the world *inshallah* (God willing). He was so proud of me. We went home, Mother made two glasses of milk, one for me another for Qader, and tea for Father.

CHAPTER 6

HAPPY NEW YEAR'S DAY

News came for Father one morning. The businessman, Ahmad Husainni, whom I had met when he came to the market store looking for father, had turned up again. He had just come from Ghazni City, and was glad to find Father alive and well because he had begun to fear that he had been killed in Kabul. Father wanted him to come to our house and stay while he was in Mazar, but he said he had made his own arrangements. They went to the *chaikhana* in the market (a kind of café) to drink chai and eat some fried chicken and rice. The man pulled some letters out of his pocket; they were from the family in Ghazni. He had been keeping them for Father for some time, so they were a bit worse for wear. There was quite a few of them. Father didn't read them right away but put them away until he had more time. They talked for a while about Kabul and all that had happened there and about Ghazni and the countryside around it, because that was where my father was born and grew up. Then he went away.

After he had had time to read them, Father said they brought all sorts of news and gossip from Ghazni from over the past year. Who had married who, who had died, problems with the animals, and so on, but the most important news was that Father's father had died. It turned out that by the time we got the news, he had been dead nearly a year. In his will, he had left Father a lot of land and the old farmhouse with a lot of outbuildings. Father said that the land was arid and was almost worthless, except for the many pine trees, which could be sold for building material. But the farm would never be anything more than a problem for anyone who tried to make a living there. That was why his father had left the place, to go to Kabul with two of his brothers and their wives to make a decent living and start a family.

Qader and I went to school regularly. We were "new boys" in that school, and so attracted attention. It was quite a rough school. We were beaten up by teachers often. There were lots of fights, mainly between the younger students, group against group, and the older students hit us sometimes. When someone hit Qader or me in the group fighting, we would remember their face and get revenge later, catching them one by one. Qader would go down behind their legs, and I would punch them in the face. And they would fall backward over Qader. This was a good lesson for them. They never hit us again. After a while, we were famous students in the school. We were accepted. We had been tested and had proved that we were able to look after ourselves. We were proud of ourselves and had a good time. Sometimes students brought their parents to resolve their problem in the school, but I never did. I had many friends, and sometimes we played football in the school area with the sports teacher.

Father often bought Qader new clothes. I was jealous and argued with him because sometimes he bought more for Qader than for me. I was thinking, why did he do that? Father said, "Oh my son! Oh my dear, you should understand. Qader is an orphan. Sit down, my son. You know he is an orphan. Their hearts are weaker, and they feel differently than us. Their hearts have been broken. I don't want Qader to feel that he is alone. Of course you are my unique son. I love you more than anything else in the world. You know that already, don't you, my son? We have to keep Qader happy. This is our responsibility. If we don't, Allah won't be happy with us."

So I tried my best to keep Qader happy because of what Father had said.

Two week before New Year's Day, my parents painted our house and bought some new furniture. Mom cleaned and prepared everything, ready for the New Year.

On New Year's Day, Father bought two beautiful suits, the same color for Qader and I, and gave us some money as *Eidi* (presents, like people give in the West to their children as Christmas presents), and Mom gave us five boiled eggs each. We had a huge celebration in the Sakhijan. Father went there for the New Year's prayers. On this day, thousands of people from all over Afghanistan congregated at the Sakhijan.

After the breakfast, Qader and I left home. We went out for a lot of fun. There was egg-fighting, a kite-flying competition, and many other games. There were lots of people on the streets, mainly youngsters, and lots of street food-sellers. People were all dressed in brand new clothes, or at least were very clean and nice, and they smelled of various perfumes.

Everything was made especially for the New Year. That was the only the day that people were not fighting, not pushing, nor discriminating between Shia or Sunni or causing any trouble. They were so nice and very friendly, saying "Happy New Year" and giving their best wishes to each other. Father said, "New Year's Day in Afghanistan is very special for everyone, and it is a traditional belief that if everyone tries their best to be friendly and polite to each other on New Year's Day, their behavior will continue throughout the following year." The whole country was sick of wars and craved for peace. I think that everyone really wanted that belief to come true that New Year.

Later in the day, we all went together to see Father's friend. His name was Wahid. He was not much taller than me, at about five foot six, and aged about forty. He was very funny, with twinkling brown eyes and long black hair. He was wearing a very old traditional vest (waistcoat) all the time because he had inherited it from his father, but it was far too big for him, he was thin and had narrow shoulders.

After lunch, Father and Wahid sat talking about work. Wahid said his truck-driving made a lot of money and suggested that if father had enough money, he should buy a truck and do the same thing. Later in the day, we went to the Sakhijan again for prayers with Wahid's family. There was a wonderful feeling of peace and happiness all around that beautiful building despite the huge crowd. The blue glazed tiles of the mosque reflected the brilliant afternoon sunshine, and the white doves rose up and flew in large flocks, swirling around in the sky every time any noise startled them. But because of the heat and the crowds, we decided to leave earlier than usual.

Wahid's words must have started Father thinking, because one night after dinner a few weeks later, he said, "I can't keep working for low wages. It is not enough for us to live on. We still have some property in Kabul and some land, trees, and a little livestock in Ghazni, which Grandfather has left to me. I can't go to Kabul because there is too much violence there. I need to go to Ghazni to sell some trees or animals or land. If I sold any of them, I could afford to buy a truck. Then I will be able to work hard to make a change in our lives."

We all agreed, but we did not have enough money for Father to go to Ghazni City, and we would need money to live on while he was away.

Mom said, "I have twelve bangles, four pairs of earrings, three necklaces, two bracelets, and four rings, and a complete set of golden jewelry."

Women love gold more than anything else in their lives. Each time they go to a party or visit family, friend, and relatives, women have to wear difference clothes and jewelry. Mom said, "People notice if you repeatedly wear the same things all the time." Mom sold her jewelry. Father promised to replace her gold. He took only enough money for the journey to Ghazni City.

Next morning, Mom made some *Yahnee* (chicken fried with olives oil) for Father to take with him. This time we did not buy any bus tickets for him because he was going to walk there or rent a donkey. He was going through the mountains. There were two ways for him to go there, one was crossing through Kabul, but he'd had too much trouble there last time. The other way was to make for Azarajad and go from village to village and mountain pass to mountain pass in a detour. This was not an easy way to go, but he had no alternative. I heard from Father, "If you want a good life, you have to work hard and take a little risk sometimes, otherwise you will never succeed. The harder things are, the better you will enjoy your success when it comes."

"You will never reach to a treasure unless you search enough, suffer pains, and work hard to go toward it." This is an Afghan proverb.

The night before Father was leaving. We prayed all night for him to come back alive, and with money. About six o'clock that morning, he was ready to go.

He said, "I have to speak with my son for a moment separately." Qader and Mom left the room. Father told me to sit closer to him. "It is not easy for me to leave you and Mom, but you know the situation and the money problems we are facing today. You don't know how much I missed you last time, when I went to Kabul. You will realize that when you become a father. My son, my dear, my love, if I do not come back, you are in charge and have responsibility for our house. You are the owner of all my worldly possessions and inheritance. Do not try to come after me. I may come back or I may not."

The going is up to you, the return up to Allah. (This is a saying in Afghanistan meaning, "You can decide when you will go, but cannot decide when you will come back.")

I was crying, and I saw tears on his face while he was telling me all this.

He said, "You are a man. Men must not cry. Do not leave your mom alone please. It doesn't matter what's going to happen. If I do not come back, Allah will take care of you. Try to go to school if possible."

I didn't like him going away, but I could not stop him because he was going to make a good life for us. He was taking risks for the family because my future was important to him. He wanted Qader and me to be educated men and become good businessmen like he used to be, and like Qader's father once was. He loved Qader as much as he loved me. Father hugged me and kissed my forehead. "God will be with you, my son."

I took his hand and touched with my eyes and kissed it. I said, "God help you, Father Jan, I will miss you. We are nothing without you. Please take care of yourself. I wish I was old enough to go with you." I was very proud of him because he would do anything to make us happy.

We walked to the door. I called Qader and Mom. She was crying and brought the Koran and held it over Father's head. He hugged her and Qader and said, "Good-bye." Mom poured some water over Father's footprints. Holding the Koran means God will save you. Pouring water after somebody makes them remember to come back fast. That's an Afghan tradition. They believe in it.

Father left home. We were all sad. Still crying, Mom was counting every minute for Father to come back.

CHAPTER 7

THE TALIBAN

Mom had fasted for fifteen days. We were all praying for Father to come back soon. We went several times to the Sakhijan (mosque) and had long prayers for him.

Qader was thinking about his family a lot. To keep his mind busy, I arranged for us to play volleyball with other friends, neighbors in our street sometimes. Qader was chosen as center forward. I was chosen as shooter for the game because I was the tallest. Sometimes after dinner, Qader and I played *jesheem bortakan* (staring contest when two people are looking at each other's eyes. Whoever blinks first, loses the contest). It was a game that we enjoyed.

Mom woke Qader and me at five o'clock every morning. It was time for *Namaz* (prayers). We had to go out into the yard and get washed, before we prayed, whatever the weather. I had problems waking up very early, because Qader and I told jokes, story, and played games until late at night. Sometimes we wrestled. Mom warned us not to stay up late night. We didn't take any notice of that. I was half-asleep when Mom's calling woke me up for prayers. It was very hard to wake up. Sometimes I told Qader to go first to pray because we had only one washroom in the corner of our yard. It took at least twenty-five minutes to get ready and pray. Then we could go back to bed, but it took a while to fall asleep again. By the time Qader came back, I had fallen asleep. One day Mom called us to wake for prayers. I told Qader to go first. Qader told me to go first. We had a lot of arguments about this problem.

Forty-three days later, Father came back from Ghazni City. At the first opportunity, we celebrated because father had arrived in good health and with money. We were so excited. We invited twenty-five people and had a sensational time. Father brought two new suits, one for me, the other for Qader, and some jewelry for Mom.

The day of the party, Qader stood on the left outside the front door of our house, and I was on the right, our job was to greet the guests. Father was sitting inside the house with Mom. One of our guests said to us, "You guys are looking great, like movie stars."

"Thank you," I said. Father brought a lot of presents for everyone at the party.

A week later, he bought a used truck, and we had another small party.

The second party was only for Wahid's family and our next-door neighbors. Father started work driving his truck. Two months later, we bought new furnishings for our house. Father was working full time, four days on and three days off, because he had to wait for loading and unloading.

After a short while, he decided to buy a taxi. While he was waiting for the truck to load and unload, he drove his taxi. Father had two jobs now. He bought a good television and two new bicycles for me and Qader. Qader and I went to *konaforoshy* (the secondhand market) to sell our old bicycles. A lot of people made offers. We sold them to the highest bidder. In Afghanistan at that time, 85 percent of the men used bicycles. If you looked at the roads during the rush hours, you would see very few cars. That's why many people in Afghanistan were fit. Now we had a good life. Father was happy with his jobs. I went to my school regularly, and boxing and Koran classes. I drove Father's taxi sometimes around our street with him sitting next to me. We were enjoying our life and began to have hopes and dreams.

Then the fighting started again. All hopes were shattered. No more peace, no more love. No one wanted the fighting. Each home, the city, the people were tired of war. Everyone was praying for their own safety. Our family already knew how terrible war could be. This time it was Mazer-i-Sharif City's turn. This time it was not between Shia and Sunni Muslims. This time it was a group of people called Taliban. They were fighting against everyone. Father sold his taxi right away in case we needed to leave the city quickly. One afternoon, he came home and said, "The Taliban are very close to the city."

Next day he didn't go to work. We heard some shooting outside. By the afternoon, the shooting got worse. Our neighbors had a basement, so we went there. The men were sitting by the door, the women a little further in. I asked Father, "Is this the same as happened in Kabul? Do you remember, in Kabul, you told me the shooting was all about somebody's wedding party?"

He said, "That time you were a little boy. I just said that to make you happy. Now you are older, you can tell for yourself what is going on."

After two days of fighting, the Taliban took over most places in Mazar-i-Sharif. They killed more than one thousand innocent people and destroyed hospitals, mosques, businesses, and even roads. Mazar-i-Sharif City had been very beautiful before they arrived.

A week after the Taliban came, Father and I went to the Sakhijan (mosque). There were too many Talibs around there, even outnumbering the civilians. More than twelve thousand Taliban came to Mazar City. They dressed mainly in black. They kept their hair and beards very long. They looked very serious and very scary. They wore large black or white turbans. The weather was hot, and they were overdressed and smelled like dead dogs. They were armed with a variety of old and new weapons. I was very afraid of them because I'd heard that they were very dangerous. Father stayed at home and could not go to work since they came, because we were Shia.

Three weeks later, shooting and rocketing began again, worse than before. I had never seen anything like that in my life. We were altogether in the basement of our neighbor's house. The explosions and gunfire and the whistling of shells overhead terrified everyone. Poor Qader was terribly frightened. It reminded him of when his family had been killed. At one time, I thought he was going to run out of the basement, and I tried to keep his attention. Later, when things quieted down, he just sat on the floor, rocking himself back and forward, back and forward. He wouldn't talk. I don't think he could hear anything either. We were stuck there for twenty-four hours. It was dangerous even to go to the washroom.

The Afghan militia had let the Taliban come to Mazar-i-Sharif City. Then they closed the border behind them. The Taliban were in Mazar-i-Sharif, but they had nowhere else to go. They were stuck there. Later when we went back to our own home, we found a lot of bullets in our yard, and all our windows had been blown out.

CHAPTER 8

ANOTHER JOURNEY

Twelve thousand Taliban were killed in less than twenty-four hours. Their bodies were left lying all around the city. Father had to go out to get us food. There had been no sound of fighting for several days, so he decided to take a chance, and I insisted on going with him. We saw a lot of Taliban dead all over the place. The whole city smelled terrible. If the Taliban smelled bad when they were alive, they smelled ten times worse when they were dead because of the heat. Father bought me a mask right away and another for himself. On the way home, we heard a rumor about someone who was searching a Taliban's pockets and found three hundred U.S. dollars and a little note saying, "If you have killed five Shia Muslims, you will go to heaven."

A week later, the international police took all the bodies to another place, about a hundred and fifty kilometers north of the city. I heard from a neighbor, he said that they made three or four mass graves, and buried the Taliban there. They dropped bodies into the pits they had dug one after another.

The beautiful clean city center was no more. It now was an ugly ruined place. Building had been burned down. The remaining houses were falling down. The shelling of the stupid Taliban had devastated the beautiful flowers and trees. It was much worse than Kabul. Three weeks later, Father, Qader, and I went to see what was going on with our school. It was shut down. We came home very quickly. Father said, "I have to work, I haven't time to teach you guys anything. Your Mom has not had enough education, but you guys can study here together."

There was still some fighting between the Taliban and the Afghan militia. Father's friend Wahid and his family came to our house for a meal one night. Wahid said, "The Taliban will keep fighting until they take over the city again."

Father answered, "We have land and a house in Ghazni province. It is a pretty remote place. We can go and live there until things become safe again. I've been there, through the mountains, not so long ago, so I know the way. What do you say? It's too dangerous to live here, and Qader is suffering badly. He's a nervous wreck. We have to go to Ghazni because it's the only safe place."

They decided it was the best plan.

We got ready to go with Father's friend. Mom and Wahid's wife made a massive amount of food. Father brought our truck, and we packed all our useful things and gave away a lot of stuff to neighbors because there was not enough space in the truck to take everything. We finished packing the next day and went to Wahid's house. We spend two days getting ready to leave Mazar-i-Sharif.

It was Monday when we were finally ready.

Father said, "Everybody, for the last time, we need to go the Sakhijan (mosque) just to ask Allah to be with us and help us to get safely to Ghazni."

We went there, and Father gave some donations to the very poor people sitting by the doors. There were a great many pitiful people there, the homeless, orphans, those who had lost their families, the poor, and the disabled, a lot of them without hands or legs.

We went for the last time to the northwest corner, where there was a big space for the doves, all pure white birds. Qader and I had been there often to play with them. They were very tame. They sat all over you if you had taken food to their place.

We left Mazar-i-Sharif early next day after prayers. Our truck was some kind of converted water tanker, green in color. It had three seats in the front; a bed at the back of the cab, behind the driver's seat. There was plenty of space on the roof for some of us to sit. Father and Wahid and his wife and Mom sat in front seats. Wahid had two boys. One was older than I was, the other was younger, and also a beautiful little girl. We would be sitting outside on top of truck all the way Ghazni City.

The first few days I was so excited. Everything was new to me. We only traveled during daylight. Our food was finished by the end of the first week. We only had some rice, oil, flour, water, and tea left. On the way to Ghazni, there were few shops on those mountain roads, and they were very expensive.

Each evening before sunset, Father or Wahid, whoever was driving, pulled over somewhere where the land was flat. We had put up two canopies; one was for us on one side of the truck, the other on the other side for Wahid's family. Father said we needed to make food. Qader and I went to collect some firewood and then lit a fire. Mom boiled water and started to cook some rice. Father found two big flat stones, which we washed and stood them on either side of fire. Mom made dough and put it on top of the stones and made some bread. So we had rice and fresh naan bread for dinner in the mountain. We had not eaten for twenty-four hours, so the bread smelled wonderful and tasted delicious.

On another day we finished the water. That was the hardest time we ever had, being thirsty. Father pulled over. We went to search for water with plastic and metal containers, all in different directions. Eventually we found a spring of fresh cold water and filled all our containers.

Further on our way. The road became very steep. "We will all need to walk because the truck may not able to make the climb. Wahid will drive the truck. We're not sure if we can get over this pass. It's not safe for us," Father said.

The road was nothing more than a rough track. I don't think it was used often. It became very steep, and everyone climbed down off the truck. The way ahead was a series of short roads with sharp bends that zigzagged up the mountainside toward the pass. The pass was the lowest point in the mountain range where we could climb out of one valley into the next. Wahid knew what to do. He put the engine into the lowest gear and started the climb. The truck made some terrible complaining noises, and every so often there was a scattering of stones from the back wheels as the tires tried to grip the track surface. We all had to keep well out of the way. We were told to sit down at the bottom of the climb and wait until the truck reached the top, and then we were to climb up to the top ourselves. But the four children and I decided to clamber up the steep slopes to get ahead and see what the view was like over the next valley. On the climb, we saw lizards and then a few snakes. They were as afraid of us as we were of them, and they moved away quickly.

Eventually the truck made it and stopped at the top to wait for Mom and Wahid's wife to come up.

The countryside was wild, with many ranges of mountains. It was also very beautiful because of the moving clouds, their shadows swept across the valleys, changing the shapes and colors of everything all of the time. Often in the sky there flew large graceful birds, which seemed sometimes to hang in the air, wings outstretched just circling. At night there were millions of stars, large and small, and a white moon, which seemed to move across the sky, plowing its way through the occasional clouds. In the low valleys, the land appeared good because the local people looked after it very well. Going from one valley to another over mountain passes for many days, we began to think we would never get to Ghazni. Every mountain and every valley began to look the same as the last mountain and valley. Overall I did not like travelling through the mountains, but Father said we did not have any choice. This was the only way to stay alive.

Our skin was not used to being exposed to weather. We had been sitting on top of the truck while it was moving, we had not felt the heat of the sun because of the cold breeze, which was strong. We all looked terrible. Our skin was burned. In the small wing mirror of the truck, I studied my face. I looked very dark and wild.

One day we stopped on open land. We found waterfalls.

"All men are going to take a shower. The women can bathe later and just wash their faces for now, and make some food until we come back. We will stay here for two or three days. We all need to take a rest after a long journey. It is sunny and warm day," Father said.

We stayed there and had a lovely time, swimming and showering, in the ice-cold mountain water. We notice there were some houses a distance away. Father and Wahid decided to go there to see if they had some food for sale. They went there the next day early in the morning and came back in the afternoon with a little lamb. They killed it, and we made kebabs. We had a cassette player in the truck, so got it out and played some music. It was a good party. We were all happy with the lamb kebabs and rice and some fruit. We all enjoyed it very much. After dinner, Qader and Wahid's oldest son said they were going for a walk. "Qader and your son are becoming close friends," Father said.

"Yes indeed," answered Wahid.

The boys went off to explore the countryside. I decided to take a shower, after a while the water was very cold. It felt very good. Father and Wahid were busy doing something with the truck. I lay down my head on my mom's knee, I was tired. Mom massaged my head. I don't know how long I was asleep. When Father called Mom, I woke up when she moved her knee. When I opened my eyes, the sun already had set. Father was calling Mom to make some food before it got dark. When the food was almost ready, Father told me to go to call Qader and Vally. "Tell them to come and eat, and tell them they'll have plenty of time tomorrow for exploring!"

"OK," I said. Atiq called me to wait a second because he wanted to go with me. We went to find the boys. We walked for about ten to fifteen minutes and could not find them. We shouted out loudly several times, calling their names. There was no answer. The sun was setting behind the hills, so we went back to the truck and said we could not find them.

"We don't know which way they've gone. There are a lot of hills all similar," we said.

Wahid pointed and said, "Go that way, probably they went that way." Atiq did not come this time. I went by myself. I couldn't find them. It was getting scary because there were noises of scuffling among the dark tall grass. When I came back, Father told me, "Eat your food. They will come when it really gets dark, they will see our lanterns."

We had our dinner. It was lamb kebabs, very tasty and delicious. It got darker and darker. Qader and Vally did not show up. Wahid's wife said, "I'm getting worried. Could you do something, Wahid, please?" He looked at my father and said, "We'll go after tea."

"OK," said my father.

By the time Wahid finished his tea, it was very dark all over. Wahid and Father took a flashlight each. Father told us to go inside the cab and close the windows. He said, "It might take an hour or two."

They went to look for the boys. They came back shortly. They couldn't find them. Vally's mom and my mom were praying for them. They went again and couldn't find them. They went again but were scared of the animals around the mountains. By the time they came back again, I had fallen asleep.

Early in the morning when I woke up, Father and Wahid were not around. I asked Mom where they were. Mom said, "They left a short while ago."

"Where've they gone?" I asked. "Looking for Qader and Vally?"

Mom made some breakfast for us. Father and Wahid showed up around midday. They looked very worried and nervous. Still they could not find Qader and Vally.

Wahid said, "They've gotten lost."

After lunch they went to the village where they bought the sheep to ask if anyone knew anything about the boys. Father and Wahid came back. They hadn't found them.

"Nobody knows where they have gone or what has happened to them," Father said.

CHAPTER 9

KOLBOWRY

It had been a whole day since Qader and Vally went missing. Father said, "We need to go to that village to ask for help."

Father, Wahid, and I went there. He paid money for six men, who knew all the mountains and the jungle, to search for the boys. There was an old man in the village who said there are some very dangerous animals in the mountains.

"A year ago, when our shepherd lost three sheep, he went looking for them, but he couldn't find them. Three days later we found them dead; they had been eaten by wild animals. We found only the skeletons in a different area. I hope nothing has happened to the boys."

After three and a half days, they had not found anything. We were all very worried, having heard the old man's story.

Father said, "We are not going anywhere until we have found Qader and Vally." We all agreed.

The people, who have been paid to search for the boys, found a watch and necklace. The watch belonged to Vally, and the necklace belonged to Qader. Mom remembered the necklace. "This is the necklace I bought for him. When we were in Mazar-i-Sharif, Qader was grieving a lot for his family, so one day I decided to take him to the Sakhijan. I told the Molla all about him. He suggested that I should buy the necklace. It has a *Davize* (a verse from the Koran) on it. The Molla said, 'This necklace will take Qader's mind away from thinking about his family,' and I told Qader he must wear it all the time."

My mom was crying and holding it to her chest.

Two hours later somebody found the boys' remains. The men who found them said, "The boys were attacked in different places by dangerous animals. Their shoes were left there, and some pieces of clothes. Nothing much was left of their bodies, only bones in different places."

We were all very shocked at this news. Mom and Wahid's wife both screamed and were crying. Father and Wahid and other people from the village went and collected almost every part of the boys' remains. They would not let me go anywhere near. Everyone was crying and shouting to Allah, asking why it happened to our poor boys. Vally's mom was hitting herself and talking to Allah and saying, "Oh, my son. Oh, my dear. Why did you take my lovely son? I want him back, Allah. You should not take him now. I can't live without my poor son." Then she was blaming his father, Wahid. "You did this, this is your fault."

Wahid said, "It wasn't my fault, it was yours."

Vally's parents were blaming each other.

Father shouted, "This is not the time for you to be fighting with each other. Let's think what to do next."

Wahid's wife said, "We'll take Vally's body with us."

"Where to?" Father asked.

"I don't know," she said, "Wherever we go."

Wahid said to her, "Could you please calm down, there are things we have to do."

Father said, "We need two white cloths."

Mom went to search in our truck and brought out two white shirts, one for Qader, the other for Vally. She sewed by hand all around the shirts and handed them to father.

"Everybody needs to come and help us to bury two young boys," Father said.

The people of the village came. About fifteen men, all dressed in a very dark *Prahan tomban* (the Afghan traditional clothes, like a very long shirt and a very large trousers.), their clothes were very old, faded, and patched. They were very upset. They also brought food and water and pick axes and spades to dig in the rocky ground.

The old man seemed to know the burial rites. He did the ceremonies. Father spoke about Vally and then about Qader and his family. The people bowed their heads and listened to Father's speech. Some of us cried. Father finished. His face was wet with tears.

We buried our boys in a very sad little grave, and Father put up a stone for each of them.

On Qader's stone he wrote, "My name is Qader. I was born in Kabul. My family was killed by Sunni fighters. I found my uncle. He took me to

Mazar-i-Sharif to survive. The Taliban came and killed a lot of people. We left to go to Ghazni City. When I almost reached my destination, I was attacked by dangerous animals in these mountains."

I couldn't read what Wahid wrote for his son. We all were very sad. We forgot about our food.

At midday, Father said, "It will take six or seven days to reach our destination. We'll stay here one more night, for the boys, as a memorial to them and to pray for them."

He bought another sheep for food for us, and we stayed up all night long, praying for the boys, asking Allah for forgiveness.

It was early at sunrise when we continued our journey. Atiq and I were sitting on top of the truck.

On that first day, I felt so lonely. I began to think about my two best friends, Qader and Vally. We had had a lot of good fun when they were alive, sitting beside us, outside on the truck. We used to play games together and tell about funny things that had happened to our parents or us and about our school. Now I missed them so very much. I was crying inside myself and thinking about Qader. I remembered when he had arrived with Father in Mazar-i-Sharif. I was jealous of him sometimes when my parents gave nice gifts to him and Father put his arm around him. Sometimes I did not treat him very well, but he was always with me, like a brother. He was always by my side when I was fighting or arguing at school or home. He was a good friend even when I was not nice to him, but I did not realize it at the time. Now he was gone, never to come back. My mind seemed to make me remember every unkind thing I had ever said to him and every mean trick I had done on him. What came into my mind was something our teacher at the Koran class had once said, it was "Remember, have respect for all humanity, men, women, and even children. Remember one thing, especially at this time, when there is fighting and killing all over Afghanistan, don't ever treat anybody wrongly, because you may never find time to ask them for forgiveness."

That was really true. Now, I couldn't ask Qader to forgive me. I was really angry with myself. I did not eat for two days. I was dreaming about him sometimes. It is very hard when you lose your close friend.

Father was concerned that I was not eating. He took me a little away from the others. "It's been bad since Qader's death, for all of us. We did our best to keep him happy, and changed his life to good. Now he has gone. We'll pray for him and his family. You need to eat now. I don't want something to happen to you. Please, I beg you, my son, eat some food. I will promise you, I will take you back there, one day, to Qader's grave, to pay your respects," Father said.

I went with Father, and I had my food.

A week later, in the evening, we arrived at our destination. It was a village in the mountains an hour and a half from Ghazni City, about sixteen miles over many hills. The village was called Kolbowry. It was a disorderly sprawl of about thirty one-story houses. Because the road conditions were very bad, it took hours to get anywhere. It also meant that we were going to be far away from all emergency services, and the police, school, shops, markets, and so on. There was no electricity, no sign of a telephone, and not even a post office.

Our farm, Father said, was outside the village, halfway up a hill. He was talking while he was driving. From what I could see, and I could see everything from our perch on top of the truck, there seemed to be nothing but hills. Hills, valleys, and very high mountains.

He was telling us all where to look to see the farm, but I could not make it out. It turned out that he was not heading toward the farm. He was going toward his uncle's house. We drove down a very bumpy track, which threatened to break the truck's axels, and we arrived at a very old, long, low, rectangular building with walls a meter thick. It was made of mud bricks and timber, and had a flat roof. It seemed that all the buildings in the area where similar to this one. The color of everything appeared to be a light dusty beige-brown, now tinged with orange, because the sun was setting. The moon was already up, and many stars were beginning to show themselves.

Father sounded the horn as we came up to the front of the farmhouse. When we stopped, people appeared from a small a door, and there was a great deal of fuss. It seemed that everyone came out to greet us, and there was laughter and chattering as we introduced Wahid and his family. The welcome was warm and genuine, despite the fact that Father had been unable to let anyone know that we were coming. My father's uncle and his family were delighted to see us, as they did not get many visitors from the outside world. He was a tall balding man, about fifty, going a little fat around his middle. He had a kind smile, as he shook my hand solemnly when we were introduced. Father had told me that he was a very religious man, and could be called a *Haji* (meaning that when he was younger he had been on pilgrimage to Mecca).

In Afghan homes, the *samovar* is always on (it is like a large ornamental kettle with a tap on the front) with boiling water for making chai (tea).

With typical traditional hospitality, it was taken for granted that we would stay the night, even if it meant that some of us were going to have to sleep in the barn. As is normal, the women all got together in the large working room toward the back of the house. Because of the extreme heat in the summer, the "kitchen" is outside at the back of the house. It usually has only two walls and a flat roof. This is so a wind can blow away the smoke and the heat from the primitive stove and oven. Water is heated in a large metal container built next to the oven, so the fire does several jobs.

The men kept to the living room. There were long mattress like cushions along each wall, where they all sat or reclined. Chai appeared right away, and sweets were passed around. Food was prepared swiftly. Fresh naan bread was thrown onto the sides of the oven, and the smell wafted into the room. We were made to feel at home. The warmth of the welcome was too much for Wahid's wife, whom we heard bursting into a storm of tears in the next room. Mom was also very upset, and I could hear her as she explained the cause of the sadness, and related the whole story in the kitchen. Father gave an account of the tragedy to the men folk and had to explain why we had traveled through the Hindu Kush. This developed into a discussion of politics and questions about the fighting and Kabul, the Taliban, and the dire state of the country. And on to Iran and Iraq. Normally the children stayed with the women, and Atiq went to them, but I was allowed to stay with Father because he wanted to show me off to the family. I was very happy about that. The trouble was I was shy. When I was spoken to, I did not know what to say. I just hung my head and waited for the attention of the room to go to someone else. Among the young men at my uncle's house was my cousin, Abbas. He was about five foot nine, with good strong shoulders, and very slim. His hair was very black and thick, and it had a shine of its own. He kept his beard like a Talib. It was so dark it seemed to sparkle. He was aged about eighteen or nineteen. What attracted me to him was that he looked like me. He worked outdoors on the farm, and the sun had given his skin a dark healthy glow. It looked very much like the way my complexion went when I played out in the sun all day. But when it happened to me, my mom did not like it. She wanted me to be of a pale color, and members of her family made remarks about her little black boy. Looking around that room, I realized that all the other young men looked the same. I felt I had discovered something important. They were all Bayats. They were all slim, tall, and dark, and happy to be so. I was the same. I am a Bayat.

Abbas was particularly kind to me because he saw my shyness and talked naturally to me so that I lost most of it. I instantly knew that I liked him. It was all very pleasant. I was pleased to be among the adults. Later, I began to get drowsy during the talking, and in my head I was back riding on the top of the truck, or eating kebabs or qand. I fell asleep. I don't remember where I slept that night.

The next day we had early morning prayers, then we all got back into the truck and went to find our new home.

The farm was on the side of a hill in a remote area. Like Father's uncle's house, it was a long low one-storey structure, with thick walls small windows and a flat roof. There was a slope up to the front door, while the back of the house seemed to be built into the hillside. It had a lot of rooms and the kitchen outside at the back. There were other smaller buildings all around. They all looked the same as the house. There was an overgrown vegetable garden with apple trees, all with red apples growing on them. Instead of wells from which to get water, we had a fast-running water supply in the form of a narrow canal built of stone, which diverted very cold water from further up the mountains. This water was used for everything, drinking, cooking, washing, cleaning, and bathing. It was part of an ancient irrigation system, which had been built hundreds of years ago. It brought a precious supply of water down to an arid land. There is evidence that many such systems were once widely in place all over Afghanistan, but civil wars, the Russian occupation, and neglect has caused them to be very badly damaged. As there was constant hot sunny weather, except in winter, the farmers were able to grow a variety of crops. The soil was poor however. An old relative had been living at the farm until he died, which had been a few months before we arrived. He had taken care of the place as best he could. The young women of his extended family had taken it in turns to go to the farmhouse and do the housework and cook his food and do his washing, so the house was in reasonably good shape. My mother had been worried about what she would find when we got there. She thought it had been empty for a long time. When we arrived, we unpacked the truck of all our belongings, but Wahid said that he had not decided what he was going to do, so his things were left packed up.

Mom soon took the house in hand. She laid out all the bedding to air on the flat roof or hung it on the clotheslines that were in the yard. She was promising to give everything a good wash as soon as she could.

If the house was in a fairly good condition, the rest of the area was not. Father and Wahid went on a tour to inspect the area nearest the house. He made me tag along and pointed out just how much land we had. To me, it just seemed to be kilometers of dry light brown earth and scrub. Along the edges of the narrow canals, where the water raced shady trees grew, but some of the channels were broken or blocked. I was a city boy, and my eyes did not know what we were looking at.

When we had left Kabul and went to Mazar-i-Sharif, I had missed my old home and wanted to go back there. When I went to work at the market, at the age of eleven, I learned a lot about how hard life was for poor people. I learned some pretty amazing words as well. Here in the country I was about to be further educated. I was a city boy in a very rural area. In Mazar, we had had a television when we could afford it. Here there wasn't even electricity. In the city, there were shops and a market and some social gatherings. Here, the mosque was the only center of activity, and that was in the village, half-an-hour's walk away. (It was not just for religious services, it was a large room, which was always kept heated in the bitterly cold winters, and all the men met there to gossip, joke, and grumble, because a lot of them could not afford to heat their homes.) Everything here was back in time. People here were doing exactly the same things, day in day out, that their parents and grandparents had done before them. There were a lot of things I was going to have to learn about life in the country.

During the next week, our relatives and neighbors came over to see us, as they got to hear of our arrival. They all knew my father very well, he had grown up there. It would normally have been a good excuse for a big party. Afghans love a party. Traditionally it is a large family get-together. All the family, men, women, children, and even babies go to the gathering. Chai (tea) is the main beverage. The men sit at the front of the large room, and the women and children at the back or even in another room. Food is served, and then there is dancing. That means that the men form a large circle and dance solo. I could tell everyone was disappointed that there was to be no party. However, Father decided to have an assembly to pray for the dead, a *fateha* (memorial party), and he invited about a hundred people. This meant that lots of my young cousins were kept busy delivering invitations to relations, some of which lived great distances away. The children knew the quickest and safest ways to travel. Some of them thought nothing of walking around carrying heavy guns and would sometimes take a shot at a distant rabbit without giving anyone any warning.

As the day of the gathering drew near, Father said that I would have to act as one of the people who would meet our guests when they arrived, because it was traditional for the eldest son to do that job. I was very happy about this. He said that my cousin Abbas was coming over to help out. He and I were to stand at the front door, greeting people with respect, and giving directions. On the day of the event, there were a lot of relatives I did not know, but Abbas introduced them to me, and everything was going well. Later, however, they started to ask me a lot question about the boys. The pain of that tragic journey came rushing back. I was missing my best friends, Qader and Vally, a lot. Abbas noticed that I was getting upset and steered me away from them. We had very good speeches and prayers, and finished by reading the Koran for them.

Two weeks later, Wahid said that he and his family were going to his brother's house, which was three or four hours from our farm. Father asked them, "Please stay with us. We have enough land that can support both families if we farm it together, and we can enjoy our lives. You can help me. I can help you."

"Thank you. You are such a wonderful man, and we appreciate all your kindness. We will keep in touch with each other even if I have to buy homing pigeons. We're going to see my brother. I haven't seen him for eight years. If there are any problems or there is not enough room for us, I will contact you," Wahid said.

Next day, Father drove Wahid and his family to his brother's house and dropped off all his goods.

CHAPTER 10

FARM LIFE

Father sold his truck and bought five sheep (two male and three females,) a donkey, two oxen, a cow, and three baby calves. He paid my cousin Abbas for a couple of months to take care of our new animals and help us when he was free. He came one day with a sheep dog called Jak. He presented him to me, saying that Jak would come in handy for the sheep and to mind the house, and that he was a working dog, "So *don't* spoil him!"

We had arrived in the middle of summer, which is not the best time to start farming. "Before we know it, it'll be winter, and we won't be able to do anything," Father said. "We should have been here in the spring to get the seeds in the ground for summer harvest."

He decided on two things. First, he would have to sell some more of the trees to get enough money to see us through until spring. Second, he would plant some crops that would grow quickly, and that we could harvest before the weather changed.

The farming work was quite hard for me because I was not old enough and because I didn't know what I was doing. Not only was there the plowing, digging, and planting, but also there were many other jobs because the whole farm had been neglected for a few years. We could not keep up with all the tasks and worked every day of the week, from dawn till darkness, when I crawled home exhausted, to eat a late dinner and go achingly to bed.

There were fences to repair, ditches and waterways to clear out, walls to build. Branches to be lopped off trees, and stone clearing from the fields. That job never seemed to end. It was backbreaking work because I was bending down all the time. I seemed to clear mounds of stones from an area one week, only for there to be masses of them there again the following week. Was there some evil spirit throwing the stones back there at night to torment me?

I don't know which job was the hardest. Trying to manage the oxen for the plowing was difficult because, they have no brains and were much stronger than me and wouldn't do what I wanted them to do. Trying to get them to go in anything like a straight line when we were plowing was impossible. They were docile enough, most of the time, to harness or lead about, but it needed two of us, Abbas and me, to do the plowing, one leading the animals and the other trying to hold down the old plow to break up the ground.

We had to grow food, such as grains, carrots, potatoes, leeks, garlics, onions, coriander, cucumber, pepper, melon, and marrow, for ourselves, for food, and to sell, to get money to buy things that we could not produce, such as tea, clothes, tools, and oil, for the lamps and heater, and all kinds of other equipment.

We settled into a farming life, which was dependent on the seasons. Summer was vibrant and very hot. Every tree bush and plant grew amazingly quickly, considering the arid conditions of the soil. The whole countryside was alive with all kinds of insects that buzzed and hummed and flew in swarms, Jak would try to catch the insects in his mouth but could not. He did manage to get stung at different times by something and ran around yelping. And there were butterflies, which flashed bright colors against the dry gold of the small wheat field, and many kinds of birds migrated in.

The dawn seemed to break at three in the morning, while the moon and stars were still in the sky. But always there was work and the heat. It was in the summer that we harvested and stored our crops.

In the fall, we were really busy collecting and storing vegetable and fruit, and we had to gather firewood for the winter. I did not know how to collect the firewood quickly, but my cousin Abbas taught me. I didn't like doing it, but I had no choice. He told me often, "If you live in this village, you have to learn some basic farming to stay alive."

I did not take any notice of him. I was busy trying to get some fun into my life. Time passed much quicker when we had fun. We liked each other's company. I don't know what it would have been like if Abbas had not come to work with me.

His ambition was to go to Iran to work. He was the third youngest son in his family, and he knew his eldest brother would inherit their farm at some time, so he wanted to get away and start his own life. He could be very serious sometimes. He liked reading. He would read anything he could get his hands on, although that did not amount to much. He was very interested in the Koran. He said that the holy book is very important in Afghanistan, especially in the countryside, because Afghanistan is wild and very mountainous. In most places there is no real law. Where there are police and officials, they are mostly corrupt. In many areas they do not exist. There is nothing to stop rich and powerful people doing whatever they like. The strong can dominate the weak. It is only the strong fear and respect held by everyone, for religion and the rules laid down, that makes the would-be tyrant think twice. The Koran is not just a holy book with a list of dos and don'ts; it is a real guide book to simple societies such as our rural one, where law and order did not exist.

From the way Abbas spoke about his Koran, I think he really would have liked to get away to the city to study, but he had no money and so could not, but it upset me when he talked about going. I said I would go with him. He laughed because his age was somewhere around twenty, and he thought of me as a kid.

We had very cold weather during the winters and lots of snow. Farming was not possible. We often saw snow on the tops of the mountains at different times during the year, but the winter snow was different. It seemed to happen instantly. One day it was fall, the next day it was winter because the snow had fallen heavily overnight, and everything was changed completely. Everywhere looked different. Everything had changed shape. Everywhere was pure bright whiteness, and silent. Trees looked black and bare against snow, and in the daytime the sky had never looked bluer. At night the moon was pale and huge, and the stars shone like massive diamonds against the black velvet sky. The air was so clear and cold that it bit your nose when you breathed in, and when you breathed out your breath came out in clouds. Your fingers froze in an instant, and the water had turned to ice. Our dog, Jak, hated the snow. It was too deep for him, although sometimes he would roll about in it and end up getting very wet and bedraggled. Then he would shake himself frantically and go and find a place in front of the kitchen fire and lie down to get dry. There is no worse smell than a dirty wet dog steaming in front of a fire.

After we had fed the animals we were keeping inside, there was nothing else to do. Father got busy shoveling, but each day he'd have to do it all again.

Sometimes Abbas and I went with the boys from the village further up the mountain for skidding. We would go very early in the morning. Abbas showed me how to cut old carpet, wood or thick plastic sheeting with a sharp knife, to make rough sledges. We needed them for the skidding. We would drag our sledges to some high place, where there was plenty of thick snow; we would take a run, throw our sledges down, and jump onto them. We went down very fast. It was great fun. We all liked doing it.

Then we would go home and have some breakfast. Later in the day, we congregated somewhere around our village and divided into two groups. We made some snow men and went around to see who had made the best one, or the funniest. We had another game called snow fighting. This was amazing fun. We all loved it. We were chasing and hitting each other with snowballs. We all enjoyed the game and forgot to go home for lunch. Sometimes our parents would come looking for us. We were hungry but did not like to go home because we were having such a good time. They insisted that we went home and ate. We would go and eat very quickly and come back and restarted the game and played it all day long, until it got dark.

Sometimes Father would go down to the mosque/meeting house and talk with other farmers, the weather stopped them from doing much else and they were bored. Occasionally he joined with some of the other men, and they all put a little money together and bought a lamb from him. They killed it and made good kebabs with half of it. The other half, they were going to use to bait a trap.

They labored to dig a pit in the earth about three meters deep, just like a little well. They did this if the ground wasn't frozen. Then they covered the top of it with black plastic sheets and some earth, and then they placed the remains of the sheep in the middle of the sheeting. They made the place look natural. This made a good trap for the wild animals that came into the village at night scavenging for food. Every night four men would stay awake and go out to check the trap from time to time. Any animal that came to eat that sheep (mainly foxes or wolves) would fall down into the pit. The men would go to the trap and shoot it with their *kalashnikovs* (Russian rifles). If they caught one, the following days they would skin it and keep the pelt until they had several of them, then somebody would go to Ghazni City and sell them for a good price. Then the men would have a good party.

There was little or no income in the winter. People did not have a lot to eat. They had only enough to keep themselves alive. You ate whatever you had saved from the food grown during the summer months. It was about this time that I notice a great change in my father. He was becoming harder. He strained his back a couple of times and could not do hard work, and this angered him. So did the poverty, the weather, the hunger, and the remoteness. Nobody really liked living there, but we couldn't go anywhere else because of the war. Everyone had problems, but there was no one, government or militia, to ask for help.

One of the more serious growing problems was the Taliban rationing, especially during the winter. The Taliban had now taken over the government of the country. They followed a very extreme set of ideas, which they said were all written in the Koran and so were Allah's holy laws. They were also Sunni Muslim, they hated all Shia Muslims. Our village was Shia. They would not allow Shias to buy food. During their regime, Shia Muslims had no rights or power. Jobs in the government were given only to Sunni Muslims. Shias were treated as inferiors. The Taliban did not even accept them as being Afghan. They decreed that Shia should go to live in Iran, because Iran is a Shia Muslim country. The era of the Taliban was bad for Shias but good for Pashton Sunni Muslims. Some of them became rich because they brought food from their lands and sold it at very exorbitant prices to the poor Hazara people. They made a very good business out of the misery of the starving millions. Hazara people are of Chinese extraction and have a distinct physical appearance, and so are easily identifiable. They are also Shia Muslim. Ghazni is populated by many Hazaras. They were cruelly persecuted by the Taliban. That is how it was. If life was hard in the country, it was much harder for people in the towns and cities.

On the farm the seasons came and went. I enjoyed the winters because of my age. Then came the spring, and the cycle began again with digging and planting and lambing. Then it began to get hotter, and summer was on its way.

One fall, Father and I were under the apple trees, in the shade, taking a break for something to eat. I was lying on one side, propped up on my elbow, eating an apple. He sat on an old plastic chair, looking at me. And Jak was lying close by, with his long tongue out, panting away. It was a scorching hot day, and there wasn't even the slightest breeze. It was far too hot to work. We should have gone to bed and come back later and worked in the cool evening. Father seemed to be thinking hard and kept looking at me for a several minutes and then, "You're getting older now," he said suddenly. "Ali, I want you to know, I am sorry you can't go to any kind of school. You should. I'd hoped that Ghazni City would have been peaceful, but it's getting as bad as everywhere else, besides we can't go to the city and live because there's no work there, and it isn't safe. What I'm trying to say is things are getting more difficult for everyone, every day. We're going to have to struggle through these times and pray that things will get better in the future. But right now, things are going to get harder. Many thousands of people have been killed, and millions have left the country and are living in tents in Iran and Pakistan. We are alive and can live here safely because this place is remote. You are young for this work, but you will be a good farmer one day if you put your mind to it. In the winter, I will really try to help you with your education."

Things did get harder, and it began to increase the change in him. When I was younger, he loved me as a child. Now I was older and bigger, I was a body to clothe and a mouth to feed, and I was probably not as cute to look at as I was when I was little. It was the sheer daily hard work that changed him. Sometimes, he and Mom didn't even speak to each other for many hours at a time, and when they did talk, it was about the farm, always the farm.

One Friday afternoon, my cousin Abbas came over. He hadn't been around for a week. Friday was the day we went to the mosque for prayers, so we were at home that morning.

"I'm going to Iran the day after tomorrow," he said to Father. "I came to see all of you for the last time before I go. Only Allah knows if I will come back or not. Forgive me if I wasn't a good nephew or I couldn't be what you expected me to be."

"You helped us more than we could have asked for. You have always been a good nephew. Allah will be with you."

Then they got to talking, and Father asked him all about his intended journey and gave him advice about this and that. I had never liked it when he had talked about going to Iran because I did not want him to go. He had become a very good friend despite our age differences. I had secretly hoped that it was all just talk, but now that it was clear he was going, I felt lost. I would miss him very much.

Mom brought him a present. Father hugged him and said "Good-bye."

Then it was my turn. We said our good-byes, and I shook his hand and wished him luck, and then he left.

I went to my room. I felt sad. I started thinking about his going to Iran. "One day he will become an educated man, with a good future." Then I had an idea. "This could be a very good opportunity for me to go with him," I told myself.

Abbas had left our house only about ten minutes earlier. I ran into the yard, took my bicycle, and went after him. I rode as fast as I could. I wanted to catch him before he reached his house. I caught him up, behind his yard, and called to him to hold on. He stopped instantly as I got off my bicycle. I threw it down and shook his hand. "Salaam," I said.

"*Alikom Asalam* (hello to you)," he said.

"I would like go to Iran with you," I said.

He was surprised and laughed.

"Ali Jan, you're too young. How old are you, thirteen? fourteen? It would be very good to have you as a companion, but you need to think about it. What did your father say? Have you talked it over with him?

"I will do," I answered. "I didn't know that you were going until this afternoon, did I? I have just been thinking about it after you left. He will let me go because he wants me to have an education, and I will never get one here. I want to go because it is boring here, and I want a different life. We could have a good time together."

"You're not really old enough, and you'll need money," Abbas said.

"I have some savings hidden away, and I will get money from my father. He hasn't paid me for months," I said.

"You need to think about it seriously. I am not going for a holiday. I will have to find work, probably on a building site. You won't get much of an education on a building site, will you? You are not strong enough. You can't come back if you don't like it. You'd have to be able to earn your own living."

We stood there talking for a little while. I could see he was thinking it over as we talked, because he kept bringing up fresh points about things that might become problems. What if I was ill? What if I couldn't find a job? And so on. But I was lucky because we had always been good friends, and I managed to talk him round. At last he said, "You need to be ready and be in the village on Saturday at 6:00 a.m. to catch the early van to go to Ghazni. Then we have to get a van going from Ghazni to Iran. It's a long trip. Think it over. If you decide to come with me, we will not be coming back for at least a year because Iran is another country."

"Don't worry. I will be OK," I said. "I will look after myself."

"I have to tell you about all the problems, but it's up to you to decide. It will be pleasure to have your company, but I cannot be responsible for you. Have a good think about it. If you don't turn up on Saturday at six o'clock, I'll know you've changed your mind and aren't coming," he said.

"OK," I said. "See you Saturday morning."

I went home, but I did not know how to start to tell my parents about it. It was very hard to get everything ready for Saturday morning. I had only sixteen hours.

First, I went to my room and took the few good clothes I owned and packed them in bag. I packed two photos, one, which we had taken with

Qader and Wahid's family, the other one was of Father. He was in the middle of the photo, on one side was me, and on the other was Qader. We were in Mazar-i-Sharif City in front of the Sakhijan. When I looked at the picture, I remembered Qader very well. I imaged, if he was alive, he would come with me to Iran. I was weeping and sweating thinking about him.

Mom had noticed that I was in my room because I was supposed to be with Father. She called to me and asked what I was doing. "I am going to Iran," I called back.

"What?" Mom said.

"I am going to Iran," I said.

Mom laughed at me. "I'll come with you, we'll all go," she said.

She didn't believe me. I went out of my room; she was cleaning the house.

"Look, Mom, I am going to Iran with Abbas, on Saturday morning." She was still laughing at me.

"You are too young my son," she said.

"You will be happy when I'm gone. We have argued since I was born because you were expecting a girl but I was a boy. You hit me because I was *seyah* (black). You did not like me. You said you loved me once when Father went to Kabul. If I go to Iran, there will no one to argue with you anymore. You should be happy about that," I said.

She did not say anything. I went out to talk with Father. He was watering our apple trees, as I was approaching him he asked, "Where have you been?"

I forgot what I was going to say, so I just said, "Home." Then I said, "Can I talk to you for a moment?"

"*Baly* (Indeed)," he said.

"Do you remember you told me once that you would let me do what I liked?"

"Yes, I remember. What do you want? Go ahead," he said.

"I want go Iran with Abbas."

"You are much too young for that," he said.

"I will be OK," I said.

I told him about my talk with Abbas, and I waited for his answer. He was quiet for a minute then he said, "I will let you go for two reason, one, because in Afghanistan there is too much violence, and two, you may finish your schooling. But, son, how can you support yourself?" He stopped what he had been doing and turned to me. "I can't tell you to go or stay. It is all up to you. You can decide. By the way, did you talk to your mom about this?"

"Yes," I said.

"What did she say?" he asked.

"She seemed happy about it."

"Happy?" he said.

"You know we don't have a good relationship. Father, I will be OK. Just pray for me."

"Have you thought about when you will come back?"

"Yes, Father. I will come back soon."

Then we went home. After the dinner, I asked Father for some money. He told Mom to bring money for me. She brought only a little amount for me. She had always been mean like that since I was at school.

CHAPTER 11

THE RELUCTANT SHEPHERD

Father was tired. He had dozed off in the living room. I took the money and went to my room. That night, I couldn't sleep well because I was thinking a lot about my education, my ambitions, and about Iran and what it would look like. I woke up very early in the morning and took my bag and went to Father's room. I knocked the door. I heard Mom say, "The door is open," so I walked in. He was asleep. Mom was awake.

"Good morning," I said. She asked me to follow her to the living room because Father was asleep. As we left the room, Mom began to talk, and she said,

"What is going on? Why are you awake so very early?"

"I am leaving now. I just wanted say good-bye," I said excitedly.

"I know that you will not take any notice if I say 'don't go,' but I want talk to you about something because I may see you again or I may not. In this situation, I only know that you are going to leave, but I don't know when you will come back. Ali, why do you think that I don't love you? My son, my love, I am proud of you. I swear to God I love you. Look, I carried you in my stomach for nine months." Mom started crying. "I never hated you, my son. What mother doesn't love her child? I will really show you that I love you if you stay with us. I will find you a good wife once you get older."

"I've got to go to now. Mom, just pray for me. I will be OK." I kissed her right hand. "Good-bye," I said.

Mom walked with me to the main door.

"Allah is with you," she said.

When I walked away from her, she began to cry very loudly. I glanced behind me; she was sitting on the ground and continued weeping. Her tears did not bother me at that moment because I was dreaming about

Iran. Father was still asleep, so I didn't wake him. I started running down to the village. I was so excited. I was singing very loudly and could not believe that I was going to Iran.

There were only two vans a day that went from our village to Ghazni City. I got there exactly on time. Abbas was already sitting in the van. I got in.

"Salam," I said.

"I thought you were not coming," he said. I could tell he was happy to see me.

He went quiet for a moment. He checked over his shoulder to make sure there was nobody listening, and then he said, "I am going to tell you something, which is very important. If anyone asks you where you are going, say we are going to Neemrose City, OK? Because if we tell them Iran, there might be a problem with the Taliban. They don't like Iran."

"OK," I said.

We sat very quiet for a while, and the car was moving very slowly because the road condition was very bad. I was so excited; my mind was full of hope and dreams and good thoughts. While we were travelling, the driver played old Iranian music all the way to Ghazni City.

When the van arrived in Ghazni City center, we got out. The city was a melting pot of people from many different backgrounds and ethnic origins, such as Pashtons, Hazaras, Tajeks, Uzbicks, and others. People there were always on their guard, and bitterness and tension existed between all of the groups. Despite this, they had to find common ground to avoid further conflict. When we arrived there, it was very busy because lots of people were arriving from many of the surrounding villages at the same time. There were many handbarrows selling different kinds of hot food and fruit. People were buying and haggling over the prices a lot. Some venders were shouting, trying to sell their goods faster. Many shops and roads were under construction. There were no traffic lights working in the city, so many of the streets were congested. There were not many cars on the roads, but there were too many handbarrows, bicycles, and donkeys. People were moving their goods around. They were shouting, swearing, trying to go faster, and pushing each other without respect. Everyone was impatient, which caused lots of trouble. People fought on the streets, often for nothing. As usual in Afghanistan, the stronger people beat up the weaker. I had been away from city life for some years now, and all the people and all the different sights and sounds caused me to wander around wide-eyed with surprise while following Abbas. The weather was nice and warm, with a fresh wind, but the city was very noisy and smelled terrible because people threw their garbage anywhere. The Taliban government did not care about public health or safety. There was a man trying to cross the street with a little black donkey, which was carrying a very heavy load. The donkey was afraid of the noisy vehicles, with their blaring horns. She wouldn't cross the road. The man was hitting her with a stick on her bony rump. I was looking at the donkey and wondering what would happen if she did not cross, but Abbas grabbed my arm and said, "We have to find the car station for anything that is going to Kandahar City."

We found out that many cars and vans went to Kandahar. Different drivers asked different prices. We picked a van, agreed a price, and put our bags inside it. It was to leave in about ten minutes. Abbas and I went and bought some fruit. The driver called everybody to get in, so excitedly we took our seats. It was about to leave Ghazni, when I was surprised to hear my father calling my name. He was searching around, looking into the different cars and vans. He found me sitting next to Abbas and came over. He told me to get out of the van. I thought he was probably going to say good-bye or tell me something important. So I got out. He slapped my face and said, "Where are you going?"

"I told you last night I am going to Iran," I said surprised and embarrassed.

"Iran," he said.

He hit me several times. I was shocked and asked him what was going on.

He shouted to the driver and told him to drive away because I was not going.

Abbas got out of the van and asked. "Is he running away from home?"

"No, he is not going anywhere," Father said.

"Why you are hitting him? If he is not going, then there is nothing wrong," Abbas said.

"You can go if you want to, don't wait for him," Father said angrily.

The driver asked Abbas, "Are you going or not? If you're not, I'll take someone else."

"Please wait for me, I'm coming with you," I shouted.

"No," Father said.

I pleaded with him to let me go and cried. I took his hand and said, "Please let me go."

"No," he said.

"Look, Father, you told me I could do what I liked. Now I would like to go with Abbas."

"Forget what I said, you are not going," he said emphatically.

That was the first time Father had ever hit me.

Abbas said, "Ali Jan. I've got to go, I'll write to you."

I felt gutted as I watched the van move off. He was leaving without me.

Father took me back home. I did not eat that night. I kept to my room. I was so disappointed.

Next day, I did not go to work with Father. I went out of the house. In the garden near the apple trees, I had my little hiding place. It was only a little hole in the ground I replaced my money. "I will need it one day," I said to myself. Then I went back in the house.

Mom tried to explain why Father did not let me go to Iran. "He thought that when you told him you were going, it was all just talk, but he wanted to see what you would do. He was waiting for you to wake him up, and he was going to tell you not to go because it is dangerous and you are very young. We don't want anything happen to you. Your safety is very important to us. When you left, I came back inside the house. I was sad and cried. When he got up, he asked where you were. I told him you had gone. He left the house twenty minutes later. We would miss you very much if you went away."

After that incident, Father became very aggressive. Mom became the opposite. She became much kinder, like a real mom. I began to get closer to her than I had ever been. I began to dislike my father. I did not hate him. He had not let me go because he wanted a farm worker, without having to pay one. He expected me to work seventy or eighty hours a week, without taking a day off. Father never appreciated any thing I did, and never thanked me after that day. I did not know whom I should complain to. My situation was hopeless.

Two months later, Abbas managed to send a letter to his mom. Inside it there was another letter for me. She gave it to me when we were alone for a moment when she was visiting my mom. She said, "Abbas wrote telling me to give it to you without letting your father see it. He said to tell you to read it when you are alone."

I didn't need to be told that. I took the letter to my room. Inside was a pen. The letter read

Salam Ali Jan, how are you? I hope you are all right. If you are wondering about me and how am I doing, thanks to Allah I am doing very well. By the way I found a good job as a construction worker in Tehran City. I am happy with my job. I am just sending you this letter to give you my address in case you come to Tehran City one day, Inshallah (God willing). Here is the information about how I got here and how much money I spent.

Your Best Cousin, Abbas.

There was no telephone number just his address. I took the letter and hid it with my money. Later in the day, riding our short white donkey, and with Jak trotting by our side, I took the sheep to the mountain to graze. The donkey was very friendly. She was used to me. I had my little beautiful Koran safe in my pocket.

I picked out a good patch for grazing and decided to sit on top of a big flat gray boulder. We were on the side of one of the highest mountains in our region. As usual it was quite windy, but I liked the view of our village and other small farms below. It all looked so peaceful, but it was not pleasing to a restless teenager who wanted some kind of a life. The birds sang. The sun shone. Everywhere was green and smelled nice. The sky was ice blue, and the weather warm, but I was bored. Very, very bored.

I noticed one of our rams was chasing a ewe. He wanted to get over her back, right in front of me. I grabbed a stone and threw it and hit him, and shouted at him to stop, but he took no notice. Even the rams were having more fun than me.

Mom had packed a lunch for me, and as usual it consisted of some bread, two boiled eggs, and some vegetables. I was very hungry, so I had my lunch early, sitting on the rock, because I could see everything from up there.

While I was eating my lunch, I began thinking. I suppose I had been brooding about things for weeks, and Abbas's letter had made me more restless. I took a good look at myself. I was a very skinny youth with narrow shoulders, about fourteen years old, five foot ten tall, and my weight was about a hundred pounds. I had long black unkempt hair and green eyes. Most of the time I wore a very old vest/waistcoat, which had about ten pockets, and a long shirt, which went down to my knees, large trousers, and a white and black cloth about a meter and half long tied around my waist. My hands were dirty, my clothes ragged, and my shoes, three years old, and I smelled like the animals. Then I considered my situation on the farm. There was no good food, no education, and no prospects. Things were not going to change because things never ever changed here. Everything went on in the same way, year in year out, and it would always be like that until *Mahsher* (Doomsday). When I finished my food, I lay on my back and looked at the sky. I looked at it for a very long time. I imagined Abbas, in a safe country, without the endless fighting, having a good job, saving lots of money, making a good future for himself. He went there only a few months ago. I imaged if I had gone with him, I would be doing the very same as him. I thought resentfully about my father. He was treating me badly. How much he had changed. He was beating me often these days. He was not the same person whom I had loved when I was young.

I lay there for a long time, comparing my expectations with the future I believed Abbas would have. There were too many thoughts going around in my head. Eventually I came up with a good idea. I decided I was going to run away from home, from Father, from being a shepherd the rest of my life, from Taliban food rationing, from my unsafe country, and from boiled eggs every day with a little bread. I hated all of it. The more I thought about escaping, the more I decided that it was the right thing to do. The next question became "When should I leave?" I'd wait for an opportunity to come, then get my money and Abbas's letter, and then run away. I would need to get clothes together and food for the journey. It was a very long way, so I would need provisions, but how could I get them without anyone noticing? I decided to wait and keep my thoughts to myself. I would be exactly the same as always because I did not want anyone to know about my decision. If Father found out, he would beat me, take my money away, and keep a constant eye on me, and give me a very hard time.

Two weeks later a chance came. One of our distant relatives was killed in Kabul City. They brought his body back to his family in the next village. Father was invited to the funeral. I thought this was a good chance for me to carry out my plan. I knew Father would be busy with the ceremony. Mom couldn't go out. "I will escape," I said to myself.

Early on the day of the funeral when father was ready to leave, he said, "I am going now, is there anything you want to know about? You need to take our sheep to the mountain to graze, and watch out for foxes. Don't fall asleep."

"OK, Father, you stay there as long as you want. Don't worry about anything. I will take a good care of everything while you are there," I said.

He looked at me for a quick moment, a little surprised by my willingness, but he had to think about other things, like what he would have to say and do and so on. Now he began to be happy because he was going to spend some time with his friends, which didn't happen often. Mom bustled about, telling him to go and not to be worried about anything. He kept saying remember to do this, don't forget that, and so on. At last he left. I watched from the window as he strode down the slope and onto the track. He was soon out of sight.

After a few minutes, I made sure Mom was busy. She was outside in the kitchen making naan bread. She was singing with some feeling, a very old

Afghani song, copying the style of Ahmad Zaher (a famous Afghani singer)
The song went . . .

> *What is this funny life, I had all the sorrow, before reaching my goal,*
> *I would die, I would die. If love is like this, if life is like this.*
> *I don't want, I don't want my eyes to see the rest of the world.*

I went outside; it was very quiet as usual. Mom's voice drifted pleasantly from the back of the house. I loved her voice. She only sang when nobody was around. Sometime I hummed her songs along with her, but not this time.

I did not take my clothes with me as I had planned because Mom could have seen me if she had looked my way, and she would have suspected something. I went to the garden and dug up the money and Abbas's letter. First, I looked about; there was no one around. Then I took the sheep up to the mountain. It was about 5:00 or 6:00 a.m.

When I got there, I checked my money again; I had enough to go to Iran. I re-read Abbas's letter and stuffed it inside my shirt. I took one last look down the valley. Then I left the sheep and ran away.

BOOK 2

Ali in Tehran, Iran enjoying the freedom.

CHAPTER 12

KANDAHAR

I was on my way, with a mixture of feelings tumbling about inside me. I ran faster and faster because it was all downhill to the village. I kept an eye out for anyone who might see me. There would be other men heading for the funeral that Father was attending in the next village, and I didn't want him to be told that I was not on our mountain but charging down the hillside as though *shaytan* (the devil) was chasing after me. I had only twenty minutes before the last van left the village that day to go to Ghazni City.

I was getting out of breath and had to slow down. I looked up to the *Kiblah* (to the north, toward God's home) and said, "Allah, help me today with my decision. Oh, Allah, I am leaving my parents and my country, and I don't know if I am doing the right thing. Guide me please."

I wanted a better life. I couldn't live this way. I wanted there to be another place where there were no wars or Taliban. I was leaving, hoping to get some education. I wasn't really sure what "education" was, but everyone said that I needed it. I had told Allah many times, in my prayers, about my ambitions to see the world and become a good businessman, like my father. I had often talked with my friends and my cousin Abbas about Tehran. This was the city of our dreams. Every boy in the Middle East yearned to go there. There, there was work, prosperity, and peace. There, if you worked hard, anything was possible. I would have a car and maybe a house. I was going to marry a beautiful girl and live the rest of my life somewhere where I could have freedom. Muslims should not be killing Muslims.

Panting and muttering to myself and to Allah, I hurried on. I should have had my cycle, I said to myself. The next thing I knew was Jak. He was running at my side. The stupid mutt. Now what was I to do? I shouted at him angrily and stopped running. He stopped and came to me, wagging his tail crazily. We often played games of running down the hillsides at speed; he couldn't have known that today was different. I shouted at him to go home. That didn't work. I told him to "sit" and "stay." He did as he was told, and I got quite a distanced from him, but the next minute, he was beside me again. I was in a panic. The dog was confused. I tried to think what I could do with him. Shouting didn't work. I threw things for him to fetch, and while he went after them, I ran and hid, thinking he would go home. But no, he found my hiding place and stood there wagging his tail wildly. He thought it was a game. Nothing worked, and I slapped him when I lost my temper. I had to move on. Now I was going to be late. So I started to run. So did Jak, but at a little distance, this time.

I knew no one would look for me all day because they would think I was on the mountain. Soon I got to the right street, but the van had gone. I was about fifteen minutes late. It was the dog's fault. I decided that I'd have to walk to Ghazni. I cursed the dog. He was still around. Then he sat down close by and was watching me. I had to find some way to keep him in the village. He could not come with me. My feelings were giving me a hard time. I loved the dog, but now I was angry with him. I called him to me, and he got up and ambled over hesitantly, his tail wagging madly again. He licked my hand, and I felt mean. I patted his head and started talking to him, telling him that he could not come with me and so on. Of course he did not understand a word of it, but everyone talks to dogs. Thank Allah, he had his collar on. A stroked him a couple of times and could feel his affection for me. He made his usual noises as though he was talking. I was looking about the street to see if there was a place to tie him. I managed to tie him to somebody's garden post, next to a small house. He didn't like it and started pulling against the wooden post. I crouched down by him, and he sat down. I wrote a little note saying . . .

My name is Jak, I am very friendly, please help me. My owner left me here because he couldn't take me with him, and he thought this house needed protection at night. I am from one of the hill farms. Please help me, give some water and food, please! Please!

I tied the note to his collar and petted his head. I loved my dog, but I could not take him to Iran. I had to leave him there. I felt sorry for him and for myself. I jumped up quickly and ran away as fast as I could, and he was barking and straining at the rope frantically. I kept going, hoping no one would release him until I was well away. I felt bad and argued with myself.

To get to Ghazni City would take hours. I knew the short cuts. The rough road did not run straight because of the hilly terrain. It twisted back and forth, this way and that, to get over the steep hills. I could cut across the countryside, climbing or dropping down the steeper parts. I had to avoid meeting anyone who knew me. News and gossip travel fast in the country.

The sun grew hotter as always, and I prayed for a stream of cold water or a pool. It was a beautiful day, and I felt elated and free. I watched large birds drifting lazily on the air. I was young and used to walking and climbing, and I felt as if I was on holiday. The sun and the clear bright sky exaggerated the rough beauty of the mountains and valleys all around me. A stiff breeze got up and I became cooler.

Over the fiftieth hill up ahead was a small village that was about halfway to Ghazni. It was after midday, and I had made good progress. I didn't want to go into that village, the people there were mostly Sunni Muslims, and I was on my own, so I would have to go around it. I was climbing up rising ground, keeping the village on my left when I came on two boys about my own age. They were Pashto Sunnis because they asked aggressively in Pashto where I was going. I had not expected to meet them. I waved my arm in the direction of the village. I was going there, I said. I felt threatened. They were not friendly. They could easily have robbed me in that remote place, and I could not expect any help from the village. Fortunately, thank Allah; I know how to speak Pashto. I answered their hostile questions with equal roughness, although I was inwardly worried. I did not mention Ghazni because they might have thought that I had money with me. I strode away toward the houses without looking back. I could hear them talking, so I knew that they were not following me, as their voices died away. I chanced looking over my shoulder and found that they had gone. I skirted the few houses. A lazy dog started barking, but I kept moving, heading for some higher ground. I had forgotten about village dogs. They are kept for protection at night and are encouraged to be vicious. Had any been loose I would have been in trouble.

I looked back, and everything was quiet again. I climbed to high ground above the village. I sat down between some large rocks. I was sweating. When I had set out, I had not thought about having trouble with anyone on my journey. I realized that I had all my savings in my inside jacket pocket with Abbas's letters. If I had been attacked, I would have lost everything. I had been lucky. Alone now, I stowed most of the money next to my skin, down the top of my shirtsleeves, just under my armpit. I left a little in my pockets. I was learning. I must be very, very careful.

It was very hard to cross many Sunni places. If I had looked like a Hazara and hadn't known how to speak Pashto, things would have been very difficult; such was the hatred between different groups in that area. I knew I could have been killed or robbed before I reached Ghazni, and I became very afraid.

It was about sunset when I reached the outskirts of the city.

I had heard that things had changed a lot in Ghazni, but it seemed unbelievable that it could have changed so much, since I was there with Abbas a few months earlier. The city did not seem to have as many residents. Like Kabul, the fighting had made it unsafe. I had heard that people were being killed randomly. A lot of the population had fled. Many men, whose businesses were in the center, now lived outside the city. They worked there during the day and made for the safety of the countryside at night.

As I walked toward the center, the streets were very quiet. Lots of shops were closed. Some of the Taliban's land cruisers passed by, with about six men in each, standing on the back, holding *Kalanishnikovs* (Russian guns) and other weapons. They were wild unpleasant-looking men with black turbans and long cloaks. They were all bearded. I had been warned not to stare at them as it might attract their attention to me. I was afraid of them. Fortunately, I did not have Hazara features nor was I a woman. Women were treated badly by the Talibs. I was so lucky because my face looked like a Sunni Muslim, and I could speak their language because when I was little, in school, in Kabul, I had friends who could not speak my language very well, so I had learned Pashto.

I bought a naan (bread). I started eating it at the same time as I was walking through the city streets, looking for the van station to go to Kandahar. I could not remember where it was and kept asking people. Eventually I found it, when it was nearly dark.

"There is no transportation to Kandahar tonight." The station man was Indian. He said, "There will be tomorrow, at 6:00 a.m. and every hour until noon."

"Oh God. What do I do now?" I asked myself. I had only one option, to stay in a hotel and take a van the next day. I found a hotel nearby and asked them for a room for the night. They refused me because I was under eighteen years old.

"The Taliban will fine us if we give you a room," they said.

So I tried other hotels, but they all said the same thing. I was directed to another one, about half an hour's walk from the van station.[2]

There, they said the rooms were full, but they did have a little space. I heard from the manager, as he guided me through the crowded main room, that he was risking being fined for letting me stay at all. Just off a passageway, he showed me to a small space like a brush cupboard. There was no bed, mattress, not even a pillow, only a blanket. I said OK because I had no alternative. He said that if the Taliban came, I was to go into the washroom, which was the next door, and hide. Although he was a big tough-looking man, his actions and the way he spoke showed that he was afraid. I paid him the money, which was not the custom, we always paid when leaving. He continued to warn me about the Talibs, while he changed one of my notes.

"They often strike people for very little reason," he said, "if anyone has shaved or missed their prayers or talks to a woman. They are especially strict toward women and Hazara people. If they find women out alone, or if the women have not covered their bodies properly, they will beat them."

He said that they sometimes came into the hotel at prayer times, and if anyone had not gone to the mosque to pray, the Taliban would beat them. He left me. I felt helpless. What was I going to do if they came? There is a difference between the way Shia Muslim and Sunni Muslims pray. If I was forced to go into a Sunni mosque, I would not know what to do or what responses to make. I would be in even more trouble if I was caught there. Fortunately my hunger resolved the problem. I was ravenous. I went out and ordered some kebab for my dinner. Once they were inside me, I felt much better.

Later in my cupboard, the place became quieter, but it seemed that all the sounds of the place funneled into that cell. I tried to settle down

---

2. In Afghanistan, at that time, I do not think that we had very many words to describe places where you could stay overnight. The word "hotel" was used for any such place. It could be anything from a large building with good private rooms with on-suite facilities down to, what I believe are called, "doss houses" (i.e., a large room without beds where everyone sleeps as best they can.) Most of the cheaper "hotels" fell into that class. The same thing applied to places selling food. They all went by the name of "restaurant." There were no words to specify "a snack bar," "café," or five-star gourmet establishment. They were all referred to as "restaurants."

with the dirty blanket. I could not sleep because people kept going to the washroom all through the night, and I cursed the manager for putting me there. Also I was worried. My thoughts kept running around in my head. Everywhere seemed much more dangerous than it used to be. How could I get to Iran? Tehran was about a thousand miles away, and I had only got as far as Ghazni. Should I go back? Then I remembered I had left the sheep on the mountain. If I went back, Father would beat me and take all my money away, and he would keep an eye on me in case I made another attempt to run away. My life would be worse than before, with no education, no love, always fearful, and working hard without pay.

Very early in the morning just as I had got to sleep, I heard the *Azan* (calling to prayer from the mosque). There was a noise at the front doorway. It was still dark. I put my head around the corner to see what it was. A Talib had entered the hotel, holding a long stick in his hand. He was shouting at everyone, telling them to go mosque for prayers. I headed straight into the washroom. There was a window, which I opened. I was out of that hotel in a flash.

My heart was beating fast as I went cautiously through the dark streets. I kept in the shadows. The air was cold. There began to be signs of the city coming to life. The wail from the mosque stopped, and the distant sound of traffic began to build. Dawn was breaking as I was nearing the van station. People, mostly men and boys, were converging toward it, coming out of alleyways and side streets. Shops vending food and chai (tea) were already open and were doing a good trade at that early hour. I bought a hot drink, and my hands were shaking with the cold as I raised it, steaming, to my lips. I hadn't realized how cold I was. My stomach rumbled as I caught the smell of fried meat as it wafted temptingly on the cold breeze.

The van station was busy. It wasn't really a station; it was just a street, and there was a kind of crowded office, with everyone asking where was the van going to Kabul/Mazar/Kandahar, and places I had never heard of. The transport available was a collection of just about every kind of vehicle I had ever seen. Old beat-up buses, transit vans, large cars, and even an old Russian personnel carrier. Adding to the noise and confusion of revving engines, each driver was shouting out his own destination and his price. I shopped around for the cheapest. Above the row, there was a driver shouting "Kandahar," but he had a murderous look about him, so I kept looking. There was a good saloon car with a large holy talisman hanging from the inside mirror, but the driver wanted too much money. Then I suddenly knew that if I was too fussy, I might not get a seat at all, and then

I thought that my father might come looking for me, like he had done the last time when I was with Abbas, so I settled for a transit van with windows. I got in and checked again that it was going to Kandahar. There were two other passengers. We nodded at each other, but no one was inclined to talk. Sometimes robbers were your fellow passengers, who would rob you on the journey, so no one trusted anyone. I was already very shaken up, having had no sleep, and I was still thinking about the Taliban and Father, so I got well down in the seat, covered my face, and pretended to go to sleep. The driver wanted more passengers, so we waited. Some other men got in. Surely we were full now, but no, twenty minutes later, we had to make room for a couple more. Only then did we leave Ghazni City.

On the way to Kandahar, I heard awful stories about the Taliban rules and regulations. The man who was sitting next to me said,

"I came from Kabul yesterday. The Taliban hacked off the hands of some men, and the leg from another person. Some women were stoned to death, and three men were hanged. It all happened in public."

The man sitting next to him asked why.

"The people who lost their hands were caught stealing food. The man who has lost his leg, he had stolen somebody's wallet. The other three men and women had had sex but were not married. They were like girlfriends and boyfriends. They pleaded that they were going to get married soon. The Taliban did not take any notice of that. They said, "We will cut off hands, legs, and hang or stone to death anyone who breaks the Holy Laws. Those are the penalties written in the Koran for people who are involved in illegal activities. It will be a good lesson for everyone."

We journeyed out toward Kandahar listening to such grisly stories. The sun came up hot and strong. The countryside flashed by. In times of war, people usually grow closer together, but the wars in Afghanistan had become civil conflicts, Afghan fighting Afghan. Travelling among strangers had once been an adventure and even a pleasure, but now, fear was everywhere. I did not know whom I was sitting next to. People could not trust each other. Fortunately several of the men knew each other, so kept up a conversation among themselves. I said nothing, the whole journey.

The driver pulled over at a roadside clearing for the noon prayers. Everyone got out of the van. Some were stretching, and one older man was in agony with leg cramp. The men started washing their faces and getting ready to pray. I realized that they were all Sunni. I was so worried in case anyone found out that I am Shia Muslim. They would not have treated me well. I knew only a little bit about how Sunni Muslims pray. I watched them carefully. I copied the way they washed their faces. When some of them laid down their prayer mats and knelt on them, they were all facing the same direction (*Kiblah*). I kept at the back of the group. They began praying. I had to do whatever they did. Everyone knelt except me. Some recited the prayer. At "citron" in the prayers, everyone bowed their heads to the ground and sat up again. I wasn't able to join in because I would have got it all wrong; I had never before heard Sunni Muslim prayers.

We got back to the van. Thank Allah, nobody asked me why I did not pray.

Four hours later, we stopped again for prayers. This time, I did what I had seen four hours before, but I made one or two mistakes. I had mixed up their way of praying with my family's way of praying. Fortunately everyone was busy, and they did not notice.

When we went back to the van, I dozed off in my seat for a short while. The distance from Ghazni to Kandahar was about four hundred kilometers, but because the road conditions were really bad, it took all day.

It was dark when I woke up. We had arrived and were driving through the suburbs of the town. It looked so dirty. The roads were not even flat. The shops, house, hotels, and many other buildings were very old fashioned. Some of the buildings were falling down. It seemed nobody made any repairs. I thought I would have liked to explore the city, but my father's voice whispered in my ears many times, "Nowhere is safe. You will be killed. It is too dangerous."

I asked Allah for help and recited the Koran from memory to calm myself down.

When I got out of the van, I asked the driver how I could I go to Neemrose town, which was the next place on my journey.

"There is no van or car going there tonight, but you can take a van tomorrow," he said.

"Where can I stay tonight?" I asked worriedly.

"I know a hotel here. They are very good people. I go there when I'm here," he said.

I got the address and the driver's name, in case I had a problem like the night before.

There was a street vendor selling kebab. He looked old and dirty, and the cloud of gray smoke from the fire he was fanning made him cough a lot, and he kept spitting phlegm into the flames. He looked ill. I was very hungry, and the meat smelled good, but the look of the vendor made me stop. I did not want to risk going into a restaurant because I was on my own and felt threatened. I bought two kebabs and some rice balls and walked around eating them. They were very tasty. I just hoped that I would not catch any illness or food poisoning from the vendor.

The hotel was not far away. I went there and told them I had been sent by the driver. They let me in easily. The hotel was very dirty. Everyone was to sleep in the one large room. It was now quite late, and I was tired. Nearly everyone was getting ready to go to sleep, so I tried to make myself comfortable. It was impossible. The blanket smelled sweaty, it was a green color because it had not been washed, and part of it had turned black. I had to use it because there was nothing else. I made the blanket like a mattress. I used my shoes for a pillow. I had never had to sleep like this before. I had not realized how well my parents had looked after me. I missed the food and my clean bed, the quiet of the country, and I would have loved a piece of qand. At last I dropped off into a kind of half-sleep. I started to dream about Father. He was yelling and screaming at Mom and asking about me, where did I go, and why did I go? He was beating Mom. She was sitting very lonely and crying. I felt very alone and sorry for myself. "Nobody knows where I am, or who I am, or where I am going." I cried myself to sleep.

I woke at sunrise. My breakfast was ready, a glass of hot green tea, with two sugars in it, and a lot of fresh naan from the *tandor* (oven), but I did not eat it all, I walked out eating it as I went. I was in a hurry, and I went looking for the van station and found it easily. While I was still asking which vehicles were going to Neemrose, some cars began driving off. I asked one driver, whose van was already full, about his destination. He was going there, and yes, he could take me. I squeezed myself into the van. The men grudgingly made room. We left Kandahar instantly.

CHAPTER 13

MERHDAD THE SMUGGLER

In the van, people talked all about the Taliban oppression. I was very uncomfortable because the overloaded van was bouncing about and throwing the passengers around because of the holes in the road. I did not get into conversation with the other passengers because I wanted to stay out of trouble, so I just kept looking out of the window.

The condition of the road to Neemrose was worse than that from Ghazni. In some places it seemed to be just a dirt track, and dust clouds rose up behind us, or covered us, as other vehicles passed us. We passed what looked like a bad accident, a body lay on the ground, and a man was waving us to stop, but the driver drove even faster almost running the waving man down. Several voices shouted him to stop, but the driver said, "It is too dangerous to stop here. It is a trick. Believe me I know this road. They are devils."

The land was mostly desert and dry scrub, very open and flat, without trees and hardly any vegetation at all. There were not many signs of life on the way. There was an occasional farm. I wondered how anyone could eke out a living from such land. It was about three hundred and fifty kilometers from Kandahar to Neemrose City; but it took us about twelve hours driving.

I had been away from home two and half days. I was sitting in that van, thinking and worrying and afraid of the Taliban. I was missing my mom, our beautiful house, my village, and my friends. And my conscience would not let me forget what I had done to poor Jak. I did not know what was going to happen next.

At sunset we arrived in Neemrose City. It was a little better than Kandahar. A lot of new streets appeared to be under construction, with plenty of vehicles everywhere, mainly old. There were many building, and most of them were in good condition, not like the half-ruined shells in Kabul. It seemed that there was a lot of renovation going on, using very beautiful colors, white, light blue, pink, and many other bright shades.

At the van terminus in the town center, we all got out. The other passengers began to disperse into the crowd of people walking about or waiting for friends. I was stiff and tired. I asked the driver how I could go to Iran.

"Do you have a passport?" he inquired.

"What is that?" I asked.

"It's like a little document. You need it to cross the border," he said, getting ready to drive away.

"Where can I buy that?"

"Not in a shop. You have to go to the Immigration Department and apply for it. Once you have got the passport, then you can go to the Iranian embassy and ask for a visa," he said, winding his window up and beginning to drive off.

I went to find somewhere to stay for the night. I found the first "hotel" in the next street. It was much worse than the hotel I had stayed in, in Kandahar City. Its best features were it was near the van terminus and it would be very cheap.

I went in. As I had expected, there was a very large dingy room, which everyone shared, and even at that time of night, they were lying all over the place. The room was lit by smoking paraffin "hurricane" lanterns, which cast strange shadows and made the place smell. There did not appear to be a fire. I asked a man squatting by the door for the manager, and he pointed out a skinny youth. Someone called his name, and he came over. He was about fifteen and had an odd appearance because his clothes were too large for him, so that the sleeves of his shirt covered his hands, and his waistcoat hung loosely around him. He had a very bad case of acne.

"Yes, agha, what can we do for you?" he asked. His voice was a strange sound because it had not quite broken, so it started high and ended low. The words were accompanied with a grimace, which I think was meant to be a smile, but his two front teeth were missing. There was a difference in the accent of the residents of this town from the way people talked in my village or even in Kabul.

I asked for a single room. He seemed amazed.

"A room? How many people are with you?" he asked hoarsely, looking about.

"Only me," I said.

"For yourself?" he said in a surprised tone.

"We don't have any of them. There are no private rooms in this hotel; you can stay in this room only. What do you want a room for yourself for?" he asked suspiciously. His tone implied that I was asking for something out of the ordinary or for some unhealthy purpose.

"How much is it to stay here, and what do I get for it?" I asked.

"Fifty rupee. Isn't there someone with you?"

"Do I get a bed? Is there a washroom?" I was getting annoyed with this spotty youth. "It says outside that you have a restaurant," I added.

"Does it?" he said. "I don't know. I can't read. We have a cook, when he isn't on drugs. You're lucky tonight, he's off them tonight. He'll cook you *somink*. Let me know what you want, and he'll go out and kill the bull." He broke out into a hoarse laugh. "He's ready to cook for you now. 'ere where are you going?"

I had started moving toward the door because I didn't like the look of the place.

"Stay 'ere, Agar. It's a laugh," he shouted after me when I was almost in the street again.

I walked around and checked out other hotels. They were all the same. Some of them had private rooms, but only for five people or a family. There was some decent accommodation to be had, but it was very expensive.

It was getting cold and late. I was tired and hungry. I decided to go back to the first one. At least it was close to the van station. When I went in, the spotty manager was not there. There was another man. He was older, about fifty. His clothes had seen better days, which gave him a shabby appearance, but then, that applied to most men in Afghanistan in his age group.

"Yes, agha?" he asked politely. I was surprised.

"Is the manager around?" I asked.

"I am the manager. What can I do for you?"

"I'd like to stay for one night."

"Of course. Have you any luggage? It is fifty rupee He swiftly added, "In advance."

I paid him. He told me to make myself comfortable, in a way that seemed to imply that I was in a first-rate establishment.

"Where?"

"Oh, you'll soon find a good space." He said this with a big smile, as he put the money into his inside pocket and disappeared through a door.

I found a place in a corner. I sat there for a short while. The spotty youth appeared and came over. "Oh, you come back," he said with a grin. "Where are your parents?"

"Home," I said.

"Then what are you doing here?" He squatted down beside me, on his haunches.

"I'm here for tonight only. Tomorrow I will go to Iran," I said.

"By yourself?" he asked, in disbelief.

"What is wrong with that?"

"No, no, nothing. How old are you?" His voice was now a high pitch.

"Nosey, aren't you?" I said.

"Being polite to the customers." Now his voice was deep. "I don't care what you do."

"When I came before, I was told that you were the manager. I thought you were too young for that," I said.

"I might as well be him. I do more work than he does. 'E goes round 'ere and talks to people as if this place was a five-star hotel."

"What do you do then?"

"Everythin', washin', waitin', cleanin'."

"Cleaning?" I said surprised. I ran my finger along the wall and showed him the accumulated dirt on my fingertip.

"Well, I don't do much of that. They don't pay me much." He paused. "So I don't do much. I'm the waiter tonight."

"You mean I can get some food here? Now I mean?" I was starving.

"Certainly, Agar. I told you before, the chef's not on the drugs tonight, so you'll be all right," he said, standing up. "How can I serve you?"

I asked what was available, and I ordered *Qabilee balaw* (some rice with meat). As he went away, I thought that I must be crazy to order food in this filthy place, but I was learning that I had to take whatever came my way. I was very surprised when I began to eat because the food tasted good. That was partly because I was ravenous.

It was about 10:00 p.m., and people started to lie down and fall asleep. I had nothing, no pillow, blanket, bed, mattress, or sheet. There was only a carpet on the floor. I looked at the other people, how they were going to sleep. Some of them had their own blankets some used their bags instead of a pillow.

In Afghanistan, most of the men carry a *Pado* (light blanket) with them all the times. They use it for many things, blanket and a prayer mat (when not in the mosque) and for covering their face in cold weather, etc. I looked at floor, it was dirty. The room smelled bad, I was not used to sleeping like this. I had no alternative. There was a semi-clean towel in the washroom. I took it and cleaned a place on the floor. I lay down thinking about the

next day, how to go to Immigration and how to obtain a visa. I thought
again about Mom, my nice, clean, warm room, my village, and my friends.
I missed them a lot. It was only my third night away, but it felt like years.
I was crying inside and felt so lonely. I wished for some company. I had
never thought it would be this hard. I could not sleep because of the cold
weather, the dirty room, bad smells, and the noises (farts, snoring) of the
people, around me.

Next morning, my body felt stiff all over. After a breakfast of naan
bread and chai, I went out to find out how to get a passport. I didn't really
know what a passport was. I had never seen one. Most Afghans don't even
have a birth certificate. After a search around the city center, I found the
immigration ministry. It was housed in a big, gray, concrete building, unlike
most of the other buildings, which were of Afghan style. This one had been
built during the Russian occupation, as a communications center, but now
there was no communication anywhere, it looked more like a prison.

There were a lot of people waiting to get passports. In a long echoing
corridor that smelled of disinfectant, I joined a queue outside an office. I stood
there all day until 3:00 p.m., eventually it was my turn, and I went in.

"What do you need?" the immigration officer asked indifferently.

"I need a passport," I said.

"What do you need that for?"

"I want go to Iran."

"How old are you?"

"I am about fifteen."

"Who have you come with? Where are your parents?" he asked.

"I came by myself, my parents are at home," I said.

"Sorry, we can't give a passport," he said.

"Why?" I asked.

"First, you are not eighteen years old. Second, you're not with your
parents. Third, if we did give you a passport, you can't cross the border by
yourself. Go home or come with your family or wait until you get older,"
he said. "Next person please."

And that was the end of the interview. I wanted to ask more, but the
official stopped me with a wave of his hand and turned his head to address
the next person who was already approaching his desk.

I went out and sat down on the ground. I was numb for a few minutes.
I had been sure in my mind that I would get a passport, and then I had
planned to go on, to find the Iranian Embassy to get a visa, whatever that
was. Now everything had come to a complete standstill. I had to try to

think. What should I do now? Where was I to go? If I went back home, Father would kill me because I had run away and I left the sheep on the mountain. I didn't know what had happened to them. I couldn't get a passport for another two or three years. "Where should I go? Oh Allah!" It was about 4:00 or 5:00 p.m. I hadn't had anything to eat except for some bread that morning. I was very hungry and disappointed. I went to a cook shop and ordered *Karayee* (eggs with lamb) and fresh naan (bread) from the Tandor (oven). Again, the food was much better than I thought it would be. I was so depressed and confused and could not make a decision at that moment. But it was getting late in the day, and from the mosque, I could hear the Azanist singing out the "call to prayers" because it was sunset. I would have to find somewhere to stay because the nights were getting colder. I could go back to the "hotel" I had stayed at, but it was not good. The other places seemed to be as bad, so it was a case of "the devil you know is better than the devil you don't know." At least I knew just how bad it would be. I decided to go there. On the way, I bought a blanket and a small pillow.

The manager greeted me again, pocketed the money again, and told me to make myself at home again. If my home had been as bad as his hotel, I would have left it years ago.

There were not as many people as the night before, so I claimed a bench and put out my blanket and pillow, and I sat on them. I was sitting there, alone, and thinking about what to do next.

An unmistakable uneven voice said, "Oh you're back." It was the spotty young waiter. He came over. He pushed his arms down against his sides so that his hands appeared from inside his long sleeves, and we shook hands. "What is going on? You were so happy yesterday. I thought you'd gone to Iran. What happened?" he asked, his voice rising up and falling.

I told him what the problem was.

"'Ere do want some chai? I'll bring some, won't take a minute." He went away and came back with a tray, on it were two glasses of green tea and a gray napkin. "We can 'ave a talk. 'Ere 'ave some qand."

Although it is a tradition always to have sweets with tea, I was so surprised by the appearance of qand. It made me feel worse than before.

"I'm Matin," he said, sitting on the floor.

We began to talk. He was somewhere around the same age as me, so I suppose that gave us something in common. He began to tell me about himself.

"I lost all my family a year ago, when the Taliban attacked Harat City. That day, I was away visiting my aunt. The next day I went home and found that all the family were dead." He said this in a matter-of-fact way, without emotion. "I lived with my aunt for about a month. She kicked me out a few times because there was not enough food for us. I was looking for a job for about three months. Eventually, somebody brought me here. I am working here about six months." By this time he had grown miserable.

His tragic story was typical of the things that had been happening to many Afghans over many years. It turned out that Matin was about two years older than me. But we were almost the same height. He was skinny, with bad skin, because of lack of food. He was born in Harat City. He was Sunni Muslim and clan of Tajik.

"Why don't you go to Iran?" I asked.

"I know people who have gone there, but I don't know where they are now. I've thought about going, but I don't speak Persian. I planned to go with friends once, but they were all talk. They never went anywhere," he said.

"My cousin went there about three months ago. He sent a letter. This is it," I said, pulling Abbas's letter from my pocket.

"Do you want to read it?" I asked excitedly.

"No. I can't read, but I would like to know what it says."

I read the letter to him twice.

"Very nice," he said.

"Would you like to go Iran with me?" I asked.

"Yes" he said enthusiastically. "If you help me."

"OK, I'll help you, if I can, but we have to wait for another two or three years until I turn eighteen," I said. "Then we can get passports."

"Ha! I thought you meant it. Two or three years," he repeated contemptuously.

"I do mean it, but we're not old enough because we have to have passports . . ."

"No, we don't 'ave to," he broke in.

"How can we go to Iran without a passport?" I asked.

"Easily. I know a way to go there."

"How?"

"Every Saturday and Wednesday, a smuggler comes 'ere and takes people to Iran."

"Here? A smuggler comes here?" I asked in disbelief.

"There are millions of people going to Iran in these days. If there weren't, this place 'ud be shut. It's been going on for years. Iran don't give out visas because Tehran is packed out with Afghans because of all the wars. If you want to go to Iran, and you'll let me come too, I can easy fix it. The smuggler's name is Merhdad. I know him very well. Today is Monday, so we have another two days to wait for him. Don't tell anybody that I going to Iran with you, because if the manager finds out, 'e won't give me my wages. I have to go now, but I will talk to you later."

Next day, I went shopping to buy new clothes with Matin because I had only the clothes I was wearing. I bought a pair jeans and a T-shirt. My jeans were black, and my shirt, light blue. After shopping, Matin went to his work, taking my parcel with him, because I wanted to go to the public bathhouse to take a shower, I was beginning to smell.

On my way returning to the hotel, I heard someone shouting out orders over a loud speaker. I noticed about six Taliban in a slow moving land cruiser. They were all in black and heavily armed. They were ordering all the shopkeepers to shut down their places of work at 1:00 p.m. They had only five minutes left to go to mosque to pray. They kept saying this repeatedly. Three minutes later, I watched them as they got out of the cruiser and started beating people and shouting, "Go to the mosque."

I was so scared of the Taliban. I had no choice but to go toward the mosque.

Oh my God! I was on my way, when one of the tyrant Talibs hit me very hard on my shoulders with his stick, and I fell down. My face hit the ground; I got up on my hands, and knees. I said, "OK." I was terrified.

He kicked me and swung a punch at me, which hit my face. His eyes were wild. He grabbed my hair, pulling and twisting it. It was very painful.

"Oh, you have very long hair."

He shouted to his stupid partner to bring scissors. He cut my hair and pushed me along the road until we got to a mosque.

"Oh, Allah help me, if they find out I am Shia and in their mosque, they will kill me or cut off my hand."

When we got into the mosque courtyard, I was shaking. I was in a panic. I watched the other men and copied all their movements. I washed my face, hands, arms. Then I followed them into the mosque. I stood at the end of a line of people. When they bowed their head on the ground, I made for the door and got out. I kept walking quickly until I was out of their sight, and then I ran all the way back to the hotel.

CHAPTER 14

THE INVISIBLE BORDER

Next morning, Matin took me to the kitchen and introduced me to his coworkers and the manager as one of his relatives. Matin said he wanted the money he was owed so that we could go out and buy presents for me to take home to the family.

"Welcome to the Neemrose City," the manager said to me.

Matin started to make tea for everyone.

"How do like it here?" the manager asked.

"It's rough. The Talibs seem to be in control here. They force the people to go to the mosque. One beat me up and cut my hair," I said.

"I am sorry to hear that," he said, as though he was the ambassador. "They beat up people randomly. Last week, I was beaten and sent to the mosque three times, on the same day. I've still got bruises. I told them that I'd been, but they wouldn't listen. Some of them are crazy."

The chef joined in the conversation, "Two weeks ago. I went to my younger uncle's wedding party. We were playing music and dancing and enjoying the party. The Taliban came in. Our wedding party turned into a funeral party because they broke our cassette player. They did not like us playing music. They beat up some of the guests who argued with them. Eventually they left, and we did our best to resume the party. We managed to get an Iranian station on the radio, so we had some music."

"But you should not have to be afraid of having a wedding party. It's not sinful," the manager said. "Why don't they like wedding parties?"

"Maybe it's because none of their mothers ever got married," Matin said. "They are all bastards."

"Shh!" the manager warned, as we all burst out laughing. "Matin, watch your mouth. You could get yourself into a lot of trouble if the wrong people hear you. Even a smile, at the wrong time, can get you beaten up."

The talk went on, and we laughed sometimes, but everything had become guarded. Later we left the kitchen.

It was afternoon when Merhdad (the smuggler) came to the hotel. Matin introduced me to him and said, "We want to go to Iran. Can you take us?"

I don't know what I had been expecting him to be like, but there was nothing unusual about him. He was average height. Aged about forty. Thin, like most Afghans, hair down to his shoulders, with a full untidy beard. Like everyone else, he wore several coats and the typical checkered scarf, stained, and the woolen Kola hat. He had a mild air about him, but he had sharp dark eyes. He was smoking a rolled cigarette, which smelled of burning rubber.

"Of course," he said as he breathed out smoke through his nose.

"How long will it take to get to Tehran?" Matin asked.

"Two weeks. Maybe more," he answered.

"How many kilometers is it to Tehran?" I asked.

"About a thousand kilometers to Tehran City."

"Why does it take so long if it is only a thousand kilometers?" Matin asked.

"Because we are going through the mountains, illegally. Do you understand? Do you really want to go? Are you serious?"

"Yes, sir," I said quickly "Yes, we are going. I should have gone there months ago with my cousin, but something stopped me. He is there now and doing OK. Do you want to see his letter?" I said, reaching into my pocket. "Just some more questions please, how are we going to get to Tehran?"

"It is easy, like everyone else I have taken before; you will need to walk a lot. By the look of you, that should not be a problem for you," he said. You can trust us because we know every stone on the mountains. Matin will tell you we've been in business for ages, since the Russians were here, since before you were born."

I offered him the letter, but he didn't take it. I supposed he couldn't read either.

"How much money do you want to take us to Tehran City?" I asked.

Matin asked him for a discount.

"Three hundred thousand Toméans for both of you," he said, "Iranian money (about eight hundred U.S. dollars)."

I hadn't enough money to pay him. I had only fifty thousand Toméans left. He told me I didn't have to pay right away. I could make payment upon arrival. His partner would take me to my cousin Abbas's home, and then I could borrow money from him.

As I had no alternative, I was pleased to accepted it.

The smuggler told us, "The two of you must be ready by tonight. I have some more people to take with us. I am going to talk to them now. I will come back for you as soon I finished with them."

Matin brought tea for him, while he was drinking, I talked to him about Tehran.

It was all so natural, as though we were old friends. He made it sound easy. It was clear that he had been smuggling people for years. I had heard some bad things about smugglers, but also a lot of good things. Weren't there relations of my mother who had gone to Europe in this way, who sent messages home now and then? We sometimes got a letter, which had taken six months to arrive because of the state of the country.

"A lot of people are going to Iran every day. It is very nice country and safe," he said.

As he left the hotel, he said, "See you later."

I asked Matin, "Are you ready?"

"I will be ready, but I need to get my money from my boss. He has not paid me for the last five months. I hope I can get it on time," he said.

It was about 8:00 p.m. when the smuggler returned.

"We need to leave now; I have some others waiting for me. Where's Matin?" he demanded.

"I am ready," I said.

I went to the kitchen and called Matin, "Merhdad is here, and we need to leave now."

"I haven't got all my money. My boss paid me only a little of it. It will take another five months to get the rest of it. This man is skinny with it. I worked here for less than one hundred Rupee day (less than one U.S. dollar). Let's go before it gets too late."

So we followed the smuggler. At another hotel, there were six people waiting for him.

We walked the dark silent empty streets heading out of the town for about half an hour. In a remote place, there was a transit van. We all got in. The van was very cold because there was no heating on, and we sat on freezing metal in complete darkness. It shook noisily with a vibrating shudder as the engine fired. It was diesel, and I suppose the gas was cold.

We drove off in silence out of the town, our frosty breath hanging in the air.

About half an hour later, the smuggler said, "There is a small bit of jungle ahead of us. I will drop all of you there. The van has to go back. Wait until I come back. Nobody goes anywhere."

We got out the van, and he drove off. We waited for him, a frozen ragged group, stamping our feet and blowing into our hands. Matin and I were excited, and our spirits were high. Merhdad came back after about twenty minutes, on the back of a motorcycle, got off, and it drove away.

"We have to run for about an hour. The border is over there about four kilometers away. We will cross it, but only when I have checked it out. Then my brother will pick us up, about eight kilometers on the other side. Everyone must follow me. We have got to stay very close together. Nobody is to talk; there may be border guards about."

We followed him. It seemed too easy. It seemed like a game. I was keen to get to Iran. Matin and I had to control ourselves to stop from laughing and shouting.

"Keep quiet!" Merhdad barked.

We were breathless and elated and eventually got to his brother's vehicle after about two hours cross-country.

"Get in and keep quiet," Merhdad said angrily.

"When will we get to the border?" I asked.

"It's behind us now. Be quiet!"

I couldn't believe it. I wanted to ask questions. Were we really in Iran? There had been no sign of the border, no wall, fence, or even barbed wire. We had crossed into Iran, and I had not even noticed.

We crammed ourselves into the vehicle, which was smaller than the transit. After slamming the doors as quietly as possible, we began to bump our way, in total darkness down some kind of track. Again the van was freezing. The journey lasted about forty minutes. Slowly we thawed out, mentally and verbally. We began to chatter, each group among themselves, in different dialects. I heard Merhdad asking why the van was so small.

"It's your fault, you brought more people this time," his brother answered plainly.

Well, we were in Iran! As easily as that. These men knew their business. I could not ask questions, and I did not know their methods. I think it was a mixture of local knowledge, who you knew, and bribery. The border guards were not well paid, sometimes they weren't paid at all. Some of them had gone into business for themselves. It seems that Merhdad had a lot of "brothers."

The smuggler took us to a house. It was about midnight. There was a very large room. We slept there that night. Matin became a good friend of mine because I really needed one. We shared everything, and I thought that it was "us against everyone else."

It seemed we were just getting comfortable, when just before sunrise, the smugglers woke us, packed us again into a van, and took us to another place. I slept on the way because I was worn out, by excitement, running, and lack of sleep. The next thing I knew, there was a huge room with about forty people inside, men, women, and children.

Merhdad said, "My job is finished here. My partner, his name is Omid, will take you to Zahedan City, and then somebody else will take you to Tehran. God save you all."

I had known Merhdad for only a day or so. He acted like a working businessman. He had done exactly as he had promised. I will always remember him. He won't remember me at all. I had thought that it had been very easy to cross into Iran, what I did not find out until later was that Merhdad had taken us through a minefield. That was why we had to stay very close together and why there were no guards. Omid brought bread and water for everyone twice a day.

CHAPTER 15

CONSTANT MOVEMENT

So we were here in Iran, in some kind of holding house. People had been brought across the border in small numbers, and we all waited until the smugglers decided it was safe to move us. More men and small families arrived the next night and again the following night.

We waited there for two days. We seemed to be in a much more mountainous country than the area around Neemrose. From the little I saw of it, I gathered that it was very remote. We were discouraged from going outside, unless it was at night, and no lights were allowed outside. Even the lighting of cigarettes had to be done inside because any kind of light would have been seen a great distance away. I only remember the millions of stars in the sky, I had never seen so many before, and the moon was huge.

The night of the second day, a smuggler brought a bus and told everyone to get in. There weren't enough seats for all of us. Some sat on the floor. The bus was very small for about seventy people. We could hardly all get in and were pushed in by the smuggler, who suddenly seemed in a great hurry.

We travelled for about ten unpleasant hours. Matin and I told each other stories about our past lives. His experiences had all been bad, but were typical of what had happened to countless young Afghans. So we became sad. My accounts and reminiscences only caused me to become homesick, so we decided to talk of our future instead. For someone who had only very recently decided to leave our country, Matin had suddenly some very fanciful ideas of what he was going to do when we got to Tehran. Only a few more days of discomfort and we would be there. The very name of that city caused our imaginations to run wild. We were poor boys from a poor war-torn country, heading for the capital of an oil-rich state. It was famous throughout the Middle East for its buildings and its prosperity. Its population was young and vibrant. Its culture and history pre-dated that of Western civilization by thousands of years. Several million Afghans had fled to Iran over the years, and many of them had made out a good life for themselves, and that is what we were going to do. Other Afghans were stuck in squalid refugee camps, but that was not going to happen to us.

At daybreak, at last we arrived somewhere because the bus stopped and we were told to get out. It was some kind of cellar-cum-cattle-barn. It was dirty and stank of animals. The bus drove away. No one was happy to be in such a place and grumbling began. Different smugglers were inside, waiting. They told us to be quiet. "You are only going to be here until dark. Tonight about ten o'clock, we are going to Zahedan City. It is not far away from where we are now. But there is one important security check left. We can't pass the security guards with a busload of people. We will drop you off somewhere before the checkpoint. There is a hill we all need to walk over. We will join the road again further on, on the other side of the barrier. We will have to walk for about two hours. A bus will be waiting for you. During the walking, no talking with each other because sound carries."

It was late at night when the smuggler told us to get onto a bus, which, thankfully, was bigger than the last one. We drove off. The driver dropped us somewhere in a mountainous area. Matin and I had been together since we left Afghanistan. We walked close to each other for about an hour. There were some old men and women and children with us. They couldn't walk as fast as we did. They lagged behind. The smuggler forced them to catch up. We had been told that there would be two hours of walking, but because of the weaker people, it took us three and half hours. We arrived at a place where yet another bus was waiting. The driver was impatient. He was annoyed with us. He said we could have been caught because an empty bus parked in that desolate place would have attracted attention if a patrol had come along.

We drove to a house. It must have been about one in the morning. When we got there, the smuggler said, "Today you are going leave here after you have had a short rest and some food. My partners will take you to Tehran City. You are all tired, but there will be no more walking. Only twenty-four hours driving."

About five hours later, two fat men arrived.

"We are going to take you to Tehran today," they told us. So we got into another bus. I had lost any idea of time. Days and night were all mixed up in my head. Every day had brought a new experience, not all of them had been bad. Matin and I were not really touched by the discomfort. We were young and full ideas and hopes. We were again packed very tightly in that bus. I was by the window this time. The sun was rising, an angry red ball coming up from behind the mountains. As the bus started to move, I fell asleep.

Sometime later, Matin woke me and said. "Get up, get up, the police have caught us."

When I opened my eyes, the driver had pulled the bus over to the side of the road. There were police with guns outside. The driver got off and was talking to a policeman. An older officer joined them, and then the driver and the senior officer moved out of sight around the front of the bus. A minute later, a policeman came onboard, looked down toward the back. He told everyone to get out. So we all got out. What else could we do?

He said, "How did you all manage to get in there?"

Nobody said anything.

Then surprisingly, the senior officer shouted, "Who is Shia? Come on! Hands up!"

I automatically put my right hand up, and so did some others.

"Shias move over here." He indicated toward the front end of the bus.

"Sunnis move down there," he shouted, pointing to the rear.

We did as we were told. I had a very bad feeling in my stomach. I was already near the front, so I moved with others. Matin moved toward the back, but turned and tried to join me. An officer saw him coming and stopped him with a blow to his face, which knocked him to the ground.

"You Sunni killers are not going to Tehran," the officer yelled at him. When he scrambled to his feet, the officer slapped his face again several times and then kicked him. I couldn't understand the language very well, and was shouting at the police to stop.

The driver forced me onto the bus. I was asking him to get Matin, but he shoved me along inside. "We got to get out of here right away. Do you want to stay? He can't come because he is Sunni Muslim. Sit down and shut up." Other men grabbed hold of me, while the driver got into his seat and started the engine. Everyone was yelling. We pulled away.

I went to the front. "What will the police do with the Sunni people?" I asked as I strained to see the small sad group at the roadside. "Will they kill them?"

"No."

"What then?"

"They beat them up and then deport them to Afghanistan," he said coldly. "I bribed the police officer, but he said there was no way he could let everyone go, especially Sunni Muslims. I managed to get him to take a lot of money, but he would only allow me to take Shia people through. There was no way for the Sunni to come with us. The officer was *Basenji* (racist)."

"Why will they beat them up?" I asked.

"So they won't try to come back again."

The smuggler was resigned to what had happened. It had probably happened before.

I felt as though I had been beaten and kicked. My mind would not work. I didn't know what was happening to my best friend Matin. Everything had seemed to be going so well. I felt sick. I went back to the place where we had been sitting, and there on the seat was Matin's pathetic little bundle of his few possessions. He had nothing with him except a little bit of money, and the police would take that from him. I felt terrible. I have never felt as bad as that.

Eventually, after hours of driving in the roasting hot bus, we arrived in Tehran very late at night. I was exhausted. We were deposited at a house, which seemed to be near an airport on the edge of the city because I heard the loud noise of a plane not very far away. The building was modern and was soundproofed. We were offered hot food, rice, kebabs, and chai, and then told to sleep. In a long room, there were a lot of clean mattresses on the floor. After what we had been through, this seemed like luxury. I dived onto a mattress and stretched out. I don't remember anything else.

CHAPTER 16

TEHRAN

Next day, I was woken by an older fat man. "My name is Sayavash, you have arrived in Tehran. How do you want pay me? Do you have the money with you?" he spoke with a strong Persian accent. He shook my shoulder hard. "Did you understand what I said?"

"Yes," I said. "My cousin Abbas is here in Tehran somewhere. I have to go and find him and get the money for you. This is what I agreed with Merhdad in Neemrose in Afghanistan. I have his address in my pocket."

"OK. Let me have it. Get ready, and we'll go and find his house," he said roughly.

Sayavash, when I got a chance to look at him, turned out to be quite smartly dressed in new clothes in Islamic style. His pants and headdress were incredibly white. He looked like a city businessman because he was clean shaven and his gray hair was neatly cut. There were other men with him, and they were sorting out what to do with the various groups of people who had arrived with me. Some had already gone away. Some had addresses of relations who lived there, and so on.

Sayavash was talking in Persian to the other men, while I went to a washroom to wash and clean my teeth. I heard the noise of planes taking off and landing as I got into the sunlit bathroom, so I opened the thick windows. The noise became deafening. And heat flowed into the room. So I pulled the window shut. There was a large mirror on the wall, and I saw myself for the first time since I left home.

What a mess I looked. I was thinner. My face had a bluish bruise on my cheekbone, and my hair was badly chopped about, and my clothes were dirty. Even after I had washed, I didn't look any better. I had a worried look imprinted on my face because I kept remembering Matin. I went into the long room and told Sayavash that I wanted to change my clothes. My other jeans and sweatshirt were not much better than the ones I had taken off. There was nothing for it; I'd have to go as I was. Back in the main room, there was chai, and I don't think I have ever tasted better.

Sayavash wanted to leave. "Come on now, I have a lot to do today. Let's find this cousin of yours. I have to go to Friday prayers."

We went out into a yard, and the sun assaulted us. It was a brilliantly hot day. Sure enough we were near the airport. A beautiful silver car was standing there in front of the door, and I heard a clunking as the doors unlocked themselves. I had never heard of a remote control. This was magic. Sayavash told me to get in and then told me to wait a moment. Out of the trunk he took out a wide roll of paper. He opened the passenger door and covered the seat with it. Then he let me get in. I didn't blame him for protecting his car seat from me because the upholstery was cream color leather. What a car. The windows were tinted blue, there was cold air coming from somewhere, and everything responded to the push of a button.

He started the engine, which hardly made a noise. The car seemed to rise about a foot, and we floated along out of the yard and onto a road. Then we joined some kind of highway, and I have never seen so many wonderful cars. Sayavash seemed to be steering with one finger. All the drivers seemed crazy. No one bothered about anyone. All of them were rushing and slamming on their brakes alternately. It was dangerous, frightening, and exciting.

There was so much to take in. I was sitting there with my mouth open. Way up ahead there seemed to be a large monument. It grew bigger and bigger as we approached it. It was a kind of arch in white stone, and it was gigantic. We drove around it, and there were fountains playing. There were many people walking around and taking pictures. They looked like tiny ants in comparison to the monument. Sayavash told me the name of it. It was called the Azadi monument, and he said that I ought to come to see it at night because it was beautifully lit by thousands of colored spotlights. In my country, we didn't even have electricity most of the time.

I think that he was enjoying showing me these sights. We headed into the city. The roads looked wonderful. The avenues were wide and tree lined, and there were traffic signals, and they worked. There were rows and rows of wonderful buildings, none of them damaged. Many of them were very tall and made entirely of glass, which reflected the sun and the sky. There were beautiful old buildings in some places and parks with stretches of grass lawns and all kinds of plants and flowering trees, and men were spraying everything with water from long hoses. And there were historic mosques and palaces and embassies with flags on them, and cinemas and great shops and bazaars. Behind all this, on the distant skyline, was a vast panorama of massive snowcapped mountains.

Here was I, a dirty farm boy with a bruised face, gliding along the roads of the richest city in the world, and enjoying every minute of it. Then we and got stuck in a traffic jam. It was a car crash. Three cars were involved, someone was unconscious. There was blood. I was shocked, but Sayavash seemed unconcerned and just kept moving forward a little at a time.

There are more than five million people living in Tehran, and I think most of them were walking around the streets that morning because I have never seen so many people together at one time. We moved off again only to get stuck in another jam, another crash. I didn't care if we got stuck all day because it was wonderful.

We eventually drove into a poorer area. Sayavash had checked his street maps before we left. So we arrived at my cousin's address. He was not there. We would have to wait for him. As it was Friday, I was sure he would have gone to the mosque. At last he showed up. I saw him coming toward us. I was sitting in the car, and I waited until he was outside the door. I jumped out, right in front of him.

Abbas got a shock. He was so surprised to see me. After a split second, his face broke out in a broad smile. "Ali jan. Where have you come from?"

He gasped in amazement. He threw his arms around me and gave me a hug. He was so delighted. This was too much for me, and I broke down crying. I was happy, and yet I was sad. I think I had been through too much in the last week, and I just gave way. Sayavash got out of the car and came around to where we were. I explained through my sobs that I needed money.

Abbas said he did not have enough money at home, but he would go and borrow some from his friend. Eventually we paid the smuggler, and away he went, in that wonderful car.

CHAPTER 17

ABBAS AGAIN

Abbas took me into his home. He had only one room and a tiny kitchen. The place was not big enough for two people, but he said we would have to manage. In his old gentle way, he made some tea, then I told him about everything that had happened since we met last time in Ghazni City.

I think I spent the most of the next day in bed. When I got up, it was three in the afternoon, and Abbas had washed and pressed all my clothes. Six articles in all. He had gone to work, but had left a note for me. I felt so much better just knowing he was around, and I was safe.

Abbas told me he had decided to take two days off work, and so the next thing we did was go to a public bathhouse because I needed a shower badly. Later we went to a park, and he took me around the town center. Iranian people called us *Afghani Kasafat*. I did not know what it meant. Later Abbas told me it meant "dirty Afghan."

"Irani people are very racist and beat up Afghans often for no reason. They are not treating Afghan people fairly at all here. You will learn more about them as you live here." He said this as we were walking back to his room. "Oh I have to tell you something about the police. They often stop people who look like Afghans, randomly, and deport them to Afghanistan. If you get stopped by police, just give them some money, and they will you let you go, otherwise you will be in trouble."

Things were difficult for Abbas because he had slight Hazara features, that is, looking like a Mongol, high cheekbones, narrow eyes, tall, and slim. I was lucky because my face and my build were similar to Iranian men. It was hard to tell if I was Afghan or Irani. People told me that if I did not talk, I would pass for Iranian, but back in Afghanistan, I had sometimes been discriminated against in some Hazara areas because they had thought I was sunni Muslim.

The third day after I arrived, Abbas went to his work. I went out to have a walk around our area. The streets were nice and clean. The buildings were in good shape, but there were many opium smokers and homeless people everywhere. They wore very old, dirty clothes, and smelled like dead animals. They could not walk properly. Some of them were totally dependent on drugs. The government did not do anything to sort out the problem. I heard from Abbas that they were the worst criminals in the province.

Two weeks after I arrived in Tehran, I went to work with Abbas. The work was on one of the many city construction sites. It was very hard and heavy work for me, but I did not want Abbas to think that I was expecting him to provide for me. Most of the physical, hard work in Tehran was done by migrant Afghanis. On building sites the money was good and the payment reliable, but in other areas wages were not paid on time. This led to strikes, particularly with city council workers. Garbage was not collected sometimes, and buses did not run. Complaints about government services were frequent.

I managed to do the job for about two months, and I made enough money to repay my loan. I stopped doing that job because I physically just couldn't do it anymore.

A week later, I found a job at a tailoring company. Its only drawback was that it took me forty-five minutes to get to the factory, and I had to leave home at 6:45 a.m. I travelled during the rush hours, and it was an ordeal until I got used to it. People were always pushing and forcing each other to get on the buses. Always the younger people and strongest got on ahead of the others. Because this was the way everyone behaved, I had to learn to forget my manners and push like everyone else, otherwise I would never have been able to get on a bus. No one was happy about the public transport. The buses smelled and were dirty. The bus ride took me about half an hour. Then I had to walk for fifteen minutes. I used to cross the fruit market if I wanted to take a short cut. I often bought fresh fruit to take for my lunch break. It was a typical market full of life and color with many different smells of fruit and vegetables, such as oranges, lemons, giant melons, and onions and tomatoes and nonah. It reminded me of the market in Mazar-i-Sharif where I once worked when I was only eleven. When I came out of the market, the streets were very crowded, with people rushing past each other with no respect. There were also many thieves, who were after your wallet or your bag or other personal belongings. You had to be very alert and keep your eyes open, otherwise you would be abused and robbed quicker than you can imagine.

The company had premises on the fifth floor of a factory building, which also housed a variety of commercial units. The building was quite new and well maintained, and every floor had an individual color scheme. It depended on what kind of business they were involved in. The businesses were either wholesale or manufacturing, which was mostly clothing. The building had a battered elevator, which was supposed to be mainly for commercial use. Every day, when I arrived, there were always people waiting to use it. Sometimes they got angry and began to swear. I did not want to walk up to the fifth floor, so I took that elevator. There was a little sign saying "Maximum six people or five hundred kilograms," but no one took any notice of it. People pushed to get in, and there would be about ten of us in it. It smelled of cigarettes and sweat. In fact the whole building smelled of different odors, particularly of cloth. Each floor had a very long hallway, and every window had different advertisements for each business. The company would not pay much until I learned the job. The first day I went to work from 8:00 a.m. to 9:00 p.m. The second day my feet became inflamed and swelled up because I had to stand up for thirteen hours, only taking twenty minutes off for lunch. I had to stand so much because I needed to learn how to press and hand-sew, otherwise I could not become a good tailor. That was very important. When I had gotten to know the work and gotten used to it, the job was perfect for me. I enjoyed doing it. At first, my wages were just enough to pay half of the rent and food. This only lasted for a short time because I learned the job quickly. I went on to make more money, even more than I had earned at the construction job. The wages depended on how fast I worked. The boss told me that I would get increases as I learned more. I worked about seventy to eighty hours a week, and I liked the work.

One day I went to the local bakery to buy some naan (bread). I was stopped by two drug users asking me for money. I told them I didn't have any.

One of them pulled a knife and said, "If you don't give money, I will kill you right here."

"I don't have any," I repeated, very afraid.

"Let me search you," he said.

I did not say anything because they were holding the knife to my throat. They found my money. It was my wages for the last two weeks.

They took it and ran away. I asked for help from the people who were passing, but nobody even asked what happened. I telephoned the police, they said, "Wait there, someone will come to help you." The police arrived after an hour. I told them what had happened. They told me,

"Tomorrow go to police station and make a statement."

Next day I went to the police station and waited there.

The police asked me first. "Where are you from?"

"Afghanistan," I said.

"Afghan! Wait here, someone will help you," he said in a disparaging way.

No one came. Nobody asked me any further question. Eventually I left.

CHAPTER 18

FINDING MY FEET

Abbas was out when I got home that night. I lay down on my bed. I was so angry and so depressed because I had lost my money, and nobody helped me, not even the police. This wonderful city, which is the dream destination of all young people in the Middle East and which I had imagined in all my fantasies when I lived on the farm back in Ghazni, was turning out to be very disappointing. Yes, there was work and a chance to earn good money; yes, there was peace and no religious persecution; and yes, it was an intact city with beautiful buildings that had not been plagued by the ravages of thirty years of war, but like many other cities, I suppose all over the world, there were some things that were very wrong. The police were corrupt and racist, and there was a massive problem with drug addicts and the homeless poor. These were the facts of life that I was learning, and I was learning them the hard way. And things got worse. A week later I went to the bank. I wanted to open an account. I decided that my money would be safer there. The bank was in the city, not far away from where I worked. It was in a modern glass and chrome building, with a revolving door. Inside there was a commissionaire in a smart uniform. The building had a beautiful marble floor, cool air conditioning, and polished light cedar woodwork. I joined the back of a queue, and when it was my turn, I approached the counter.

The bank clerk said, "Salam, how can I help you, sir?" He was smartly dressed in brilliant white robes.

"I want to open an account," I said hopefully.

"How are you today?" he said.

"I am fine, what about you?" I answered. I liked his polite manner.

"Where are you from, handsome young man?" he asked with a smile.

"Afghanistan," I said.

"Oh . . . Afghani boy, you want to open an account?"

"Yes, agha (sir), I do."

"Affy, here is not your country. You can't have an account number."

I asked, "Why?"

"Dirty Affy boy, get out of here before we force you to!" he said nastily.

There I stood, a young working class boy in ill-fitting clothes, and his sudden change of manner made me feel ashamed to be myself. It hurt. I suppose it was the boxer in me that made me respond.

"Sir, you should show me some respect, I am human like you or anyone else. The difference is I was born in Afghanistan. I am leaving now, but Allah will punish you."

I went home, and I spoke to Abbas about it.

He said, "You will have to leave your money with your boss if you think you can trust him. That is what I do. You can take it when you need it. That is the best way. Some Irani people are racist. Today after work, my boss told me that a bus driver killed six Afghans yesterday morning because he was going to lose his job and was being replaced by an Afghan driver."

Three months passed, and I had become a good tailor. Every Friday I usually went to the park to have fun and play football, but because some Iranian people were openly racist, I did not feel safe there. We heard reports daily of beatings, robbing, and deportations to Afghanistan. Sometimes, after work, on my way home, there were a lot of people (opium smokers) sleeping all around the city center and in the small side streets. They attacked anyone they thought was Afghan. They knew the police would not bother to intervene.

One Friday, Abbas and I went shopping. We left home about 10:00 a.m. and returned at 4:00 p.m. When we came back home, the door to the room was broken, and the window smashed, thieves had ransacked the place. They had taken everything, our clothes, money, and even the rug. We phoned the police. When they found out we were Afghans, they did not help at all. Abbas and I had lost everything, all of the possessions we had got together since we arrived in Tehran. I cannot describe just how bad it felt. It was not only the loss of all our hard-earned possessions, it was as if we had been physically assaulted and our personal privacy had been violated.

Fortunately, we had some money, which we had left with our employers. We got over the shock. We had to. We got a few things together and managed to rent a small apartment in an old house and bought everything new that we could afford.

I decided to go to boxing classes again and to join a gym, just in case I need to defend myself against these people.

Six months after my first day at the clothes factory, I became one of the best and fastest tailors in our company. The job was piecework. I was paid for each garment separately. The more garments I made, the more I got paid. The staff at the factory consisted of the boss, two managers, fifteen tailors (men and women), three footboys, and six girls for general help. The boss not only owned the factory but also had several retail shops. Most of my co-workers were Iranian. They were jealous of me because the boss and I had a good relationship. He liked me because I was much faster and cleaner than the others. So I was working six days a week from 8:00 a.m. to 11:00 p.m. or the middle of the night, sometimes even until 1:00 a.m. My boss, or a manager, dropped me off at my home most of the time because of the trouble with drug addicts.

After a short while, I was making a good amount of money, and my boss held it for me. I was still living with good old Abbas, but our apartment was really too small. He was wonderful because we were always in each other's way. He never complained, but I knew I was getting on his nerves a lot of the time. He liked to study, but he had to put his books under his bed because there was no room anywhere. And then there was the cooking. We agreed to take turns each in making the food, but I hadn't really learned to cook. So I usually burned everything or undercooked the meat or put in too much salt. The burned food was the worst because it left a smell in the house for days after, and some of the pans had to be thrown away because I couldn't get the burned food off them. Most of the time he laughed about it, but I felt bad. He had hard manual work to do, and the food I served up was uneatable. Also he was older than me. I was a teenager, and I expected him to want to do the same things as I did. A lot of the time I must have been unreasonable, with my loud music, especially when he wanted to read.

Once, when my boss had dropped me home after I had worked late, he made a sort of comment about the size of our home and the area we lived in, it was not a nasty remark and he may not have realized what he was saying, but it put an idea into my head. He often said things that made me think, and I started to see what he meant.

When I had arrived in Tehran, I had been a kid straight off the farm, afraid of my own shadow, although I would never have admitted it. I thanked Allah for Abbas being there. Now with my boxing and visits to the gym, I was much more confident. I knew my way around, where to go, and where not to go. The boss treated me as an adult, and that made me even more confident. From then on, I began to think about changing things. As I was now making good money, I decided that it would be best if I moved to a place of my own, where I could be free to do whatever I liked, but it bothered me because I did not want to hurt Abbas's feelings. After turning things over in my mind for a week or two, I thought the best thing to do was to discuss it with him. One Friday, our day off, we were in the park hoping to get a game of football. We were sitting on a bench, and I suddenly said, "What do you think about me getting a small apartment of my own?" He didn't answer. "You must have felt sometimes that I was getting on your nerves. There isn't enough room for the two of us." I felt terrible. Was I ungrateful? I looked into his face. He looked surprised, and then he started grinning.

"What? What's funny?" I asked.

"Ali Jan, you are a mind reader. It is exactly what I was thinking," he said.

It was my turn to be surprised. I had been dreading telling him. I imagined he would have thought me ungrateful or been hurt that I wanted to move away from him, but he seemed very pleased at the suggestion.

I talked a lot about it at work, asking everyone if they knew how I could get a place of my own. One night, when the boss was running me home, he gave me the name and phone number of a Mr. Husain, an acquaintance of his from his mosque, who owned property, which he rented out. "You can use my name as a reference because I know how much money I am holding for you. I have been unhappy for some time about where you live because there are too many drug addicts around here. Half of them are crazy, and they will do anything to get money, as you know. They could kill you. And I don't want to lose a good worker," he said laughing, "and flowers for funerals are expensive."

That is how I came to get my own place.

I phoned Mr. Husain, as recommended by my boss. He said he was expecting a call from me. He said he had several properties, but most of them were already occupied. We arranged to meet.

He was about five foot eight, and very skinny, in his late forties. He had brown skin, humorous blue eyes, and a very big fat nose. He kept his beard long. He had lost nearly all his hair, except for a small amount of black hair at the back of his head. I liked him and felt easy with him. He drove me to see one or two properties that were vacant. The first one was too noisy, while another was well out of the city. Another was beautiful, and I would have liked to have taken it, but it was far too big, and the rent was more than I wanted to pay. We had seen half a dozen properties, but I was unsure. Mr. Husain did not seem to mind my indecision. He did not try to push me into anything. He drove me toward my home and simply said, "Take your time. You have my number if you need to call me, and I will tell your boss if anywhere else becomes available." I thanked him and apologized for wasting his time. He smiled. "I have a son a few years younger than you. You remind me of him. It must be hard for you to be in a big city on your own, I don't think he could do what you have done." I told him that I was not alone, but with my cousin. In our street, I got out of the car, and we shook hands. After he had gone, I thought that maybe not all Iranians were bad.

Later, I talked to Abbas about it. I hoped he would agree to coming with me, and we could have afforded the beautiful apartment I had seen, but he said he didn't want to move. He was settled, his work and his friends were close by. I was disappointed. Was he really glad that I was going?

At the factory, everyone was given a notebook to write down how many garments they made. Every Thursday afternoon, the manager came around and asked us for our totals. Most of the workers had sewn about thirty to fifty-five dresses maximum per week. But I had sewn ninety to one hundred in the same amount of time. There was a big difference between me and the others. My boss called me "ingenious," and so did some of my co-workers.

I was beginning to design stylish new samples, and the other tailors had to copy me. It was clear that one or two of my co-workers were unhappy that I was doing so well. Even the boss noticed it. We had a meeting every month. One day in the meeting the boss asked me to sit beside him.

"Afghanistan is our neighbor. That means we are like brothers and sisters. We need to respect Ali. He is like our brother, and he is an ingenious and intelligent tailor. I am proud of him because he works hard. Our productivity is up, so everyone here is going to have lunch for free," he said. So we had a good party.

Next day, when I went to work, everyone treated me differently. I was always respectful to everyone. I never acted like an "ingenious tailor." I really liked my job, but I never like Iranian racists and how they acted and how they were disrespectful to Afghans.

Eventually, I rented a neat house. It had two small bedrooms, a big living room, and a large basement. Abbas helped me to move in, although I did not have much to carry. He said he liked the house and wished me all best wishes. We agreed to see each other on Fridays, which was everyone's day off. He said that one of his friends might be coming to live with him, but if I was not happy with my new home, he would always find room for me. That was just the way he was, thoughtful, considerate, and tactful.

Mr. Husain was a good landlord. He collected the rent from me monthly and was always ready with advice and suggestions. If he was busy, his wife came instead. She was a short, plump, happy lady. She dressed in a long tight black *monto*, which reached to below her knees, and a pair of jeans, which did not seem to suit her because she had a heavy seat. One day she arrived with a beautiful girl, her daughter. My heart missed a beat when I opened the door and first saw her. (She was a university student. She was very beautiful, about five foot six, and very slim. She had white skin and brown eyes.) She was dressed exactly the same as her mother, but the monto and the jeans looked fabulous on her. We were both shy with each other, and I am sure she was blushing. Her mother noticed this too and was going to say something but laughed instead. Rent days did not come around quick enough; I wanted to see more of Yasmine, that was her name. I had seen plenty of young girls before but never really noticed any of them. It was like an electric charge that ran through me when she smiled directly at me. She began to be on my mind all of the time.

I had been at the factory for a year and had become well known to everyone there. I got on very well with my boss; in fact I was becoming his favorite worker. He reviewed my year of work and was very pleased with my progress. Next day, he bought me a brand-new sewing machine and other tools.

On a Thursday afternoon, the day before *Eid*, I was working as usual when my boss came beside me.

"Ali I have a problem," he said.

"What is it?" I asked.

"I have been paid a very good price for an order of forty monto (lady's shirt), the ones you helped to design. They are not ready. The material has been cut to the pattern, and it is ready for sewing. I need them for tomorrow by 4:00 p.m. The order is from one of our best customers. He is coming tomorrow from another province to pick them up. If I don't have them ready, I will lose my business with him. He will be really mad at me. Tomorrow I will have to be at our retail outlet all day. Today is Thursday; everyone is going to leave early because tomorrow is Friday, and it is *Eid*, everyone's day off. Can you help me please? Stay all tonight and finish the order before he arrives. I will pay you double for each one. I will bring lamb kebab for your dinner and lunch," he said.

"But the time is 6:00 p.m. now," I said. "I am almost ready to go home, and tomorrow is my day off. My cousin Abbas and our friends are off too. We have plans for fun. I have worked eighty hours this week. I am so tired I need to take time off. I have to do my laundry by hand, shopping, and go to my boxing class," I said.

"Please, you are my best worker and 'ingenious' tailor. The only person who can finish them in this short period of time is you. Please, I beg you," he implored.

Eid Fitr is one of the great Islamic festivals. Its importance can be judged from the fact that Almighty Allah Himself ordered the believers to celebrate it. It is celebrated at the end of the month of fasting (Ramadan) and has a special significance for the Muslim society. I was really looking forward to the holiday and had made plans with Abbas, but my boss was very worried.

Eventually I agreed because he was very persuasive and very flattering about my work. He wanted me to do the job because I was super fast, and I always made things more beautiful than the sample.

"I am going to order food for you from the best restaurant in Tehran," he said excitedly.

He went out. The boss had asked two other tailors to stay and help, but they were just messing about, laughing and wasting time. I sent them home. Eventually everyone had left, and I was alone. I tied a red cloth on my forehead to keep my long hair from falling over my eyes and said, "Oh, Allah, help me to finish this job before 4:00 p.m. tomorrow."

I worked until 5:00 a.m.; I took a little nap and woke up again at 7:00 a.m. I had tried my best and worked fast. I broke three needles and kept pressing the accelerator on the machine all the way down all night. I did not take a break except for ten minutes for dinner and ten minutes for breakfast. Eventually I finished completely. I even packed them in plastic.

About 1:00 p.m., I took the red cloth off from my forehead and said, "Thanks, Allah, you helped me today, and I helped my boss."

I made tea for myself and waited for the boss to come in. He arrived and greeted me worriedly "Salam. Why are you sitting drinking tea? What has happened to the dresses?"

I did not say a word. I just looked at him and then raised my eyes to the shelf. He jumped to the shelf and checked everything over.

He said, "I can't believe it. It's finished before 4:00 p.m. You are amazing. I don't know how I can say thanks to you. I will write a notice on main door that you are the most ingenious tailor in world."

He drove us to one of his retail shops. He gave me two T-shirts and suggested I might like a suit or some dark trousers. I said that I would never wear them, and jeans would be better. He looked at me for a moment and said, "You wear jeans for work, you should think about changing your styles. Clothes can make a lot of difference to a person. You have seen that when we have had the models in, to wear our new designs. Clothes can make an ordinary girl into a princess. A suit would make a man of you, still if you are sure that you prefer jeans, take your pick."

And so I did. And then he gave me a cash bonus as a reward.

CHAPTER 19

MORE THAN I EVER DREAMED OF

I went home and took a shower. I watched the television for about twenty minutes. I was so tired and I went to bed at 8:00 p.m. I woke the next day at 6:00 p.m. I had slept 'round the clock. I cleaned my home and went shopping. I finished the laundry and cooked enough food for a week.

I went back to work after the holiday. I was about to start doing my job, when my boss arrived in the workshop and said, "Salam, Ali agha (Mr.), I have very good news for you. You know the forty monto (lady's shirts) you sewed. They were excellent. The customer loved them. He was so excited and has ordered about three hundred more montos. He also said to give it to the same tailor. He wants to meet you. You helped me to honor my promise to him, my business is safe. Today, I will take you to a beautiful restaurant. I will pay for your work today, but you will have the day off. Later we'll go out and have good fun."

At lunchtime, we went to a restaurant. I ordered some kebab with rice and salad. The food was delicious. During the meal, he had a phone call from the factory.

"I have to go somewhere. Have a great day, and see you tomorrow," he said.

I walked around the town center. It was very busy, and crowds were moving in all different directions. Too many motorcycles were passing by at very high speeds, but the traffic was moving well. The sun was shining, and the weather was nice and warm. I went to Abbas's home to see how he was doing. He was not in, but I left him a good message.

After a while, my boss hired three Afghan tailors. I helped them a lot to learn the trade. Some of the Iranian workers were very jealous because I did not help them as much as I helped my countrymen. They are racist and have two faces. They said some good things about me when I was present. In my absence, they said the opposite.

One day I decided to buy a sewing machine and tools for my home, and to start working one or two days a week for myself. I withdrew some money from the boss.

"What are you going to do with all this money?" he asked suspiciously.

"My mom is sick. I have to send some money to her in Afghanistan," I said.

If I had told him I needed it for my own business, he would have given me a hard time.

At work, I kept up the number of garments I made. My boss told his business friends about me when they came to visit sometimes.

I decided to work two days for myself and four days for the company. I told my boss I now needed to take two days off a week. He did not agree with my decision.

When I promised I would sew the same amount as before, eventually he said OK.

I put some notices around my area and gave my business cards to people. My notice read

CHEAP, FAST, EXCELLENT TAILORING SERVICE. READY AS PROMISED. and my name, address and phone number.

I was surprised; my first customer was Yasmine, my landlord's daughter.

She arrived with her mother on the second day of my business.

"Salam to you," I said.

Yasmine had brought her own favorite material.

"I want you to make this cloth into a beautiful dress for my university party."

I lost my confidence and was shy because she was a really beautiful girl. I took her measurements and discussed her design and other details, and told her to come back the next day.

Her mom asked, "Tomorrow?"

"Yes, madam, tomorrow."

She looked at her daughter and said, "That's fast, isn't it? How much will it cost?"

"Because you are my landlord and the first customer, I won't charge any money."

"That's not fair, because you are paying rent to us and you have your own expenses," her mother said.

"Just for this time, I don't charge any money, but if you bring any more work, the standard charges will apply."

Yasmine was looking at me from the corner of her eyes while I was talking. When I looked at her, she quickly looked away.

"See you tomorrow then," her mom said happily.

I had only her dress to work on. I tried my best to make it as beautiful as possible.

It was finished the same day. I also made two shirts, one for myself, another for my cousin Abbas. I had two phone calls that day regarding making clothes.

The next day, Yasmine came with her mother and her younger brother, Mortaza. He was about five foot three, and aged about thirteen, very skinny, just like his father, with narrow shoulders. He kept his black hair long, and it had a natural sheen. He had bright blue eyes, and brown skin, unlike his sister. And there was the beginning of the growth of a moustache and beard on his cheek, but he had not started to shave yet. We shook hands formally. He was shy and awkward, but we were both teenagers, and so I understood him.

The dress was on a hanger, and I handed it to Yasmine.

She asked, "Do you have a fitting room here?"

"Yes, I have," I said.

I had two bedrooms, and I'd made one of them into a fitting room.

She went in, put the dress on, and then came back into the room.

"I really like it. It's so beautiful. Thank you very much," she said very excitedly.

"You are very welcome," I said. I was so pleased.

Her mother was smiling broadly and telling her to turn this way and that. Then she said, "It is a very good fit. You certainly have been quick. We really should pay you . . ."

"No," I broke in, "we agreed yesterday. You are my first customer. It is a present. OK?"

"That is very kind of you."

Yasmine went and got changed. When she came in again, her brother jumped up from the sofa where he had sat in silence, and then they left.

That was the beginning of my business. I served my customers well and charged them less than other tailors. They told their friends. One person told another, and so my reputation grew.

I was thinking a lot about Yasmine. A week later she came to my workshop with three of her classmates. She was excited, and they all were giggling a lot and saying things to each other in slang Persian that I could not quite follow, but I knew they were talking about me. Yasmine saw that I was confused and said, "I really love my dress. I wore it at the university party. Every single person passed a comment about it. Some of my friends asked me who made it. A lot of my friends want to meet you and to order dresses, but I did not know if you are available. I've brought three of my classmates, they want dresses."

They were all laughing and teasing each other. I did not know how to deal with it because in Afghanistan, sexual feelings had to be repressed. Such a meeting, between young girls and a boy, would not have been possible without a chaperone. As you can imagine, boys fantasize about girls in their dreams, and here I was with three beautiful girls all teasing me as they waited to get measured, and they were enjoying themselves. I felt as though I was blushing from head to toe. One girl, Asma, who was bigger than the others, deliberately caused the tape to slip, so that I had to do the measuring several times over. I was trying to write the figures down, but my hand began to shake. Another girl got behind the girl I was trying to measure and was putting her bag against her friend's back so that the measurement was twenty inches more than it should have been. They were merciless. I was lost, and Yasmine was embarrassed. The trio continued laughing.

"Let's measure him!" one suggested.

"He's got a big chest . . ."

"And big arms. He's a boxer, aren't you?"

"One minute," I said, and almost ran out of the room. I could hear them laughing hysterically, as only teenage girls can. Wow. If my business was going to be like this, what was going to happen to me? I was not used to being harassed by *girls*. I headed for the washroom because I couldn't think of what else to do. It gave me a minute to think. What should I do? Run away? Call the police? A man is supposed to be in control in his own business, but I had lost it. Then I became angry. I had to get them out of the place.

I could hear Yasmine telling them off. I came out of the washroom and headed back into room. They were quieter now.

"The best thing . . . The best thing is for you to come another time . . ." I said shakily, "but not all together," I added quickly.

"He wants to see us alone," Asma quipped. And the giggling began to break out again.

"Right. That's it. We are going," Yasmine shouted angrily. "I am sorry for their behaviors, Ali."

"It's only in fun, Ali," Asma said. "You've got to have a laugh sometime, haven't you?"

"That's OK," I said, trying to gain control "Next time you come, bring your mothers."

"He's into older women, that's it," Asma again, and the laughter broke out again.

"Out," Yasmine commanded. She was at the door now, holding it open.

Samera was the first to go. "Bye, Ali. Nice to meet you."

Amna was next, "Bye, Ali. See you again soon," and she blew me a kiss. "I've got your number. Bye."

"Bye, handsome." This was Asma, walking with exaggerated style. "We'd all like to see a lot more of you," she said with a wicked long wink, and the laughter broke out again outside the door. Yasmine was following them and turned to apologize. "I should have known this would happen. I'm sorry, very sorry."

"Are you coming, Yasmine?" Asma shouted.

"They really do want dresses, really. They just don't know how to behave. Look, I brought you some CDs of Iranian's music, I hope you like it." She left them on the table and walked away. I could hear the girls laughing as they went. I'd never come across anything like this before. Did I need a chaperone?

My little house suited me perfectly because it was just about the right size for me to start working for myself. Mr. Husain and his family were supportive. I told him my plans, and he was very interested. I had grown to like him and his wife because they were a very happy couple and enjoyed being together, and so of course their whole family was a happy one. I noticed almost immediately how different their marriage was from that of my own parents. My father would think nothing of hitting my mom over trivial things. He encouraged me to criticize her and to spy on her when he was away. She deceived him over money, and he deceived her with other women. I had seen it for so long that I thought all marriages were like that. Now here in Iran was a lovely middle-aged couple with a fine family, and I thought it was great. They liked me too, I could tell. Mrs. Husain was especially friendly because I flirted with her a little, and she liked that. One day, when she came to collect the rent, she asked me if she might ask a favor of me.

"Certainly," I said, wondering what was to come next.

"It's Mortaza, our boy. What it is . . . You have met him when he has been here with me, well, he seems to like you. He has mentioned you sometimes. What it is . . . We have too many women in our family, there are my sisters and our girls and Husain's poor sister, Clovinda, She has never been the same since her betrothed threw her over. She cries at every little thing, and there are our nieces as well. And then there is only Mortaza, and baby Omar." She stopped and looked at me as though she had explained everything, but I had only just been able to keep up with what she had said. My Persian was not wonderful.

"Mortaza," I repeated. "What is the matter with him? Is he ill?"

"No. He's fine. A bit skinny, but most teenage boys are, aren't they? Maybe that's part of it. What it is . . . There are too many women at home . . ."

"I am not understanding what the problem is with Mortaza. What do you want me to do?" I said, trying to find out what the problem was.

"He is painfully shy. We have spoiled him too much. Iranian women are like that. Daughters have to get on with things and learn house crafts. Sons are put on a pedestal. You know what I mean. It is the same in your country. He is very precious to us . . . As he has started to become a man, he has become terribly self-conscious. He thinks everyone is looking at him all the time. Can you help us?"

"How?" I said.

"You go to the gym and boxing classes. Would you take him with you sometime? At the moment, he is frightened of his own shadow. I know you are a busy man, and we'll pay all expenses . . ." she said, her eyes growing wider as they search my face.

"Oh is that all?" I said, I thought there had been a real problem. "How old is he, twelve, thirteen? I'll have to think out a plan. He can't go straight into boxing. I started when I was eight or nine with kids the same age. I'd have to train him up . . . He needs to sharpen up his reactions . . . Build some muscle." I was thinking as I was speaking. I was only about fifteen or sixteen myself, but physically I was much bigger than he was, and more mature, I thought.

"It would take time. He has to come often at first . . ."

"I can bring him as often as you want. If I can't, Yasmine can, she can drive now."

Well, that was it for me. If Mrs. Husain had been a saleswoman, she had just made the selling point, and she didn't even realize it. The beautiful Yasmine was going to bring her brother, and my prayers were being answered.

Mortaza was in a bit of a state when I had a good look at him. But everyone has to start somewhere. I got through his defensiveness almost right away and tried to give him confidence about his slimness. I told him he would make a good flyweight boxer in time, if that was what he wanted. I had good friends at the gym and asked for their help and warned them not to give him a hard time. They were a rough and ready bunch and normally would have given him a ribbing and had a laugh at his size, but good enough, they behaved themselves. There was to be no boxing for him just yet, but I started him with a basic workout of eight exercises, which would build up all parts of his body. The weights were fairly light, and I kept an eye on him. Over time, he did put on a bit of muscle, and he began to get more confident.

My thoughts were constantly on Yasmine, and though she was guarded and shy, I was sure she liked me, or was I mistaken? Was her mother encouraging us to meet?

After a short while, I got more customers. In fact, I began to get more and more customer every day. I worked only three days a week at the factory. I made much more money working for myself. And I had a lot more fun. Yasmine often dropped by, usually with her mother or her brother. Mortaza began to get friendlier; he couldn't have known that I wished he wasn't there sometimes.

I signed a contract with a businessman. He and his partner told me that they wanted to order more than a hundred monto (lady's shirt) a week. I decided to stop working at the factory all together. I gave two week's notice and told my boss, "I have started my own business. There is no point for me to work for you anymore."

He was so disappointed because I was leaving. He was holding a lot of money for me. He promised he would give it to me when I needed it. I was sorry to leave. I had worked hard at that company, and the boss had always treated me fairly. I had a lot to thank him for because I had learned a trade there. Sometimes he came to visit me to see how I was doing. He told me,

"I always thought you would be a good businessman one day, but I never thought that it would happen so fast. It is amazing how successful you are. You deserve it."

My business got bigger and bigger. I couldn't handle it by myself because I took single orders from the public and bulk orders from businessmen. I worked six days a week from 8:00 a.m. to the middle of the night. Sometimes I even worked on my day off because I was behind with the orders. I employed someone to clean my house and do some cooking, and I was able to go to the boxing class more often. I bought another sewing machine and hired a tailor. Still I couldn't keep up with the orders. I did not like it when people shouted at me if I had not finished the job on time. I was so busy that I had to refuse to take some order. Some customers asked me to start a waiting list. I had some customers waiting for two to three weeks. I could not buy any more machines because my place was too small. I saved a good sum of money since I started the business. So I decided to rent a bigger place. I phoned Mr. Husain, and he helped with finding it. He had a larger house available. I saw it and decided instantly to take it. He was more excited than I was. I bought three more machines and hired five people, three men and two girls.

CHAPTER 20

MINDING MY OWN BUSINESS

I was very busy running my business. I had met a lot of good and bad people after I opened the workshop. I kept in touch with the good ones and got rid of the bad ones as soon as possible.

One Thursday afternoon, after my employees had left the workshop, I was busy checking over the figures. I had a phone call from Yasmine. She said she wanted to meet me. I told her I was busy doing my accounts. She said, "I can help with them."

Fifteen minutes later, she arrived and brought me a coffee. We sat down on the sofa in my office. We started checking the paperwork. She took the calculator from me, and I read out the number of dresses from the book. We worked for more than an hour and were about to finish when we stopped for a moment, I looked into her eyes, and she looked into mine. She dropped the calculator and touched my hair and said,

"You are handsome, Ali agha (sir)."

I kissed her and said, "You are very beautiful."

I kissed her some more, and we left the counting for another day. I took her to a good restaurant and then went to a cinema. When the lights went down, we kissed each other.

Next day we went to a park and shopping. I bought her some presents and then went to a restaurant again. After we had ordered, I asked, "Do your parents know where you are? In Afghanistan, we would have not been allowed to be together alone."

"I am eighteen years old. I don't have to give an account of my movements" was her answer.

"Do they know you are with me?"

"Yes, of course. We are adults. There isn't anything wrong. They know you, and they like you, and Mom thinks you are marvelous, I don't know why. This is Tehran, not Kabul or wherever you are from. Women have rights here." After the dinner, she said, "Thank you so much for everything. I really enjoy your company."

After that Thursday, I decided to work a little bit less and to spend some time with her. In my free time, Yasmine and I went everywhere together, to the parks, cinema, zoo, the mosque, theatre, shopping, restaurants, and skating. On one occasion we went to see a water-fountain show. It only took place at night. It was held in a beautiful park. In the warm evening air, we strolled together under wonderful illuminated trees, breathing in the perfume of the blossoms and flowers. The fountain show was very spectacular. Massive jets of water shot up into the air, they were lit by wonderful colored spotlights. Orchestral music played, and the fountain rose and fell as if the water was dancing to the music, to me it was the most magical thing I had ever seen.

One Friday Yasmine came to my house. We watched the television. We kissed each other and got very hot. We couldn't have sex because she was a virgin and kept to the stupid Iranian traditions. We were afraid of the government's rules and regulations. That rule was that if people had sex before marriage, the man would hang, the woman would be stoned to death.

"You need to come to my home and talk with my parents about *Khastekary* (to ask them to give my hand to you)," she said, "that is, if you want to."

I kissed her and said, "OK, my darling," I couldn't believe my luck.

We arranged the time for the following Friday at 6:00 p.m. I was to meet her parents formally at their house.

I went to a hair salon and had a haircut. I had made a beautiful suit for myself. I was ready to go to Yasmine's home, but I did not know what I should take with me. I thought for a moment. I remembered when Father and I went to Ghazni City to the wedding party, Father bought a bunch of flowers and some sweets for the woman he loved. I did not know what the Iranian tradition was. I decided to buy the same things as my father had done.

It was about twenty minutes before 6:00 p.m. I called *Achanse* (taxi agents). I went to Yasmine's home. I got there at ten past six o'clock. I knocked the door. Mortaza and Omar, her young brother, opened it. He was grinning broadly. I went inside the house. There was a family crowd. Fortunately I felt very relaxed and confident because I had been dealing with different people every day, and I knew Yasmine's family by now.

"Salam, gentlemen and ladies," I said smiling seriously.

"You are very welcome, Ali agha," Mr. Husain said happily. There he stood dressed immaculately in his Iranian clothes, his blue eyes twinkling, and he had a massive grin on his face. Everyone stood up for a moment. Yasmine was standing by the door. I handed her the flowers and sweets.

First, I shook her father's hand. We had been on friendly terms for some time, but this was a sort of formal occasion. He led me into the room and pointed out the sofa. I sat down, and Yasmine came and sat beside me. I started greeting people one by one and holding my right hand to the middle of my chest and moved my head down and up, which was the Afghan tradition. Yasmine introduced everyone. There were Yasmine's two aunts, three sisters, two brothers, one brother-in-law, and three nephews.

"Nice to meet you," I said happily to everyone. I noticed that her aunt Clovinda was smiling and weeping at the same time.

Everyone said, "Nice to meet you too, agha."

Yasmine's sister brought tea for everyone, while we were drinking it, we ate the sweets I had brought.

"How is the business, Ali agha?" Husain asked, smiling.

"Very busy, agha Husain," I said.

"I have heard all about your company and the service you provide. People pass many compliments about you. It is a great pleasure for us to have you here. You are a very young man. It's an excellent achievement for an Afghan man in Iran. It's unbelievable to me that you have a good business in Tehran City. If I had not known you since you started at the beginning, I would not have thought it possible. I will be honest with you, we did not like Afghan people before we met you. Millions of refugees came here from your country, and many of them were desperate and resorted to criminal ways to get by, but since you became my tenant, we have found you to be a nice person, and you are well respected in the neighborhood. I really like Afghan people now."

"Thank you so much for what you have said about me. It's hard to make judgments about different nationalities when you don't know them. Every nation has good and bad people. Everyone is different," I said.

He was quiet for a short while. I whispered to Yasmine, "Why is your aunt crying?"

"She is happy to see us together."

"Happy?" I asked. She did not reply.

"Do you want some more tea, Ali?" Yasmine's mom asked me.

"No thanks, *Khala Jan*," I said.

Husain stood up and spoke to everyone and then said, "Ali is our guest tonight, we are not going to talk about Yasmine this time. We will talk next time about this matter. We want to make him welcome and to feel at home. Shortly, I will be going to the mosque for prayers, also we have a meeting there."

I talked to everyone a little bit, after Husain left. Baby Omar climbed on to the sofa, wanting me to play with him. Everyone began to relax. The welcome was warm and natural, and I did begin to feel at home.

Yasmine's sister said, "I bought a dress a couple of days ago, it is a little big for me. Can I bring it now to see if there is any way you can alter it?"

"Leave it now, it's not the right time," Yasmine's mom said sharply.

"It's OK, I don't mind," I said.

She brought it, I looked at it, and I said, "Can you bring it to my workshop tomorrow? I will alter it for you."

We all watched television.

About an hour later, Husain came back from the mosque and said. "Yasmine, go to the kitchen and help your mom to bring the food in for dinner."

At dinner, there were chicken kebabs, beef kebabs, rice, minced meat, churned sour milk, naan, greens, yogurt, pickles, and salad.

After dinner, they brought tea. It was about eleven thirty when I left. I went home feeling lightheaded and very, very happy. I watched boxing movies because I did not want to go to bed.

Next day I got on with the work as usual, but I was singing, and the workers joined in just to tease me. It was about ten o'clock when Yasmine and her sister came for the alteration.

I told them, "Come back this afternoon or tomorrow, it will be ready by then."

On Friday Yasmine and I went to the park. We talked about our future and then went to our favorite restaurant. We made plans to meet her parents the following Friday regarding our marriage.

The following Friday, I bought a bunch of flowers and some more sweets, and a toy for baby Omar. The same crowd was there.

I told Husain, "You are like my parents, you can decide about me and Yasmine."

"I have already made my decision, which is I am not going to intervene. Yasmine is an adult and an educated girl. She can decide for herself because she is going to live her life with you, not me. My job is to make sure that you are a Shia Muslim and a nice person, and have a good career."

Yasmine said, "I have known Ali for a long time. He's the one I was looking for."

Everyone clapped their hands and said, "*Mubarak* Ali! *Mubarak* Ali! (Blessing congratulation)"

We made arrangements for the engagement party.

CHAPTER 21

WHICH WAY THE WIND BLOWS

I think it is a well-known fact that many women go crazy over weddings. Men do not. Our party was only to celebrate our engagement, but the way the women in Yasmine's family behaved, you would have thought that it was the most important event of the year.

We had decided to have the party three months after the *Khastekary*. I was all in favor of it. Maybe it was time to show off a little. I had done very well for myself with my business. I was young and very much in love with this beautiful girl, and I couldn't think why she was very much in love with me. I remembered I had once asked my father what "love" was, and he had said, "It's a kind of insanity. You do all kinds of crazy things, and when you look back on it, you wonder why on earth you had been so mad." that was his opinion, but then, he had fallen out of love with my mom (if he had ever loved her. He had had at least one girlfriend (*Zenee—Zagha-ee*). He always thought that he knew everything.

So the women chattered excitedly about anything to do with the party. Every aspect of it brought up accounts of other weddings and engagements. Who had worn what, who had said this, who had said that. How much this had cost. What had happened to "him." Where "she" was now. What had gone wrong there? How many children they had had, what scandal there had been. and so on, and so on. Aunt Clovinda was crying most of the time. She had been very much in love with a man who jilted her on her wedding day. She was heartbroken ,and young people's romances always reminded, but her frequent crying over a little things like a piece of wedding cake or a floral bouquet took on a comical aspect.

Yasmine and her student friends were in constant high spirits and seemed to be able to laugh and giggle at everything. Yasmine tried to

140

involve me in all of the craziness, asking my opinion on many things and then pretending to be very annoyed when I could not give her an answer. She used her usual feminine logic on me, but it did not work. She would ask questions like "Is my green dress the best color for me to wear, or is purple better?"

If I said purple was the best color, she would ask what was wrong with green, and vice versa. I couldn't understand her logic.

I made a very special dress for Yasmine. It was in a rich cream-colored satin with an over layer of lace into which gold thread had been hand-sewn. I also had made suits and dresses for other members of her family. I made three suits myself, one for me, the other two for Abbas and his housemate.

We were to hold the party in Yasmine's father's house. I invited all my Afghan and Iranian friends, and my employees, my former boss, and other businessmen, whom I had worked with. I spent a great amount of time and money. Abbas was surprised and pleased by it all. Yasmine's family had invited about a hundred people. Our guest list numbered about one hundred and forty altogether. Yasmine, her parents, and I went shopping. We bought everything for the party, such as beef, rice, chicken, naan, and other foods. As is the tradition, our neighbors and Yasmine's parents and my cousin Abbas cooked the foods to serve to our guests.

On the day of the party at six o'clock, I was sitting with Yasmine in the garden of Husain's house. It was much larger than their biggest room, and the whole family had decorated the trees with red Chinese lanterns. The trees were full of blossoms, and their perfume drifted in the air. There were candles everywhere, and all the tables had large flower arrangements on them. Our guests began to arrive, and Yasmine held my hand tightly.

"Now we're in for it," I said, getting ready for the ordeal. Most of the guests I already knew, and so the formalities were limited. Some Iranian music began to play.

There were many people in the middle of the garden by now, and they began to dance, and I encouraged them. As is our tradition, everyone danced alone. Some of them were good dancers, and I threw money at them. Other guests, who were not dancing, clapped rhythmically, keeping time with the music.

After the engagement ceremony, we served people with dinner. Some of the relatives stayed until 1:00 a.m. They were dancing and enjoying themselves. Toward the end of the party, Husain came to me and said, "*Murak Basha* (congratulation), Ali agha, I wish you all the best and an excellent life." He kissed me on my cheek and handed me a present.

"Thank you very much, Mr. Husain, for everything," I said.

Every one of their family got in a line and gave a gift for me and Yasmine and wished us "every happiness." I was so excited during my party.

After Yasmine's family had finished their presentations, Abbas took me to one side and said, "I think it is my turn now."

He seemed sad. "How are you doing?" I asked.

"Fine," he said. I shook his hand. We kissed each other on the cheeks.

"I can't express my delight. I am proud of you and wish you all the best." He handed me a present and also one for Yasmine. A little later he left. In the early hours of the morning, the party was finally over, everyone had gone, and I said a long good night to Yasmine.

When I got home, I opened Abbas's present. There was a picture of my parents and a letter. I looked at the picture for a moment and cried. In that picture was my beautiful mom standing next to father, holding his hand and smiling. Father looked very serious and tired. Abbas had taken that picture the day before he left Afghanistan, when he came to meet us for the last time. I felt so sad, and I was so sorry for what I had said to my mom. I now missed her so much.

Abbas wrote in his letter,

> First of all, I want to say congratulations on your engagement. I wish you all the best. I was so depressed, when your father did not let you come to Iran. Now I am glad that you are here with me. I am proud of all your achievements. I have been thinking about your present since you told me you were getting engaged. I could not think what I should buy. I decided on the photo of your parents because you have everything else in your life except this picture. I just want you to remember them please.
>
> Remembered Allah first, and don't ever forget your parents, your country, and your culture. You have never talked about your parents since you met Yasmine. One day we will all go back home to Afghanistan to visit them. Inshala.
>
> Yours faithfully,
> Abbas Rahimi.

Yasmine dropped her university courses because she loved tailoring and working with me. We were running my business together. Her family called in often. Yasmine was my secretary, and even took a hand in the sewing sometimes. I began to improve as a designer and made new styles of clothing for my market. I visited the museums and the libraries for ideas. I looked at the traditional Persian costumes and fabrics, and I tried to think how I could bring them into modern-day fashion. The use of jewelry and beading was also very interesting. But it was the subtle use of colors, the matching, shading, and contrasting, which I found most impressive.

One Wednesday afternoon, Abbas called in at our workshop. I was not in there. I was in my designing room. It was not as grand as it sounds. It was a small room at the top of the house, where it was quieter and cooler, and there was a big window, which, even when shaded against the fierce midday sun, let in plenty of light. I had a small sewing machine there and a large secondhand drawing board and a basket full of samples of cloth. I also had fashion magazines, which Yasmine found interesting. I had plenty of ideas. Some of them might work, and some of them definitely would not. I was trying to concentrate on men's fashion. It needed a boost, but people seemed to be so conservative. I had tried many different ideas, but nothing was working.

Yasmine came to me and said, "Sorry to disturb you, but your cousin Abbas is here. What should I do?"

"Oh, let him come up," I said.

When he came in, he looked very unhappy. He said, "Salam Ali agha."

"*Salam, bacha kahala* (Hi cousin), why did you say 'agha' to me? How are you?" I asked.

"Fine, what about you?"

"I can't complain," I said.

We went down to my office because there was nowhere to sit in the top room. I asked Yasmine to bring tea.

He began, "You have a very beautiful business and nice fiancée. She is a very nice girl. Ali Jan, you are very lucky. I don't want take your time because you were at the middle of something."

"Abbas, I am glad you came, I was stuck for ideas up there. I have got an idea at the back of my mind, but it won't come out. I needed this break. Now how are things with you?"

"That's why I've come. The construction job has finished. They don't need us workers anymore. I've been trying for days to find another construction job, but I can't. Wherever I went, there were too many people after the same job. They don't pay as much as they used to. I have decided to follow your way; I have to try to get into a different trade." He stopped for a moment and then burst out, "I would like to start working for you. Can you give me a job? You know, I have always enjoyed studying religious books and would love to become a Molla someday *inshallah*. But I need to make money, while I study."

"Abbas, of course I can. Why didn't you let me know before now? You are very welcome to start at any time. I have not asked you to work here because this work is so different from construction work. You are used to working with strong men, and this is totally different. It might take a bit of time, but if I can do it, so can you. I will teach you how to sew. Once you have learned how to do that, I will teach you more and more, step by step. Is that OK?"

"Fine," he said cautiously.

There is other work here besides sewing. There is checking, delivering, packing. The best thing about you coming here is I know you. I can trust you. You know what people are like. We, Yasmine and I, we have to watch the people, who are supposed to be watching the other workers. Things go missing. Money doesn't balance. You will be . . . I can't tell you how glad I am about this."

And so it was settled there and then. Yasmine brought the tea, and we drank a toast to Abbas. Good old Abbas. I would never have offered him a job because I thought he would have been too proud to work in a workshop environment for me because I was much younger than him. He was a big guy, well over six foot; with a beard, and it may have been the look of him that had caused me not to think of asking him. But he would be perfect in many ways. I was delighted. After he left, I took Yasmine into the office, and we closed the door. And then we discussed how we could alter his appearance. Even doing that was fun. But then, everything we did together was fun. Next day Abbas came to work. He was dressed the same as always. Well, he *was* a construction worker. I knew that he did not have a big selection of clothes, he had never needed them. I made him some shirts and trousers for the job. I tactfully said that all the girls would be after him, if he didn't have a beard, and he took the hint. A few days later, we went to a proper hair salon to get him a special cut and style. He had only ever had the most basic of haircuts; sometimes he had just let it go wild. You would have thought that he was going to have his head cut off, instead of just his hair. I have never seen anyone look more uncomfortable. I thought that at one point he was going to run out of the shop. And he would have done if we hadn't had an appointment booked, and a chair was ready and waiting for him. He was not used to having his hair washed by another person. He thought the young male hairdressers were effeminate and was nervous about them. It was no use asking him what style he wanted. I gave the instructions that I thought were best. The combing and the blow-drying he submitted to unhappily. Eventually it was all over. What a difference. He had a smart short style, which, I'm sure, he secretly liked because he kept looking at himself in any available mirror. The cologne was a different matter, and he complained that he smelled like a woman. He told me later that his flatmate pulled his leg about it, until he had washed the scent away. However, he liked his new hair cut because it always fell back into place after he washed it without him having to do much to it.

I went every Friday to Yasmine's house and stayed the night. After a short while, I made Abbas the supervisor in my workshop and gave him keys so that he could open and close the premises when I was busy. I went to my boxing classes three times a week because I now had more time. We had boxing competitions in our club every two months. I had won several times. My coach liked me very much and taught me new tricks every time, because we made a bargain, he would teach me and I would make dresses for his wife for free.

One Friday, the weather was glorious, and after going to the mosque, my fiancée and her family and Abbas and I went on a special excursion, which Husain had been planning. We went through the mountains to the North of Tehran to the Caspian Sea. The mountains were very high, and the vegetation changed to pine forests, and there was snow, and skiing was the local sport. We carried on to the seaside, to a beach for a BBQ. The fresh sea air was wonderful, and the sight of the sun dancing on the sea was a delight unfamiliar to an Afghan's eyes. We made some kebab, and sent Abbas and Yasmine's younger brother to buy some beverages. I had grown to know Mortaza much better, he was a very funny boy, and he seemed to like me very much, and vice versa.

He came back very worriedly about ten minutes later and said,. "When we went to the shop, on the way, there were four guys. They stopped us and told Abbas, 'Affy, where are you going?' Abbas did not say anything, and we walked away. We were about to reach to the store, one of these guys hit Abbas from behind. Abbas told me to call you."

"Where are they?" I asked.

"I'll show you," he said.

We ran to where Abbas was. I saw he was on the ground. These stupid people beating and kicking him. I shouted at them, "Stop. Stop." They did not take any notice of me. They started swearing at me and said, "Who the hell are you?"

I was really mad at them. I wanted to find out what had happened. They did not let me. They started punching me too. I hit the big guy first on his face as hard as I could. He fell down instantly. Abbas and Mortaza were fighting with them as well. The big guy was bleeding and shouting for help. Two of them were fighting with Abbas, another one with Mortaza. I helped Abbas. I hit another one to his kidney very hard. He screamed and fell down. There were two left. One was smaller than Abbas.

"Abbas, put him down," I said.

I ran to the one who was fighting with Mortaza. I grabbed his hand and twisted very hard and punched his arm. Mortaza punched his face. Eventually I broke his arm. There was only one left. He looked at his buddy whose nose was bleeding, he ran away. We followed him and were about to catch him, when the police arrived.

They took us to the police station. We explained to them what had happened. They let Mortaza and Abbas go home. One of the police officers asked me, "Where are you from?"

"Afghanistan," I said.

"Do you know what you have done to these people?" he said.

"I just defended my cousin and myself. You already know what is going on."

"What I know is you have broken one man's arm, two ribs, and knocked out four teeth. Who are you? Are you Bruce Lee?"

"What do you do?" a different officer asked.

"I did not mean to break parts of their bodies. It happened accidently. My name is Ali, I have my own business. You know every day Irani people beat up Afghan people, and no one helps them," I said. "When can I go?"

"You will be here until we find out about this incident," he said.

I was in jail for thirty-five hours. I prayed all night. At about 2:00 a.m., I was just about to fall asleep, the police officer woke me up and told me, "You are going to leave here now."

"Thanks, Allah, you accepted my prayers. I am going home now to see my fiancée," I said to myself.

Instead of releasing me, they took me to another jail where I was badly beaten, and then they sent me to Tehran City. I was kept there for a while. I received visits from Yasmine, Abbas, and Husain at different times. They were trying to help me, but it was decided that I should be deported. They beat me up again and again, and shouted. "Who do you think you are, fucking Bruce Lee? You are a fucking boxer. Affy, we will teach you some boxing here. Fuck off, Affy. Go back to Afghanistan, and kill the Taliban. You are a good fucking fighter."

After a long while, they deported me back to Afghanistan.

BOOK 3

Ali boating at night.

CHAPTER 22

OLD HAUNTS

I arrived in Herat City, Afghanistan on the deportation bus from Tehran. The government of my country had changed. I heard Ahamed Karzai was now Afghanistan's president.

The bus had been full of unlucky Afghan men. (Most of them were Hazaras because they were easily identifiable, but there were some Tagic and Usbeks) All of them, like me, had gotten caught without papers. We presented a sorry sight, my fellow passengers and I, as we got down into the street at the bus depot. All of us had been beaten up, time and again, by the stupid Iranian guards, and some of the others still had bruises and black eyes to prove it. The policy of ill-treatment was carried out to act as a deterrent, to make it clear to us that going to Iran would not be a pleasant experience for refugees, but the civil wars, the Taliban and the Russian occupation of my country, had caused a steady exodus of Afghans over many years. Literally millions of people had been killed and displaced by the troubles.

I certainly did not want to return to Iran until I could be sure that I could not be deported again. I would have to try to get a passport and a visa. I suppose I had been lucky, although it was a sad kind of luck because Abbas had got a good lawyer for me, who was able to produce reliable witnesses to prove that I was not guilty of causing the fight in that seaside town on the Caspian Sea. If things had gone against me in court, I would certainly have been sent to prison, and Iranian prisons are notoriously bad places. But as good as he was, the lawyer could not dispute the fact that I was an illegal immigrant, and so I had been detained for some more months, while waiting to be sent back to Afghanistan.

The journey from Tehran had been swift, and it only took about eighteen hours to get us to Herat. It had taken me two weeks to get there, cross-country, with the smugglers, when I had left my country ages ago with poor Matin. This time we had driven at speed on the main highway, on excellent roads through the mountains. At any other time this would have been an exciting experience. The scenery was spectacular and, of course, the weather was brilliant, but none of the passengers was happy. Some were relieved to be out of prison, but all of us were apprehensive about our immediate future. I am naturally of an open nature and make friends easily, but on this trip I had too many things whirling around in my head, Yasmine, and all our plans, my business, which was now nonexistent, my future in Afghanistan, and so on. To tell the truth, I was not in good of health because of prison food, lack of exercise, and the beatings. I had lost weight and even muscle bulk. When you are feeling down, even small things seem massive, and I couldn't see any way forward. Thank Allah for Abbas! He had done as much as he could for me. His concern was evident, even when I got off the deportation bus, because somehow he had arranged for me to get some of the money from the sale of my business, at the main city mosque. This was an amazing achievement, given the state of things in Afghanistan, where even a simple phone call was a minor miracle.

I had decided that I should go home and see my father. Well, where else was there for me to go? I had missed my mom very much when I had first arrived in Tehran, but other things had taken over my life. Now that I was back in Afghanistan, I thought I would journey to Ghazni City and on to our village and stay there for one or two weeks. I would tell Father about my fiancée and my business. Knowing him, he would have something to say about that. It is our tradition, that our parents have the right to arrange our marriage partners for us. People as young as twelve years old are often married, but I had decided who I was going to marry, and if things had not gone wrong, I would have been already married. I was no longer the boy I was when I left. I was an independent man. But I was beginning to feel uneasy because I had neglected to keep in touch with home. Communication of any sort was almost impossible in my country, and that had been the real reason for not doing so, but I began to have a pang of remorse and began to worry.

Once I had thought things through, I would get that passport and go back to Iran legally. I bought some beautiful presents for my parents.

So I made my way home to our village. I had forgotten how crazy transport was. I found the street where cars, vans, and buses were parked ready for journeys to other cities. Everyone was shouting out destinations and prices. I got into a van, we drove to Kandahar and then on to Ghazni City. The journey was long, hot, and unpleasant, and I changed vehicles several times. The people seemed happier with the new government, the Taliban had been removed from the main cities, but they still attacked people in outlying areas. There was lots of construction work on the way. Everything in the country was improving.

Eventually I got out of the van in our village. I stood for a few minutes at the side of the dusty street, just looking at the scene, then I walked through the cluster of mud-walled houses, among the few people who lived there, I realized that I did not know anyone, and nobody recognized me. I was much taller and more mature than when I left. I had on a smart jacket and slacks, but I looked out of place. I had forgotten how village people were. The men regarded me with suspicion, it showed in their faces. Children followed me at a distance, but were afraid or too shy to come near. Then I hurriedly took the track that led to our farm. I called in at our old neighbor's home, which was on the way. There were different people living there. Everything had changed a lot from the way it used to be. I moved quickly on. I was looking forward to seeing my folks. I was so excited and thought everything would be wonderful.

When I reached the farm, it had a neglected air about it. Weeds were growing all over the place. There was no one around, and none of the usual signs of life, no smoke from a fire, no washing drying in the sun, no smell of cooking, and no singing coming from the windows. I went to the side of the house to the apple trees where I used to hide my savings and remembered how Father watered them. The trees were bigger now. There were many apples on the ground going bad. No one had collected them, the place was deserted. I sat down on the ground with my back against one of the tree. I sat for a while, trying to think what to do. This was not the homecoming I had expected. Everything had changed. I was tired because of the journey, and I was turning things over in my mind. I thought about my life and how it had been before I went to Iran. There, life had taken hold of me, and I had had to deal with the reality of just staying alive. I had done well for myself, but only because of my determination to get on. Then I went away to find my parents. At last I found some people who knew me. I was told, "We haven't seen your father lately. Your mother will be on the mountain, with the sheep,

you know the place, and it is where you left them, when you went away."
Country people never forget anything.

I made my way there, and the memories came flooding back. The brilliant daylight was the same, the scudding clouds passing in front of the strong sun, cast great moving shadows over the hills and down the valley. The scene changed constantly. And there was the wind, I had forgotten the wind. It pulled at my clothing and tugged at the rough grass that clung to the mountainside, and it caused the trees to thrash about in a frenzy. I remembered Father said it came from China.

I could hear the stupid sheep bleating even before I saw them, they were exactly the same, but I could not see Mom. I climbed my way up to my old vantage point on the great gray boulder, and I spotted a small figure, her clothes billowing in the wind, just over toward my left, a little in front of me. She appeared to be praying. I got closer to her. She did not notice me at all because of she had covered her face. I could hear her speaking. She seemed very upset. She was crying and talking to Allah.

I was very affected to find her like this. I was now very near to her.

"Salam, mother Jan," I said. There was no reply. I moved a little forward and said again, "Salam, mother Jan (Hello, Mother)."

"Who's that?" she said.

"If you take the cover away from your face and look at me, you will know me."

She pulled her scarf up to cover her hair and at the same time looked in my direction. Fear showed in her face.

"What do you want from me?"

She didn't recognize me.

"Who are you? What do you want? I have no money."

"I am here to see you, mother Jan. I am Ali, your black boy, don't you know me? I left the sheep here behind me, on this mountain. Where is my father?"

"Is that you Ali Jan, my son?" She stared at me suspiciously. "I can't believe this, oh Allah."

She stood up and came to me and hugged me, crying. We sat down right there for a short while and then went toward home, talking breathlessly as we picked our way down the steep path, shouting against the wind.

"Where is my father?" I asked.

"He is in Kabul."

"Why are you here then? Did he leave you?"

"Yes, he did, he went on business."

"Why didn't you go with him?"

"I couldn't leave here because of you. I knew that you would come back one day." She stopped walking and turned to me, smiling. "Oh my son, you are so handsome, exactly like your father when he was young."

We got to the farmhouse. She put fresh water in the samovar and lit it, and while she got the tea things together, I began to get the full story.

"When you left, he went away from me. I was crying and thinking all about you. My son, when you left us, everything else left us too, happiness, love, peace, and your smile. We searched for you for about three months. We couldn't find anything. Your father changed. I don't think he ever really loved me. He began to neglect things. I knew he was going away from me. Things got worse. He treated me as bad as he could. We argued a lot. He beat me. He decided to go to Kabul, to work and live there. When he comes, once or twice a year, he just comes here for our land, to see how things are, to check that the trees haven't been stolen. Then he leaves without even saying bye to me. He has never brought anything since you left. My brother Nasser sends money from the England to support me, because I'm living here by myself. Sometimes when Nasser's friends come home to visit their family, they drop off your uncle's presents to me. I am alone. I am very lonely, my son. Please don't leave me again . . . I go to that mountain, just to pray to Allah, for your health, and that you would come back home soon."

It was clear that things had been neglected inside the house as well as outside. There was no food, except for eggs, some poor vegetables from Mom's patch, some fresh naan bread, and apples. We talked well into the evening, that is to say, Mom did most of the talking. It was like releasing a coiled spring. She had not had anyone to talk to for some time, and so I got all the news about the family going back over the years since I had left. Mom had had a bad time of things.

I lit the paraffin lights as darkness came. I felt so sad. I had been expecting a hard time, from Father. I had expected an argument, and I had hoped for reconciliation, and even, just possibly, a small celebration at my homecoming. I had hoped to have time to be able to get my health back. When I got off the bus in Herat City I had thought I had problems enough, they faded out of view when I saw the way things had gone here at home.

"I have had enough crying and sadness, and enough worry," she continued. "My father died when the Americans attacked the Taliban. Three weeks later, my mom died because of her illness. I could not help her because there was no man to go to the doctor with us. During the Taliban time, you know that women weren't allowed to go out by themselves," she said, crying.

"Forgive me, Mom, I did not know that all these bad things were happening to you. I should not have left you. That was my fault. Oh my poor mom," I said sadly.

It grew late, and I was really longing to go to bed. She kept looking at me and smiling. I gave her, her present, which was a bolt of some silk material in a deep shade of blue. Father's present I left in my bag. She began to feel happier. I felt worried; we agreed not to make any decisions about what we should do next until the morning.

Waking up that morning on that farm was a strange experience. All the sounds I ever remembered were around me. The rooster crowing, animals lowing, and the wind rattling, everything. More cups of chai and then we sat down to talk. All decisions in families in Afghanistan are left to the men. Women are not used to having to decide anything. So Mom was looking to me to tell her what to do. I had just arrived. I did not know anything about anything. Father had always kept everything in his own hands.

Women had no rights. She kept looking at me, was expecting me to sort everything out. As her son, it was my duty. I had money from my business, which would have lasted me a couple of months, but now I had responsibilities I had not expected. Things could not continue as they were, but I did not know enough to make any decisions. I wanted to go back to Iran that had been my overall plan. I told my mom about my business and my fiancée and only the good things that had happened to me since I left her. I eventually made her smile, and she laughed when I was telling her about Yasmine.

We decided at last that we had to find Father. We would go together because it was clear that she was neglecting herself. The farm was too much for her, there was hardly any food, and she had no money, and so on. She said she couldn't leave because Father would not want her to. I said she could not stay there as things were. She said she thought that I would start to run the farm again, for her. That was not my intention. The situation was impossible. We went on turning things over and over. The answer had to be "to find Father."

Next day we went to Kabul. I had paid a cousin to look after the sheep. Mom looked older now, all her hair was gray, and she seemed to have all sorts of pains.

It was about 7:00 p.m. when we arrived in Kabul. We went to the house where we used to live. I knocked the door. A young man of about thirty opened it, and he looked at us blankly and said, "How can I help you?"

"We are here to see my father," I said, looking past the man into the hallway.

"Who is your father? Why would he be here?" was his reply.

"He owns this house. I lived here when I was a boy," I said.

"We bought this house, oh . . . a long time ago, from Mr. Satiq Akbari," he said.

"That is my father's name. He sold this house to you?" I asked in disbelief. "Did you know about this?" I asked Mom. She shook her head.

"I have been away in Iran, and my mom was in Ghazni province. We don't know about this—"

"I have been living here for years. Everything was done legally," he said.

"Do you know where my father is now?" I asked.

"No, I am sorry," he said. "Many people are looking for relatives. I have not seen him since we bought the house, a long time ago. I am sorry," he repeated, as he shut the door.

"Mom, did you know about it?" I asked again.

"No, my son," she said. "He didn't tell me."

"Father sold our house and did not tell you about it? I will find him, dead or alive. I promise you, Mom," I said angrily.

So we went to a hotel that night. Thankfully, it was much cleaner than those I had stayed in on my journey. Mom looked at me constantly and kept hold of my hand.

"Thanks to Allah. He brought you back to me. You have improved your personality a lot," she said very happily. Now her troubles were over. Mine were just starting.

CHAPTER 23

SEARCHING

I had not been in Kabul since I was a child. We had fled from there, for our lives. We went to Mazar-i-Sharif as the Taliban invaded the city. I had no real memories of it, except that the area we lived in was in a semi-derelict state. At the time, I did not know that it was so badly damaged because I had never known it to be any different. Now, after all those years, it still seemed to be in the same condition. The ring of high sharp mountains surrounding the city still pointed up into the clear sunlit sky, giving an impression of peacefulness. I remembered that it was from those mountains that we heard the rumble of the artillery as the deadly shells were launched. A minute later they came whistling into the city, and the explosions followed. I remembered the wave of panic that took control of me because we knew the shells were coming, but we didn't know where they would explode. Now we were back again, but now I had had the experience of living in Tehran. Now I knew what a modern city should be like. And I wanted to know if things in Kabul had improved. I had heard that there were special people from abroad who were working to remove the thousands of land mines and cluster bombs left over from the civil wars and the Russian occupation. These murderous devices littered the cities and the countryside, maiming the children who played with them, or the farmer who ploughed them up. I knew from the TV in Iran that a lot of money had been sent as aid by foreign countries, so things should have been improving. Some areas were amazingly modern, with great luxurious houses surrounded by security railings and high walls, but many other areas remained devastated, and there were no signs that anything was being done about them. The rich were clearly getting richer, and the poor, well, I don't think they could have got any poorer.

The day after visiting our old home, we went to find my grandfather's house. We thought my father might be there. The old man had been fairly well off for money, I had memories of his pleasant old house, which was of a stately style, in a quiet neighborhood of tree-lined avenues.

When we got there, the trees had been hacked down years ago for firewood during the severe winters, when the city had been under siege. The shelling from the mountains had wrecked the area. We found the house, but there was nobody there at all. It was damaged, everything from inside was missing, and even the timber of the doors and doorframes had been stolen. It had been completely looted. Mom was very upset. We looked around for a very short while. She cried a lot. "This house used to be very nice. My parents lived here for years. I grew up here. When I had problems, or your father was away, I used to bring you here to see your grandparents. Do you remember? This is awful, awful." She started to sob. "Now they're dead, and nothing is left in the house."

"They are with Allah now" was all I could think to say.

She was very miserable. I led her away from there as quickly as I could. One bad thing seemed to follow another. It took time to get Mom to calm down.

We went to a café. After the lunch, Mom said, "I need to see a doctor; I have a pain in my chest. It is hurting a lot."

"OK, we will go now and find one," I said. I was worried. I had noticed that she had been in pain sometimes, but she always said it was rheumatism, or old age.

We found a doctor nearby and got an appointment for the next day.

My original plan, when I arrived, had been to stay one or two weeks with my father and mother in Ghazni province to get my strength back, but it had now been many weeks. I had not expected to find a lot of problems here. I desperately wanted to see Yasmine again soon. I had tried phoning dozens of times, but I was never able to get through. She was in my thoughts and my dreams all the time. Damn this backward country. A phone call was all I wanted.

Next day we went to see the doctor. There were a lot of people waiting for him. We arrived on time, but waited for an hour. Nobody called us. I spoke to the receptionist. I explained that we had an appointment for that day at 9:00 a.m. Nobody had called us. "What is the problem?" I asked angrily.

"Follow me," he said.

We went outside the room. He said, "You did not give me any money."

"For what?" I asked.

"Is this your first time visiting the doctor?"

"Yes," I said.

"If you want see the doctor quickly, you have to give me some money, otherwise you have to wait for several hours."

"Is this the doctor's fees?"

"No, you will pay him when you finish the appointment."

"What is this for then?" I asked surprised.

"Oh Allah, you don't understand, what I mean is, you will have to wait for several hours."

"Do you want a bribe to let me in?" I asked sharply.

"Yes. Look, I don't like asking people for money, but the doctor is not paying me much. I have three kids. How can I support them?" he said.

I gave him some money. Five minutes later, we went to see the doctor in his room.

He checked my mom and took some X-rays. He told the nurse to take some samples from her, and wrote things down on a clip file. The nurse helped Mom to dress and took some tiny bottles out of a cupboard. The doctor called me to come to another room.

"Sit down," he said.

I sat. "What is wrong with my mom?" I asked worriedly.

"Who's in charge, I mean who is supporting her?" he asked.

"My father should be, but he is lost now. I am taking care of her."

"Has she been unwell for some time?" he asked.

"I have been in Iran until about a month ago, so I don't know. She is living in Ghazni province, and there is no doctor in the village."

He studied his notes and began, "There is nothing wrong with her heart. She appears to be malnourished, if that continues, it affects the whole body. If she doesn't eat regularly, or does not eat properly, that will cause flatulence, wind, which in itself is painful and will cause chest pains. She is not very old, but her condition is common these days. Her condition is not life-threatening as it is . . . Her diet will have a lot to do with her progress. Also she needs to rest. She is now having urinary and a blood samples taken by the nurse. The results of the tests will be ready the day after tomorrow. They will give me more information." He looked up from his notes and smiled. "For now, I am going to give you a prescription. Get the medicine as soon as possible. It will help her to feel better."

She took her medication the same day. I told her that the doctor said she did not have a heart problem. The following day she felt better. We saw the doctor again, and he explained the test results. Iron deficiency, slight anemia, and a few more terms that meant nothing to me. He gave me another prescription and a detailed written report of what he had found. He said she could see a doctor again in a month's time, to check everything was OK. There was nothing seriously wrong with her, and we had no need to worry.

We searched Kabul for my father for about a month. It was still a busy city, and the suburbs covered many kilometers. We tried to think of anywhere he might be living. We looked for any relative he might have gone to stay with. We couldn't find them.

One day, I left Mom in bed and went looking on my own, so that I could cover the ground more quickly. I found myself down by the river, in the old market area of the city, but I could hardly recognize it. It was nothing like it used to be. However there were still traders shouting out their wares, shoppers ferreting for bargains, and noise and bustle. Life had to go on, even under these dreadful conditions.

I found myself somewhere that seemed familiar. I half-remembered it. Once there had been several streets where carpets were made by hand. I was sure that this was the place. The carpets that were made here were very special carpets. My father said that people used to come from all over the world to buy them. He loved this area and often talked about it. He described it vividly and said that some of the carpets had designs on them that made them magic carpets. Many merchants had shops here, outside of which, many wonderful carpets were displayed. Strong young men were on hand to unroll each carpet or rug for anyone's close inspection. Inside the buildings were large weaving looms, and even children were employed to work on them. Everywhere there would have been noise. Everything would have been in motion. That whole area had been very colorful because long ropes had been stretched across the streets, from buildings on one side of the road to those on the opposite side. On these ropes were masses of fabric threads hanging down. These threads had been dyed in a variety of bright fast colors. They were mainly in reds, blues, yellows, and greens, but there were smaller amounts of different shades, such as browns, olives, and black. They were hanging there to dry in the strong sunlight, and they swayed gently in the wind. It had been a bustling area. It had been so vivid that it had remained in my memory since the days of my childhood. Had it really been like that? Had I remembered it wrongly? Now everywhere was changed. There were no colored fabrics and no carpet businesses. Everywhere looked drab.

I was getting depressed because things had definitely changed for the worst and my mind was elsewhere. I was so worried about things in Iran. I did not know what had happened to my fiancée. My business was definitely over, and what about the house I had been renting from Husain, it would be empty now. I thought of Yasmine and imagined her being there. I'd have to get back to Tehran soon, but things here were not getting sorted out. I turned everything over in my mind. I couldn't leave my mom alone in Afghanistan. She was an old woman. She had had enough bad times and lost everything. Most of our extended family had fled, scattered; only Allah knew where. I was the only the person responsible for her. But she could not make her mind up about anything. Not only that, but also she disputed any decision I tried to make for her. The money was getting low. I was rationing it carefully, but it would not last forever. The only solution was to find my father and ask him why he left my mom alone. "He has to face up to his responsibilities," I said to myself.

A few streets away I wandered into what had once been the busy spice market. There were some traders there, and in front of each stall were the mounds of spices laid out on rush mats. Most the spices came from India or Pakistan, and the vendors were mainly Indian. But here also, the place was nothing like it used to be. The aromas were there and customers haggling over prices, and even children playing, but it was depressing. I was just about to wander on, when I noticed one trader in particular. He had a familiar look about him. As I got closer, I knew it was my uncle Mahmood, my mom's older brother. At least I thought it was him. He glanced at me and looked away again. He certainly didn't know me. Now I wasn't sure, because he had changed. He was much older. When I had been a child, he would have been about twenty. So by my reckoning, he should have been about forty. This man looked fifty at least. And to be fifty in Afghanistan meant you were really old. I stood in front of his stall, and he looked at me again.

"Salam alikom," he said expectantly. "What would you like, agha?"

Yes, it was my uncle's voice. But he did not know me.

"Uncle Mahmood, it's me," I said, "Ali."

He inspected my face closely.

"Ali who? There are many Alis. I know about seven."

"My mother is your sister. My father is Satiq."

His face broke into a big smile, and he came to me, and we threw our arms around each other, laughing.

We both asked each other questions about our families at the same time.

He kept stepping back and looking at me. I was much taller than him.

He told me a little about himself and his wife and children and asked about my parents. I gave him a brief account about my living in Iran, while Mom and Father were in Ghazni. He said he had heard that we were living there. He had been there one summer many years ago and thought it was a wonderful place. And so we had a sort of reunion. He seemed delighted to see me and wanted to see his sister. To see any family member alive and well was a big event because of the terrible things that had happened to our country. I asked if he had seen my father, but he hadn't. And so we talked and laughed and cried. He insisted that I bring Mom to see him as soon as I could. I said we would come that evening. He gave me his address and directions how to get there. We arranged a time so that he could finish his work, lock up, and so on.

I gave Mom the news about finding Mahmood. I tried to tell her quietly, but her reaction was instant. She cried and praised Allah alternately. Then she asked many questions, which I could not answer. Her excitement grew. She was talking and laughing at the same time. She had been a picture of total misery for the last month, now that was forgotten. She had a new strength, and I was thankful for it.

I asked the manager of the hotel about the district on the address Mahmood had given me. He frowned when I told him that we wanted to go there that evening.

"It is quite a rough area. You'll need to keep your eyes open all the time. Robberies are regular round there. Take a taxi, that's your best bet. It's not a good place to go for a stroll."

At about eight, we were on our way. The manager was right, the area was very run down, but then so was much of Kabul. We arrived at a mean-looking house in a sad little street. I got out first and knocked the door, which was opened instantly by Mahmood. He stood there smiling. I helped Mom from the cab and then made a deal with the driver to come back for us at nine. Mom and Mahmood had gone into the house, so I followed and closed the door behind me. The room was small, spotlessly clean, with a bright atmosphere. There were signs of children. From the next room I could hear them talking. Mahmood called to them to come and meet their aunty Zahra, and in they rushed, followed by their mother, my new aunt. The three kids were sweet. Having run in, they were now standing shyly staring at us. I noticed how thin and pale they were. Mahmood made the introductions and motioned us to sit down on rugs.

Aunty Zoliha brought in chai, and we relaxed into an easy conversation. Mom and Mahmood reminisced about things I had no remembrance of. They laughed sometimes, and sometimes they were sad. Neither of them had had much of a good time. Mom told him about everything since we had gone to Mazar-i-Sharif. And all about my running away, and on and on. Mahmood scowled at me from time to time. Were we still enemies? His story was one of difficulties and trials, fairly typical of most Afghans during that time. Although he put a good face on things I could see that he had had a bad time. Money was short. He had been robbed several times on his way home from the spice market and all his money taken. His store was broken into regularly. They were barely managing for food but were getting by. They had to. But his main worry was for the children. There was the eternal threat of land mines, so the children had constantly to be warned about where they could play. There were desperate men in the area, and there had been reports of abductions. The evening became subdued. The sound of the taxi motor horn brought us back to the present. I got up and went into the street. I returned to see Mom and Mahmood embracing. She was crying and smiling.

We promised to meet again soon, and left the house. The children came out and waved as did their parents. As we drove away, we waved until they were out of sight.

"Poor Mahmood, my poor Mahmood," Mom kept saying.

We had found a relative, but still no sign of Father.

Later, back at the hotel, Mom said that she wanted to go back to the farm and that I had to go too and take over running the place. We had our first dispute since I had arrived back, and I saw a side of her that I had forgotten. She could be cruel with the things she said. If I went back, I would be trapped possibly for years. I had to find father. Mom then decided we should go and see her brother again the next day. She pleaded that she was ill and needed a woman to be with her, which was true, but I knew what she really wanted was to get me there, so that he could put pressure on me to "do my duty" and so on. I remembered how they had always ganged up against me when I was a child, when Father was away. I remember he and his brother Nassir used to slap me. So Mom and I argued until it was time to sleep.

On my own, I tried to think. I had to get out of the trap that was closing on me. Money was becoming a problem. Maybe, if Mom stayed with her brother for a couple of weeks, it might give me time. Mahmood had said that Father had gone to Mazar-i-Sharif. I could go there and find him if Mom would stay with her brother.

In the morning I told her of my plan. She eventually agreed although she said that she didn't like it, going to Mazar-i-Sharif was too dangerous. We went to see Mahmood and, of course, he agreed with her, that we should go back to the farm. When I offered him money to let Mom stay for a couple of weeks, he changed completely. And so it was agreed. I felt that I disliked him even more because, in our tradition, hospitality is of great importance. He should have offered Mom a home without having to be bribed. To be fair, he had obviously been having a hard time for years. Anyhow it was agreed. Mom was genuinely pleased to be in female company again, and I was glad of a break.

I arrived in Mazar-i-Sharif in the afternoon. First, I went to Sakhijan (mosque) where once I was Molla's assistant. It was the only building that was the same as when I was last in the city. I think it might even have been the only building that had survived intact in the whole of Afghanistan. Everything else was damaged, roads, houses, hospitals, schools. The city was a ruined place. Also here, people had lost whole extended families, and all their friends. Many children had been orphaned. They were pitifully begging around the Sakhijan. I gave them some money and asked them to pray for me to find my father. In the Sakhijan, I prayed earnestly for some time. That beautiful holy place seemed to breathe peace on me.

For about a week, I searched for Father in that city. I went to the markets where he and I used to work. They had been destroyed by the Taliban. People were trying to rebuild them. In desperation, I decided to go to the police, although I didn't trust them. I thought there might be a slight chance that they could help me.

They asked, "Was he Shia Muslim or Sunni?"

Here again was the same old question. What had that to do with it?

"Shia Muslim," I said.

"A short while before, America attacked the Taliban. The Taliban took Shia Muslims from some cities and sent them to Kandahar. They might have taken your father. You will have to go there and ask the Kandahar police about it. They might have more details about what happened to the Shia Muslim people. Thousands of people are missing. Many have been killed. I can't help you more than this," he said resignedly.

So was this it? Was this the reason he had vanished? Why no one had seen him? Why he had left Mom to nearly starve to death? If this wasn't what had happened, then I was sure it would be something like this.

I went back to Kabul and stayed in a hotel that night. In the morning, I went to Mahmood's house. Fortunately he was at the market. I wanted a serious talk with Mom. She had changed a lot. She was much better. Color had come back into her face, and even her voice had more strength in it. I told her that Father would be in Kandahar, and I had to go there and find him. The truth was that things looked bad, if he had been taken by the Taliban, but I could not tell her that. I did have to tell her that the money was running out. We would have to raise some somehow. We would have to sell something, land, sheep, anything. No, I said emphatically, I was not going back to the village to take up farming. It was the last thing I intended to do. Despite her protests that the farm had belonged to my father and my grandfather, and one day would be mine, I steered the conversation back to money. What were we going to sell? There was no use her saying that Father would not like it. Where was he? I did not want to say that he might be dead, but death in Afghanistan was all around us. I hinted that we might not see him for some time, and at last, I could see that I was getting through to her. "I am a man now," I said, "I will have to decide what to do for the best for you. When Father comes back, I will explain everything to him. I will ask him to explain why he treated you so badly."

"He won't like you questioning him about that. I am against selling the land," Mom said.

"We have got to do something to sort things out for you. Then I can start to sort my own problems out in Iran. We have got to sell something. Father sold trees sometimes, I will sell them, or the sheep or anything anyone will buy."

At last I got her to agree. If she had not agreed, then I would have had to start selling things whether she liked it or not. But she was not beaten yet. Out of the blue she said,

"There is my gold, my rings and bangles and necklace. We sold them once before when we lived in Mazar city. Do you remember?"

I was dumbstruck for a moment, then I could have gone crazy at her. She had been almost starving on the farm. She had suffered from her self-neglect, doing without this and that. She would not even have sold one of the sheep, or killed one for food, without Father's permission, now she was telling me about her jewelry. Seeing how things were when I arrived, I never thought about her jewelry. Surely she would have sold it to make her life easier. I will never understand Afghan women.

She produced her jewelry, magically, there and then. I was amazed. She had had it with her all the time. It would raise a good amount of money. I swore to myself that whatever we sold, I would replace, down to the very last piece of it for her, if I had to sell everything I owned in the world. My old boss was still holding a lot of money for me. I had planned to use it for the wedding. When I got back to Tehran, I would work night and day, either for myself or in my old job, to put things right. I knew things were going to be OK in the future.

Mahmood, when he arrived, greeted me warmly. I was surprised. Mom had been telling him all about my business in Iran, and she must have embroidered the story, because he seemed to think I was well off. The truth was I had no business. I had spent money on traveling from city to city, paying for separate accommodation for Mom and myself. Food, doctor's fees, and medicine, and other expenses had all been chipping away at the money I had.

We were sitting on the rugs waiting for chai, which his wife and mom were making, when he smiled and asked what my plans were. I told him, in a lowered voice, that things did not look good about Father, and that I needed to go to Kandahar because there was a chance I might find out what had happened to him. Mahmood knew from my tone what I meant, and nodded.

"What about the farm at Golbowry?" he asked. "Your mother wants to go back there soon."

"It is very run down. He neglected it. I am not going back there." I thought I would make that clear in case this was the beginning of a lecture. "I have prospects and a fiancée waiting for me in Tehran."

"Your mother has been telling me. You are lucky to have the choice. Why don't you bring your wife to Afghanistan? That would solve the problems." He was studying my face for my reaction.

"It is Father's farm. Everything belongs to him. I am not meant to be a farmer. It is too remote for me, I can make a good living as a businessman, besides I cannot sell or buy anything there, it would not be legal."

"You're definitely not interested in farming then?" he asked cautiously.

Mom and Aunt Zoliha came in with the chai and a bowl of sugar and qand, which they put before us. He stopped talking until they had left us. It was strange, I thought, I had expected an attack on Mom's behalf, but I was only getting a gentle questioning.

"What about your mother?" he resumed. "She wants to go back. She tells me she is unwell."

"She is my responsibility, and I will take care of her . . ."

"She says she won't go to Iran," he broke in. "She is too old to be expected to be uprooted. She doesn't speak the language, nor know anyone there," he added.

"She must have discussed this with you while I have been away. The answer lies with Father. We can do nothing without his say-so. He is really responsible for her. I will look after her until I find him."

"What happens if you don't?" he paused "What if he's . . . if you never find him?" he corrected himself and went on, "You have been looking for him for two months now, is it?"

"I'll know more when I have been to Kandahar. I need Mom to be able to stay with you for another week, that was what we agreed, wasn't it?"

"Oh that is fine with me, Ali Jan. We hardly know she is here, she doesn't eat much and the children and she are inseparable. We have been talking over old times."

I took the van to Kandahar and arrived late at night. Next day I went to the police station. I told them everything about my long search. They told me to go to another police station. I went to five different police stations. Eventually I found some information about the Shia Muslims who were arrested by the Taliban. I stood at a high counter, in the drafty outer office of a down town station. The place had a bleak impersonal air about it. A lot of notices were pinned to the wall, and the benches and the table were screwed to the floor.

The burley police sergeant cleared his throat and looked across his high counter, straight into my eyes. "All we do know is they killed more than half the men. We found some still were in custody. We released those people right away. We don't have any records of their names or where they came from. We have no way of checking if a Mr. Satiq Akbari was one of them."

I left the police station and walked toward the town center, not knowing what to do next. I had to face the fact that Father was dead. If he were alive, I would have found him, or at least a trace of him, by now. I was still far from feeling fit. All the travelling, being thrown about in all kinds of vehicles on atrocious roads, a strange diet of food on the journeys, and only half-decent accommodation, all contributed to my feeling unwell.

There was no transport going back to Kabul that night, so I would have to stay in Kandahar. I was suddenly cheered up by the thought that this city was in the west of Afghanistan. I could try phoning Yasmine from here. The Iranian border was not far away. Maybe, it was just possible there would be a phone line connection. I found *mohaberat* (telephone center), and my heart leapt in my chest when at last I heard the phone ringing out at Husain's house. "Answer it! Answer it!" I shouted down the receiver. Ring. Ring. Then I heard a nervous voice say, "Hello. Mr. Husain's household." It was Aunt Clovinda.

"Hello, Aunt Clovinda," I almost yelled down the phone.

There was a pause, then, "Who is calling please?"

"Aunt Clovinda, it's me, Ali. I'm calling from Afghanistan," I said, laughing.

"Ali. Ali, is that you?"

"It's your almost brother-in-law."

She spoke to someone else, "It's Ali. It's Ali calling from Afghanistan." Then to me, she said, beginning to cry, "Oh, Ali, oh my poor Ali," and then she started sobbing.

"Can I speak to Yasmine? Clovinda, is Yasmine there?" Clovinda was her usual overemotional self, but I was desperate. "Can I speak to Yasmine? Or Husain?" I shouted.

There was the faint sound of talking, and Mortaza said, "Is that you, Ali?"

"Mortaza. Mortaza, how are you?"

"Ali, I am fine. It's been ages. You said you were coming straight back . . ."

"Mortaza," I broke in, "I don't know how long this phone line will hold out. I've tried calling you many times. Can you put Yasmine on the phone?"

He paused and spoke into the room, then, "She's not here, she's out."

"Is your dad there? Put your dad on."

A muffled sound of talking followed then, "He's out. At work." His voice was faltering. "There is only me and Omar here, and Clovinda. I have to go."

"Mortaza," I yelled. "Talk to me. Don't go. I cannot call from Kabul. I've been trying for weeks. I want to say a lot of things. How is Yasmine? How are your mom and your dad? Please. I am in Kandahar."

"I've got to go. Call tomorrow. Bye," then he hung up.

I could have smashed the telephone. The stupid rat, two months I'd been trying to get through, and now this. I was so angry. I desperately tried calling again, but the phone was off the hook. What did this mean? Mortaza was my friend. Why did he ring off? I was sure he was talking with Husain when he was talking into the room. Why didn't he come to the phone? I didn't understand. I just didn't understand.

I tried again early the following morning, but the receiver was still off. I had to get into a van back to Kabul before eight o'clock or I would have to stay another day. The journey began. I sat there so depressed. Father was dead. I would have to tell Mom the news. Something was wrong in Tehran, but what? What options did I have? I felt like running away again. One thing I was certain of, I was not going to become a farmer, no matter what Mom said. But what was I to do about her.

"Look, we have searched enough for Father and not found him. We have to face the fact that he is dead." I had prepared what to say as I rode home from Kandahar. "Let's go to Iran and meet your future daughter-in-law, and Abbas. I had a good business there, I can start it up again. I will be able to take care of you there."

I said this to Mom and Mahmood when I got to his house. There was silence for a minute. Mom seemed to have accepted the fact that Father might be dead, she had probably thought so for some time. It was me that had been wanting him to be alive. I wanted to go back to Tehran leaving things nice and tidy with Father back home looking after Mom, and me free to go my own way. Then she surprised me.

"You are missing your fiancée?" she asked with a smile.

"I don't know what to say, Mom," I said a little shyly. "She is a lovely girl. You will love her. There is no chance of me taking over the farm. We will sell it. I will go back there and close the place down and sell off the land, then we are going to Iran."

"No, we're not!" she said emphatically." Then she got up and left the room and went into Aunt Zoliha's bedroom, where I could not follow her. Mahmood motioned me to sit down, which I did reluctantly.

"Have some chai. The samovar is boiling. Let us talk," he said. He shouted to his wife to make some tea.

I was tired out with thinking. It had been nothing but worry for many months. I was not sure of anything anymore. The last thing I wanted to hear was a lecture from Mahmood. I had never forgiven him for hitting me when I was a child. Was I being childish to remember it? I had nothing to say. I looked at him, he obviously had something to say to me.

"We have been talking, your mother and I," he said.

I bet you have, I said to myself. I just kept looking into his face.

"I have made her understand that you will not work the farm." I was surprised. "That is right, isn't it? You have just said so again, just now." He went on. "She is adamant that she will not go to Iran. We have decided . . ." he paused here. "If you agree," he added, "We thought it would suit us all if, if I went there, with my family, to take care of everything. What do you think?" Now it was his turn to look into my face to see if he could work out what I was thinking.

In came the chai and qand. This was sudden news, and I was trying to think. I naturally distrusted him. I didn't like him, and he didn't like me. What he was suggesting would have solved my problems about Mom. I did not want the farm, but I did not want him to have it. I paid attention to putting sugar in my tea and staring at it, saying nothing.

What followed was, he explained how difficult life was in Kabul, how he feared for his children, how his business was failing, and the robberies, and so on. I really began to feel sorry for him. Then he pointed out the advantages to me, which he slightly overdid, because he made it look like he was doing me a great favor. He ended with the same question, "What do you think?"

"Let me have time to think about it. There are things to consider," I said, trying to think what they were.

"I don't know what the legal situation is. We do not know for certain if Father is dead. If he is, am I legally the owner? He does not seem to have left a will, unless Mom knows about one."

"She doesn't," he said quickly. So they had already talked it through. "It doesn't matter anyway, so long as we all agree. I am not trying to buy the place. To be honest, I have not got any money. She has given me her permission. She wants us all to go there. She says it will be wonderful for the children. You are not losing anything. If it is to be your farm, you will be having it run for you. I have not said I will charge you for my going there," he added.

No, I thought, you would spoil your argument if you started to expect to be paid for going. I had been a market trader at the age of eleven, so I know a good sales pitch when I hear one. But he was really bad at it.

He went on a little more, but I wasn't listening. My mind was working.

"I will think about it, Mahmood," I said.

"What are your first thoughts though?" he asked expectantly.

"To be honest, my mind is all over the place. The last few months have been an ordeal. I will sleep on it. Thank you for your offer," I said politely. "I am staying in the hotel. It is quiet there. I will rest, and then I will think things through. Then I will let you know." He looked at me. "Tomorrow," I said, getting up.

"Tell Mom I will call in the morning." I made for the door, shouted, "Good-bye, Aunt Zoliha," and left the house.

I agreed. Mom was delighted and so was everyone else. Things moved rapidly. We all had our different reasons, but our aim was the same. I thought privately that Mahmood was in for a nasty shock, when he had to get down to working the farm. He had been there once, but that was many years ago in summertime. Everything is nice in the summer. What was he going to do in the winter? Still that was what they wanted. It was what I wanted too. I helped them as much as I could to get them away as soon as possible. Meanwhile, I applied for a passport, and two weeks later, I went to pick it up. Then I went to the Iranian embassy to get a visa. A few days later, they presented me with one.

Mahmood had bought a beat-up lorry, and they piled everything he owned on to it. The day came at last when I waved good-bye to my remaining family. They were in high spirits, and the children were laughing and waving and even singing as they sat on top of everything, and for one moment I caught a sight of myself of many years earlier, on the top of a truck going to Ghazni from Mazar-i-Sharif, with a little girl and the two little boys, who never completed the journey to that same farm.

CHAPTER 24

BACK TO IRAN

"Ali, the wedding is off!"

Unbelievable words coming down the phone line hit me like a prizefighter's punch. It was Husain.

I was shocked, stunned for a moment.

"Husain, what do you mean?" I shouted. "How can it be? We are engaged. We are in love."

"You've been missing for more than twelve months. We haven't had a word from you since you were deported. Yasmine was terribly upset. Abbas sold your business. What were we to think?" he asked.

"I have tried contacting you hundreds of times," I shouted back. "You don't know what things are like in Afghanistan. There isn't even any electricity. Husain Jan, please. Let me talk to Yasmine," I begged.

"She's not here . . . She is away on holiday. I—I—there is something I have to tell you. She is in at her aunt's house." He seemed to be making it up as he spoke. "You cannot talk to her. I had to think of her future . . ." he went on. "The truth is she is married."

These words hit me hard. I stopped listening to what he was saying and started shouting "No . . . no."

"You are lying! You are Lying! We are promised. You know the traditions. The engagement party we had at your house. She is engaged to me. I don't understand. Why have you changed? You wanted me to marry her . . ."

"There is nothing to say," he said fiercely, "I decided that it would be best for her to marry an Iranian man. You cannot get Iran citizenship. You can be deported at any time, there is no stability. How can you bring up a family if you are liable to be sent away at any time?" His tone hardened,

"I will tell you this. Yasmine is not for you. She is married to her cousin Ahmad Kafashiyan. He is of our family. He is well respected."

"No!" I yelled.

"I have work to do. I must go."

He cut the phone off. I redialed the number. It was *eshghal* (busy).

I could have gone mad. His words made my mind stand still. Yasmine was my fiancée. We loved each other. I was certain of that. How could she be married to her cousin? All our future plans were based on being together. She was all I had thought about for months. Our wedding was planned. My ex-boss was holding my money, which was going to pay for it. What was Husain talking about? I'd kill him. I had to talk to Yasmine. I could not doubt her. We had to be strong. She loved me, and I loved her. I was certain about that. My thoughts whirled around in my head, but I had to hold on to what I knew to be true. We loved each other.

I was in Mashhat, a city in Iran over the border from Afghanistan. It was the first stop on my way back to Tehran. Having taken care of my problems in my own country, I had set off excitedly to get back to my fiancée as soon as was possible. First, I went to the beautiful mosque, Hazrat-e-Imam Raza, and it reminded of Sakhijan in Mazar-i-Sharif, Afghanistan. The mosque was beautiful very colorful and very crowded.

I remembered the one call that had gotten through to Tehran was from Kandahar, and now I understood why it had been so crazy. Other calls I had made from just over the border were never accepted at Husain's house. I was sure now that I had only got through this time because I was calling from inside Iran. If I had been calling from Afghanistan, he would never have accepted the call.

I was in the coach terminal building. My coach was due to leave for Tehran in half an hour. I vacated the phone kiosk and gathered up my bags and belongings from the floor. I had left them where I could see them while I was phoning. There were many people milling about, just as in coach stations all over the world. The day was unpleasantly hot. The smell of hot diesel fumes hung over everything. All sorts of vehicles were roaring in and out, horns blaring. Flies were everywhere. Vendors shouted their wares. Children were getting fractious and running all over the place. Mothers were scolding, and no one seemed to know which coach was going where. There was one official with a clipboard. He was a short fat man in a uniform tunic and a long dirty white shirt. He wore a turban, which was almost over his eyes, he was being bombarded with questions from a crowd of people of all ages, shapes, and sizes in a variety of languages. He was sweating and smoking a black cigar, trying to refer to his notes from time to time. Added to the local people were tourists of several nationalities. Scruffy long-haired teenagers wearing beads and kaftans smoking drugs and listening to tiny tinny radios. Their fair skin had turned to blotchy patches of angry red. The Germans were complaining, the Chinese impassive, and the Americans seemed to be drunk.

By now my mood was murderous. I was lucky enough to be able to read the signs and timetables, and made directly for the Tehran bus stand. My coach was in and boarding. I checked that my luggage was stowed and climbed on board. The inside was dark and cool. I pulled myself along the narrow aisle, found my seat, and threw myself into it sulkily. All I wanted was for the journey to start and for us to get to the capital as soon as possible. I also knew it would take sixteen hours at least to get to Tehran, with a couple of stops on the way.

Tehran. The coach crept smoothly through the sleeping suburbs of that fantastic city in the early hours of the morning. There was hardly anyone about, except men coming home or going to work. There was the odd bus and road sweeping machine doing the rounds. Most of the passengers in the coach were asleep. I was wide awake. I felt stiff in my joints, and I promised myself a much needed shower as soon as I could get one. The brilliant sun was coming up as we neared the city center, driving down the familiar palm tree-lined avenues. My plan was, first, to call on Abbas at his old address. He had always been my rock in troubled times. He was not there, but his ex-roommate had his new address. He now had rooms in one of his beloved mosques in one of the central city areas. He worked there, running an Afghan refugee facility. I couldn't wait to see him. He had been my only true friend nearly all my life. I was glad that at least he had been able to settle down with some sort of security. His friend said he now had official permission to stay in Iran. This had been achieved with the help of the Mullahs, who recognized his valuable work.

With Abbas's new address. I got into a taxi and was there in a flash. I had never been to this mosque before, and I was surprised to find that it was a beautiful building of great age. It was designed in perfect proportions, adorned with ornate plasterwork, and surmounted by a traditional turquoise, onion-shaped dome. It was surrounded by large old palm trees and a high outer wall.

By luck, even at that early hour, I found Abbas standing at the main door by the trunk of one of the trees. I shouted out very loudly, "Abbas," as I got out of the cab. He was so surprised to hear me so close to him. He ran toward me, as I was paying the driver. I turned to meet him. We both automatically opened our arms and held each other for a while. Our happiness and excitement was too much, we couldn't control ourselves, and we both had tears running down our faces. It was such a pleasant meeting for both of us. We had missed each other very much. Abbas welcomed me and asked me to follow him to his quarters. We went along many small passages and alleyways; some were flagged with large well worn stones, while others were inlaid with beautiful old mosaics in bright coloured gemlike stones arranged in intricate patterns. We passed under many ornate archways, and I began to wonder where he was leading me. The mosque had a very big courtyard at its center, with beautiful flower beds around the sides. The colors of the flowers were vibrant, and as we got closer to them, I began to inhale their fresh sweet fragrances. The mosque itself had been built many years ago, and while we were walking, Abbas told me its history and all about the beautiful renovation work, which made it look brand new. Then he enthusiastically began telling me all about his job and the refugee center. So we walked for some time. When we got to the back of the complex, Abbas suddenly opened a door and said, "We are here, this is where I live."

His apartment was on the same level as the mosque and was of the same age. He had two huge rooms lit by tall windows, which had dark wooden screens carved with complicated designs to keep out the sun's glare, and two smaller rooms. The walls were very thick, which endowed the rooms with silence. He used one of them as a bedroom, and the other one as his living room. His new apartment looked a lot better than the last one he had. He must have a good job, I said to myself, because all the furnishings looked brand new.

Whilst he made chai from his samovar, he kept telling that I had got taller and bigger. We had so much to talk about. When we were settled, our talk turned to my own situation. I explained what had happened when I had called Husain, and how he had told me that I could not marry Yasmine. I was expressing my disbelief, my anger, and my confusion, and so on. It all came flowing out in a jumbled tirade. I eventually stopped talking, and we sat silent for a moment. I had expected some words of sympathy, I suppose, but Abbas said nothing.

"What do you think?" I asked. "Has the family said anything to you?"

"I have not seen any of the family for some months since you were here in prison, before you were deported. I have not seen Yasmine since that time because they live far away, and I live here in the city center. I knew something was wrong because I had to phone Mr. Husain about your business. I found that he was still charging you rent on the house you had, even though he knew you were going to be sent back to Afghanistan and would not be using it again and that it was empty. I had a row with him about it, but he blamed me for not telling him what he already knew, that you could not carry on with your business. He said that he wanted formal notification, and that he expected to be paid the rent arrears. I had to write a formal letter, telling him you were giving up the property. I told him straight that I did not think that he was acting like a future father-in-law. It was then he told me that he was not going to let you marry his daughter. And that she was to marry her cousin. I am very sorry, but you know, if you remember, I have not really liked that man for some time. Here at the center, his name has been mentioned by some of the refugees who were tenants of his. They said he was a man who evicted people violently. I did not tell you all that I had heard."

"Husain always acted like my best friend, he made me welcome, the whole family made me welcome."

It didn't seem as though we were talking about the same man.

What Abbas was saying was not really what I wanted to hear. I wanted to hear something that would give me hope that there had been a big mistake somewhere. I was still in love with that girl, and I was not going to give up on anything. Abbas could read my mind because he tried to change the subject. He asked about my time in Afghanistan, how were my parents. This was not what I was ready to discuss. I told him his mother was well, and gave him her messages, we both told stories about all that had happened since we last met. I was so glad that good things had happened for him. He had found his dream job in the mosque. And he was now engaged with a Mullah's daughter. His life had changed a lot in a very short time. I was really happy to see him looking so much better. The way he dressed, the way he talked, and even his personality all seemed to have improved. We laughed when he reminded me about the things I did in my childhood in our village. I began to forget my problems.

His favourite saying had always been "Life has its ups and downs." This seemed particularly true at this time, because before I was deported to Afghanistan, I had been rich, and he had almost nothing and had begun to work for me. Now I had nothing, and he had everything that he wanted. I love his proverb and use it to this day. He insisted that I should stay with him, and when I suggested payment, he would not agree to it, only saying that I could do some work with his refugees if I felt the need to earn my keep, but that it was not really necessary. I spent the rest of the morning in a restless state. Abbas said he needed to go to work, and I was to make myself at home. He tactfully got out one of his clean shirts for me to wear, just as he had done the first time I had arrived in Tehran many years earlier. This time I did not need to borrow it because I had my own clothes in my bag. He left, and I took a well needed shower and used some of his cologne. I felt very refreshed. Despite being tired out, because I had not been able to sleep on the coach, I could not relax. I would have liked to have explored the mosque because it was very beautiful, but my wandering about might have been resented. I did not think that I would be able to find my way to the front entrance because when we had entered, I had blindly followed Abbas through a maze of passages. Fortunately his apartment was at the rear of the complex, and when I opened his door, I could hear noises from a street. Sure enough when I had gone through a stout wooden door set in the wall, I found myself in a narrow mud-baked, back lane, which ran between high whitewashed walls, over which towered the large green palm fronds of the trees. The stout door had shut behind me, so I went on. At the end of the alleyway was a road. I carefully took notice of everything as I went, so that I could find my way back again, and within a few minutes, I was walking along the sidewalks of the busy city avenues. The contrast seemed unbelievable. I had stepped from the old world into the modern day. From tranquility into a kind of hell. Everywhere became familiar. I knew I was back in Tehran all right, thousands of people, most of them young, hundreds of new cars, the smell of auto exhaust, and the noise. Every car seemed to be using its horn, all the street vendor seemed to be shouting at the tops of their voices. Yes, I was back. But everything I saw reminded me of Yasmine. We had been on these avenues together, been in the cafés, on the trams, in the taxis, in the cinemas, the restaurants, and bazaars. Even the smell of coffee reminded me of her. It was impossible not to think of her. It was painful, almost physically painful. I was wandering around. Nothing seemed to have a point. Where was I going without her? My mind was split. One side of me knew I wanted us to be together again despite what Husain had said. Then a wave of panic would surge up, and I found myself thinking that she would never have wanted to marry me, a poor guy, without the right to stay in the country, without a job, and at that very moment, nowhere to live. And so I passed the hours in this way, reminiscing, being negative and then positive in turn. I returned to Abbas's place, had some chai but nothing to eat. Food was the last thing I wanted. I resolved to go and see her.

CHAPTER 25

CLOVINDA SAW IT IN THE TEA LEAVES

After five thirty that evening, I was walking down the familiar roads in the area where the family lived. There, looking exactly the same as when I last saw it, was the house. I stood in the same welcoming glow of the porch light and rang the same bell. Its sound reminded me vaguely of my boxing. I had that tense nervous feeling at the bottom of my stomach. "Seconds out."

The door opened. It was Mortaza. I found myself smiling.

"Ali," he said. He was surprised and didn't know what to do. "My father is not in, he hasn't come home yet."

I was pleased to see him. He had changed a lot since I last saw him. His shoulders were broad, he was taller, his voice had deepened, and he had a dark comical moustache. I recognized the unmistakable results of his weight training.

"What's going on, Mortaza? Is Yasmine in? I need to see her," I said as evenly as I could.

"No, she's out. She's gone to the cinema," he stammered. "I thought you were in Kabul or Kandahar."

"That's where I called you from a couple of weeks ago, but you hung up on me. You remember?" I said. "I thought we were friends. That was not friendly."

"Ali, I'm sorry about that. It's Father. Things are altered." He was serious now. "He decided that he didn't want you to marry Yasmine. He said you're too wild."

"Mortaza, you know me. You know what happened. I stopped you getting flattened that day," I reminded him.

There was scuffling behind him, and the head of little Omar appeared around the side of his leg.

"Ali, Ali!" he shouted delightedly. He pulled himself in front of Mortaza and reached his two arms up to me for me to pick him up.

"Omar," I said and held out my hand to shake his, "Salam alaikum, Mr. Omar."

"Salam, Ali Agar," he shouted excitedly. "In, in," he said. He had kept hold of my hand and was pulling me with all his might.

"I'll come back later when your father gets home," I said, patting Omar's head.

"Now. In. Come in."

"Not yet, Omar Jan. Well, no one seems to have told him that things have changed," I said to Mortaza.

"Go to Clovinda," Mortaza said, picking him up and putting down further up the hallway. "She wants you."

"No. I want Ali." Omar's tone was altering into a whine. He was going to start crying as all kids do when they can't get their own way. He threw himself at Mortaza's legs, which were blocking his way. He started to punch him, and when that didn't work, he kicked him.

"Do you want a good slap?" Mortaza asked, grappling with him. "I'm sorry, Ali, I'm going to have to shut the door," he said to me.

"All I want to know is what . . ."

"Ali, oh poor Ali!" suddenly there was the high tearful voice of Aunt Clovinda. She came quickly to the door and pushed past Mortaza. The next minute, she had her arms around my neck and started to sob. "Ali, oh poor Ali. Why didn't you come back?"

Before I could answer, she continued sobbing and kept repeating, "Ali, Ali."

Omar was struggling with Mortaza who could not hold him, so the next thing I found him clinging tightly to my legs. I could not move at all. Omar was holding my legs like a rugby player, and Clovinda had her arms around my neck. I started to stagger then lost my balance. I was falling sideways toward the ornamental plant pots at the side of the door. Clovinda fell with me. Omar thought this was funny. Clovinda tried to disentangle herself, but because of her flowing clothes and her long scarf, this was not easy for her to do.

"Mortaza! Clovinda! What are you doing? Who are you fighting with?"

I was flat on my back with a broken plant pot shard sticking in my butt, and plant and soil in my hair. Mrs. Husain was standing at the door looking down at me. "Ali? Is that Ali?" She was asking Mortaza. Then as I was scrambling to get up, to me, she said, "Don't come here making trouble, or I'll call the police, and you know what they will do."

"Poor Ali," Clovinda wailed. "Poor Ali. I knew everything would go wrong. I saw it in the tea leaves. Didn't I tell you? This is what happened to me. This is what happened to me! Oh Ali, Ali."

I managed to get to my feet, but by now Clovinda was up to her usual standard of hysteria. She was attempting to put her arms around my neck and was drenching me with her tears. Omar was now alarmed and started howling. Mortaza was trying to brush me down, and there was blood coming from somewhere.

"You'll have everyone out of their houses," Mrs. Husain was saying, ever conscious of her neighbors. "Come inside for Allah's sake."

Clovinda dragged me through the door while I was still trying to get her arms from my neck. Omar now started laughing again.

"Clovinda! Clovinda!" Mrs. Husain shouted. But Clovinda was in a world of her own, "Oh for heaven's sake, Clovinda, let go of him. Mortaza, do something. Clovinda stop that noise. Right now!" she shouted. But Clovinda couldn't hear her. She was hysterical. Mrs. Husain disappeared into the other rooms. I was shaken but could not stop Clovinda grabbing me. "Mortaza was trying to help me, I think, and Omar was running up and down the hallway."

"My poor Ali. Poor, poor Ali." Clovinda's sobs started all over again. "I know what it is like. It happened to meeee!" She seemed to have more arms than an octopus, as soon as I got one away from my neck, another one seemed to replace it. The wailing increased. Next thing, I got a shock. A bucket of cold water hit Clovinda and myself. That did the trick. Clovinda released her grip but continued her deep sobbing. Omar wet his pants, laughing. "'Gen, do it 'gen," he shouted. We stood there dripping.

"Clovinda, go and dry yourself." There was no response. "Now! Go and dry your hair, and cover it." Sobbing still, she allowed Mortaza to lead her away.

"Omar, look at the mess you have made, go and get a cloth." This was Mrs. Husain as I had never seen her before. She was very angry. "Ali, why have you come around here causing all this? Look at the mess. It's lucky for you that Husain is not here. Don't move, you'll have soil everywhere. And stop dripping on everything!"

"I came here to talk to Husain, that is all, Clovinda went hysterical," I tried to explain.

"You're not trying to say that she knocked you down? She is too thin. You are twice her size, don't be ridiculous!" Not only was she angry but also there was contempt in her voice.

"Ask Mortaza. Clovinda saw me at the door and started crying, and things got out of hand," I said.

"You should not have upset her. Well, I have had just about as much as I can take of this. She cries for the least excuse. It will take me all night to calm her down after this," she said accusingly.

Omar came back with a cloth, and Mrs. Husain snatched it off him and started to wipe up his puddle.

"I came here to see Husain. I want to know what is going on. About twelve months ago, here in this house, you and Husain welcomed me like a son. Yasmine and I had our engagement party here with all your family. I want to know what happened to change everything. You know how much we love each other," I said this with some feeling because I was angry, and I was in the right. I think this had the effect of changing her attitude because she looked at me for a moment as though she had only just seen me.

"Didn't my husband explain everything to you? He told me he had." she asked.

"You know that I have not been able to get through on the phone for the last week or so."

Husain only said that the wedding was off and that Yasmine has married her cousin," I said this sharply.

She looked at me for a moment. "Go into the kitchen and clean yourself up, then come into the office, and I will answer your questions." She got up from where she had been kneeling. I did what she said and headed for the kitchen. Clovinda continued to sob loudly. I did the best I could to get rid of the soil and wash a cut I had on my hand.

In the office, Mrs. Husain was at the desk, and she motioned me to sit down as soon as I came in.

"There is not a lot for me to say. We decided that you would have been unsuitable to have as a son-in-law." I opened my mouth to say something, but she held up her hand.

"Listen to me first, and then I will listen to you. First, you are not Iranian, that means that you are not allowed to do many things that Iranian men can do, like buying property. You can be deported at any time. You have no income, and all your savings are gone. We did not want our daughter to go to Afghanistan to live because your country is a wreck. We would never have seen our grandchildren. These are just a few of the reasons that made it impossible for you to marry our daughter. We had no idea of what had happened to you. We heard nothing from you. Yasmine is now happily married to a member of our family. She cannot be un-married. Think about it for one minute."

"I don't need to think about it. I have been thinking about nothing else. I have nearly gone crazy thinking about it. We love each other. Very deeply," I said with all the feeling I could express.

"You are wrong. We have talked this over and over with Yasmine, and she has seen sense. She could never have gone to live in Afghanistan, we know how they treat women there, and so do you. She is not in love with you anymore." This was a slap in the face for me to hear.

"You have made her think this way," I said accusingly.

"Yes, we have persuaded her," she agreed unapologetically. "We are her parents. It is our duty to see that we get the best for her. You would do the same for your own daughter. It is traditional for parents to arrange the marriages of their children. You will not believe me if I say that I am sorry about this, but I really am."

Outside the office was some noise, I could hear Clovinda wailing again, and it was getting louder.

"I am sorry, Ali, but will you please go. You . . ."

The door was flung open, and Clovinda let out a scream and came rushing in, making a direct line for me with "My poor Ali. My poor Ali. They are breaking your heart, just like they broke mine!" She wailed.

"Oh I have had just about all I can take tonight of these hysterics," Mrs. Husain said, beginning to lose her temper."I cannot put up with it any longer."

I was trying to avoid Clovinda's arms, and Mrs. Husain was getting angry. "This house is becoming a mad house. Ali, Please go. You can see how upsetting this is for her, and we have children to consider. I have given you our reasons, so now please go!"

I thought she was right this time, and I went through the door. I think I have never been so glad to leave anywhere. I quickly passed through the muddy hallway, out past the broken plants and pots, and down the driveway. I walked slowly away. What an evening. What a crazy house.

CHAPTER 26

MAKING MY MIND UP

In his apartment, Abbas had company. There were two young people of about my age, a beautiful dark woman and a tall bearded youth who got to his feet as Abbas introduced us. I soon realized that this was his new fiancée, and the youth must have been her younger brother. They were very pleasant, and it was obvious that they were all in a happy mood. At the earliest chance, I excused myself and went into the little spare room. I threw myself onto the bed. I wanted to have a think.

That night Abbas asked me what I thought I would do next. I answered that I just did not know. As we sat drinking chai after our evening meal, Abbas gently coaxed me to consider my options. He listed them.

"One, you could go back to Ghazni and the farm.

Two, you could restart your tailoring business.

Three, you could stay here with me and help expand the refugee center.

Four, you could get a job at your old place of work.

Five, you could get a job doing something else."

I was sure that he had my best interests at heart, but I did not want to think about it, but to go along with his train of thought, I considered his suggestions. I really wanted to get back with Yasmine, but I was beginning to realize that I was not going to get what I wanted, she had really hurt me, and possibly I thought that if she could do this to me, after all we had meant to each other, then maybe I would be better without her. This last thought came as a shock to myself.

"No, I did not want to go back to the farm. Starting my business again would be a struggle but was possible. Working for my old boss would not be possible now. Working at the center would be difficult for me because

182

I thought that most of the young men there were not trying to help themselves (but I did not say this to Abbas). Anyhow all these last options were dependant on me getting Iranian citizenship. The government was not issuing papers because of the sheer numbers of Afghan applicants. I had a temporary visa, but when that ran out, I could be deported at any time, and the experience I had had last time was too unpleasant to even think about. I did have one germ of an idea, and that was to go somewhere else. I had uncles in the UK, and from the little contact I had had with them, they said it was a wonderful place. So the idea had taken a hold. Having answered Abbas's questions, I thought I would make a suggestion of my own. I surprised him by saying "How about us going to England?"

"Us? You want me to go to England with you? But I have work here. It is important to me. And you know I am considering getting married. I don't want to leave. I am settled," he said gravely.

"It was just an idea. I thought it would be good fun. I have nothing to stay here for, have I? You have your own life now. I will take a day or two to have a good think," I added.

I slowly got over Yasmine. It was taking time because she was in front of my eyes at unexpected moments, and some nights I was talking to her in my dreams. I told myself that there was no future for me if I stayed in Iran. I wanted to forget Yasmine, and I hated Iran the way everything was. The only option was to contact my uncle in the UK. I phoned him, and he said, "Ali Jan, if you ever get here, it is a safe country, and there are jobs going. Tailoring is a good trade. If you ever do set off and get as far as Turkey, call me. I will send you some money."

"Thank you, uncle," I said. He sounded as though he thought I would never get there.

I eventually decided that I should go to England. I told Abbas. He seemed sad about the news. He said, "I believe that everything is predestined. Sometimes it is good and sometimes bad. It might be your fate to have had this upset in your young life. Maybe the future will be much better for you when you get over Yasmine."

I went to the Turkish embassy to ask for a visa. They refused to supply one. I decided that I would have to find a smuggler again, which would not be difficult.

He said, "Be ready in two days."

Abbas had hoped I would be around for a few months longer. He wanted me to be at his wedding. He unhappily accepted that I was going.

He simply said, "Allah is with you Ali agha. You got all your problems because you helped me that day at the seaside. Allah will never leave you alone because you have never done any wrong. You are a kind and helpful person. Keep in touch with me. Write to me here. If you come back, I will still be here. I wish you all the best. Please call me whenever you can.

CHAPTER 27

IN CALLOUS HAND

It was about 4:00 p.m. when I left Tehran, hoping to have to a better life and promising myself to forget everything that had happened. I was tired of having problems here and there. I wanted a peaceful life.

The journey was kind of the same as when I first left Afghanistan for Iran illegally, but I soon realized that the smugglers who I was paying to take me to the UK were very different from those who brought me from Afghanistan. They were not professionals at all. They turned out to be little better than gangsters. They did not care about people's safety, and people died on these journeys. No one cared. Once the smugglers had got our money, we were in their hands. We had no choice to decide anything for ourselves. They knew we would not dare to complain to the police because they would deport us. We had to wait here and there until the smugglers thought it was safe, then we continued the journey. We waited somewhere for about one week in a mountainous area. During daylight, we were allowed outside. There were lots of trees in a nice garden and amazing fresh cold water. When it got dark, we were taken back to a very large room. It was painted in white but smelled sweaty, it was dirty and had broken windows.

One afternoon, the smuggler said, "We have checked our way ahead. It is now clear to cross the border. We are going to leave about eight. We all are going to have to walk about twenty-five hours." Everyone in our room said, "Twenty-five hours is a lot."

"We will sleep during the daytime on the mountain. We will walk during the night."

I was beginning to have second thoughts about this trip. I was changing my mind and would have liked to have gone back to Tehran, but that was not possible.

They brought enough food for everyone to take with us. There was no way for us to go to Turkey without walking. We slept until nearly sunset, then we started our trek. That night the mountain was cold, windy, and very dark. After several hours, I sat next to a huge stone, which was a little warmer out of the wind. I was feeling tired. I had not had good food for a while. I must have looked like an orphan boy, who had been neglected, and there was no one to help or support me. That night was unforgettable. It was the worst night in my life.

We were ordered into a very large truck. After several hours, we got out and went to a house. Different smugglers divided us into the three rooms, all the men were separated from the women.

Later, two smugglers and a beautiful girl brought food for us. When she came to our room, I couldn't take my eyes off her because of her beauty. She was tall and slim with long black hair. Her beauty made me forget everything else in my world of sadness and start to think about her. I can't find words to describe how pretty she was, but all I can say, she was very beautiful. She was carrying a big bowl full of hard-boiled eggs, which she handed to everyone. When she gave me my eggs, I said, "*Tashakor* (Thank you)."

She looked at for a moment and smiled and said, "Are you from Afghanistan?"

"Yes, what about you?" I asked.

"I am Afghan too."

"What are doing here?" I asked, smiling back.

"I have to go now to serve the smugglers. They will leave shortly, and then I will come to see you. We will have a good talk."

I was surprised because she was an Afghan, and I wondered what she was doing there with the smugglers, who were all from Iran and Turkey. My heart was beating for her to come back. She came after a short while. "Salam, they have gone now."

"Who has gone now?" I asked.

"The smugglers, they will come back very late tonight. Can we sit outside the room, in case they come back, I will be able to see them. They don't always keep to what they say."

I went with her outside the room.

"Sorry, I couldn't answer your question before because it is a very long story. I am going to tell you briefly why I am here. One year ago, my family and I planned to go to Germany. I have two younger brothers. One is ten years old. The other one is twelve. I am the eldest, I am sixteen years old now. My mother is dead. We had only my father, who was looking after us. We came here, the same way as you did, I think. The smugglers separated me from my family. They sent my father and my two little brothers with others people somewhere else. One of the young smugglers took me to his house. I cried and asked where my father was.

"He said, 'We have sent them to Istanbul City. I will take you there soon.'

"'Why you brought me here?' I asked.

"He started to touch me. I did not let him do it, and he forced himself on me. He abused me, and then he took me to another place to his friend. They did very bad things to me. They never took me back to my family. I cried and pleaded to be taken back to my family. They said they would take me soon, soon. Every time I asked, they told me the same thing. But they never have taken me back to my family. I ran away once, from the house, but they found me and brought me here. I wanted to go and find my family or go to Germany, because I have some relatives there. I am really tired of my life. I want to run away. Help me," she pleaded desperately.

"I am depending on someone else to take me to England. How can I help you?" I asked.

"I have a plan," she said. "Different smugglers will take people away from here at about 3:00 a.m. When they come, they will bring a truck with them. They don't have much time to stay. They are always in a hurry. If I wear a man's clothes and cover my face and do not talk, will you help me to get into the truck? You talk instead of me if anyone asks a question. You know people are going to push each other to get in faster. Nobody will notice anything because they are busy taking care of themselves. I will stay awake, make myself ready."

I said, "I have heard about the smugglers keeping beautiful girls sometimes for themselves. You are a very beautiful girl. I don't know how we are going to make this work. We don't even speak Turkish. I don't know if I want to get involved. It could be hard to get away from these people. There could be a lot of trouble from them."

She started to cry and said, "You don't know what they have done to me since they took me away from my family. They rape me and abuse me. You are an Afghan man. You look like a good person. Do you let these people to do these things again to me? I will be yours. Allah will reward you. Today I need your help. Please help me. I have tried to kill myself several times. Do you think it is right that they make a business on me? Help me please," she said and cried a lot.

I felt really sorry for her, and I said, "I don't know if I can help you, but I will try. There are three Afghan men with us. I will tell them about you, they might help."

We heard a car coming. She went to her room. I went to back inside. I told the other three Afghan men. They felt angry about it.

The smugglers came in and said,. "I have called the truck driver who is coming to pick you up. But it will take him a day and a half to get here."

Then they brought food for us, and the girl was with them. She winked at me and whispered, "I can't talk right now."

I winked back at her and whispered to her, "OK."

They did not give us a lot of food, just about enough to keep us alive.

After the pathetic dinner, Sahar brought some good food for me. I shared it with the other Afghan men.

We made a good plan for her. First, we changed her name to a boy's name. Her name was to be Jafar. Then I gave her a shirt out of my bag. There was a short man with us. He gave trousers and a hat, someone offered a jacket. She brought us more food several times. At times we were able to sit outside the room and talk when the smugglers were not around.

Later, two of the men came into the room; they were in a happy mood and said, "Early in the morning, we are going to leave here."

Some of the people began getting ready. I thought it would be better to get some sleep, but I could not. I was laying and thinking about tomorrow what's going to happen. At about 3:00 a.m., the smuggler told us, "Fucking drugs, get in the truck very quietly."

Nearly everyone moved out at the same time. About sixty people pushed each other to get in the truck. When the room was empty, a smuggler turned some lights off, making it almost too dark outside. I and the three Afghan men were looking for Sahar, and pushing people in different directions to cause a bit of confusion. Everyone was pushing to get into the truck. We were pushing them away from it. We wanted to make a delay until Sahar came. There were only two smugglers, one was behind the vehicle, and the other was patrolling outside in the road. About 25 percent of people got in. She still did not come. People started to use abusive language to us because we were hindering them. Someone ran into the crowd. My Afghan friends told me to go and help her to get into the truck. It was very difficult to get back to her. Most of the people were pushing forward. I kept pushing them aside. Some of them stood on my feet and hurt me. Eventually I got close to her and tried to pull her to me. My friends, who by now had managed to get into the truck, shouted to me to hurry up. I bent down a little and took her hand. I was pulling her, the other three started pulling me. Eventually we all got in. The smuggler, who was patrolling outside, came in and said, "Fuck," and kicked the people who still had not got in. At last everyone was in, and the gang placed a lot of sacks of plaster inside the truck to hide us, and slammed the doors shut and locked them.

CHAPTER 28

OUR PLAN BEGINS TO WORK

There was very little room for sixty people in that truck, and it was very uncomfortable, everyone was crammed close together. People were pushing each other, fighting, swearing, and making a lot of noise. I was jammed in the corner. Sahar was next to me, trying to hold my hand. She was getting crushed, but she couldn't complain or argue because of her voice. She was wearing men's clothes and had covered her face. People took no notice of her at all. I struggled and managed to change my seat with her because the corner was much more comfortable. I pushed people to get a little more space for her. The confined space got warmer and warmer. People started to sweat. Sahar whispered to me, "I am getting really hot and feeling so bad. I can't breathe, I want to uncover my face."

"Wait for a moment," I said.

The other three men were sitting in the middle of truck. I stood up and called them to come and sit beside me. They pushed other people aside to get closer. I helped them to get next to me. Eventually we were all together. I said to Sahar,

"You can take your cover off your face a little bit. Don't look at people."

She was facing me, so she was able to uncover her face. I looked at her in that dark little place; she was shining like the moon. I could read in her eyes that she was scared.

I whispered, "Wow, I am so happy that you here with me."

She looked at me, smiled, and whispered, "I am so glad to be free."

The truck smelled bad because too many people were in that small space, some of them had not taken a shower for a couple days. There was only a little space above us for the air to circulate.

After several hours, the truck pulled over. We made a plan to cover our faces because it looked more natural if all of us were covered almost completely. We left a little space around our eyes. It was hard to tell who we were.

The smugglers opened up the doors and hurriedly started to take out the sacks of plaster. Then they shouted at us, "Get out fucking drugs, quickly!"

People started pushing each other to get out faster. One of the gang directed people to different rooms. Our small group and about fifteen other men, all went to one room. The five of us sat at the far end of the room.

I told Sahar, "When the smugglers come in the room, for any reason, just lie down. If they ask what is wrong with you. we'll tell them that you are just tired."

We all had taken our scarves off but were not facing anyone. Someone came in with food. Sahar lay down to face the wall. They gave us our food and left quickly. Sahar got up, and we ate. We were pleased that our plan had worked well so far.

At about 2:00 p.m., Sahar said she needed to go to the washroom.

"Can you hold on until it gets a little darker?"

"OK," she said.

Two hours later, she said, "Ali jan, I can't hold it anymore."

"OK, wait, I'll go and find out where the washroom is."

I went outside the room, and I called a smuggler, and I said, "I need to go to washroom, where is it?"

He answered from the other room, "Can't you go and do it outside in the yard?"

"I can't do it there because people are watching me."

"You are a man. Come on. Why are you being shy?"

"I am Afghan. I never did it in front of people before in my life. I want the washroom!"

He came out and handed me a key, pointed down a passageway, and said, "Hurry up, shy man."

I went back to the room, and I shouted. "Jafar jan, I've found the washroom, you can come with me now."

We half covered our faces and made our way down the passage to a door. She went in. I waited outside. When we returned to our room, some of the other men seemed to be getting suspicious. I think it might have been because we covered our faces, or it might have been the way Sahar looked. She wasn't very manly. Every so often people kept looking in our direction, and I knew they were talking about us. Suddenly someone recognized who she was.

He said, "Is this the same girl who brought food for us the other day in the smugglers' house?"

"You are wrong. He is a boy. His name is Jafar," I said.

Everyone else in the room noticed what was going on. This man from Bangladesh said, "I will tell the smugglers about it."

"Don't do that. She is like our sister, they rape her and beat her up."

"Oh, she is a very beautiful girl. If I had the chance, I would have done the same."

"You can get your mom and do the same things to her. You are mother fucker. You are fucking illegitimate," I said angrily.

We argued a lot and got angrier. Everyone started shouting and arguing. Eventually it led to blows. One of the Afghan men and I beat up the troublemaker and threatened him that if he told the gang about it, we would kill him. There were other Bangladeshi men travelling with us, they took his side and started to fight with us. Men took their belts off and fought using them. They beat us more than we beat them because there were more of them, and we were only four. One of the fighters on our side pulled a nail-trimmer from his pocket and jabbed the man who started this fight on his shoulder. He screamed and cried and asked for help. One of the smugglers ran into the room, yelling, "What's going on? Why are you fucking screaming, dirty man?"

Everyone was talking at the same time, but the man said, "Someone stabbed me with a knife, and there is a girl with them."

"No, he's lying," I said.

They pointed at Sahar. The gangster went to her and pulled her scarf off and recognized her, and said, "I was dreaming about you. We have been looking for you. We never expected you to be here. Where do you think you going, beautiful girl?"

"He is one of them who raped me!" Sahar shouted to us.

He was trying to take Sahar with him. I started to struggle with him and said, "You can't take her away from me, you will have to kill me first. Don't you have your own family? What would you do if someone else did that to your sister?"

The other Afghan men took my side and shouted the same thing.

He pushed me and said, "Get out of my way, fucking black man."

"She needs to be returned to her family," one man said.

"You are human. You should have some feelings," someone else yelled.

"I hear a lot of that shit every day. I am telling you to get out of my way."

Sahar was crying and pleaded. The smuggler took no notice. He slapped my face and started punching hard.

I got mad and lost my temper and started fighting in earnest. He stopped fighting, he had blood running from his cut lip. He pulled out a gun. Facing me, he said, "I am going to kill you right here, fucking black man, if you don't stop fighting."

Sahar jumped in front of me and said, "Kill me please, shoot me now, I am the sinner. I ran away. Why do you want to kill him?"

Other smugglers heard the noise. They ran in, shouting, "What are you doing? Why are you pulling gun on him?"

He put the gun back in his trousers. He grabbed Sahar's hair and pulled her away from me. She was crying and hitting his hand, trying to release her hair. I tried my best to stop him taking her away, but the other three beat me up, and then left the room, slamming the door and locking it.

CHAPTER 29

UNEXPECTED NEWS

When they had gone, I looked for the man who had caused all the trouble. I jumped up very quickly and ran at him. I grabbed his neck under my left arm and kept punching his face. He was bleeding. The rest of the men did not want any more fighting. They tried to intervene. I was shouting, "I hope Allah will teach you a lesson because of what you've done."

He was screaming and yelling for help. Smugglers came back in and took him out. I sat down. I was sad and depressed; the Afghan men were sitting next to me.

"Well, we tried," one of them said.

"They have all the cards. They are too many," another said.

"Sahar needs our help. We shouldn't ignore that. They have abused her very badly and will go on doing it," I argued. "I can't accept it. I'm going to stop here and do something about it. My father has been lost in Afghanistan. I have lost everything. I have nothing to lose. I am going to get Sahar away from them, or be killed in the attempt."

"I am staying with Ali to resolve this problem. It's not his responsibility alone. It's the responsibility of all Afghan men," said one of the men. His name was Fawad.

The other two said, "We don't want to die here. We have to go to Europe because our families are waiting for us."

"I didn't ask you to stay or die here. You can do what you like," I said.

I shook Fawad's hand and said, "We'll get Sahar back to her family."

We sat apart from the other two.

"Haven't they got any guts?" Fawad asked angrily.

We discussed what to do for about two hours. We worked out a plan. We were going to wait for the some of the smugglers to leave, as they usually did when we were waiting for another vehicle to come. That should leave only one or two of the gang. We thought we could then challenge them and ask them to return Sahar to her family. If they refused, we would go to the police and tell them about it. We hoped to Allah our plan would work. We ran the risk of being killed by the smugglers if they thought that we were going to report them, and the police might deport us back to Afghanistan if we went to them. There was not much else we could do. Sahar was at risk, so we had to do something. Fawad and I prayed a lot, and asked Allah to give us power to return Sahar to her family.

Next day after, we had had the usual chai and naan bread, I lay down, closed my eyes for a short while, and thought about our plan. I heard someone come into the room. I did not pay any attention to them. I thought it might be someone bringing more food. Whoever it was came closer to me.

Still I did not open my eyes. I was thinking about Sahar. I heard her voice, she said, "Ali Jan, are you sleeping?"

I thought I was dreaming. She asked again and again, and then she shook my shoulder. When I opened my eyes, she was sitting next to me and holding a newspaper in her hand. I was surprised because she seemed very happy.

"Oh god, am I dreaming now? You look happy, Sahar Jan. What's going on?" I asked.

She handed me the newspaper.

"What should I do with this?" I asked.

"Look at this page. There is my picture," she said.

I looked at it, not comprehending. I couldn't read it because it was written in the Turkish language. The photo she was pointing at was like her, but someone who looked younger. "What does it say?"

"My family went to Germany. My father and my uncle came back to Turkey. They have been looking for me for a long time. They have been advertising about me in the newspapers, giving my picture and their telephone number. They have offered twenty thousand U.S. dollars as reward to whoever knows where I am. No questions will be asked. The smugglers brought this newspaper. They want the money and are going to return me to my family. I was there when one of them called my father and told him, "Bring the money and take your daughter." My father did not believe him, so they handed me the receiver, and I spoke to him. We both cried for a short while. He said he will come today. They arranged a meeting somewhere far from here. The smugglers told him to be there late this afternoon. "I am leaving here shortly, but I don't know how I can thank you. I will miss you very much. I will remember you for the whole my life." She put her hands up, prayer-like, and said, "You helped me a lot. You might have been killed because of me. I promise you I will pray for you forever. Allah will be with you."

I told her about our plan and added, "I am glad that you are going back to your family. Now I am going to continue my journey. You don't have to thank me. Whatever I did, that was my duty. I will remember you in my life too. I wish you all the best. Have a great life in Germany," I said.

"I have some feeling about you. But I can't tell because it's not the right time, and I am not a good girl."

"What you do mean that you are not a good girl? You are a very nice girl. Don't think about yourself in a negative way."

"You know about the smugglers, what they have done to me. It was very bad. In our traditions, girls . . ." She stopped talking.

A smuggler came in and told her they had to go right away. He looked at me and said, "Do you want to try again to take her away? Did you know her before somewhere else?"

"I had planned to return her to her family. Now I am glad that you are going to do that."

"We are not returning her voluntarily. Money is involved, that's what make us return her."

We had only known each other for a couple of days. But it seemed we had known each other for years.

I looked in her eyes. "Good luck, Sahar Jan. Take care of yourself."

I followed her to the yard. I felt I wanted to give her a good present just to remember me by, because it is our tradition. I searched my pockets, and I couldn't find anything. I had only my watch on my wrist. It was very useful to me, but there was nothing else. So I gave her my watch as a memento. She wanted to say something, but before she opened her mouth, I said, "Please accept it as a friendly gift."

"Ali Jan, you will need this."

Then she gave me a letter and said, "Read it please, when you get to England."

She got on the backseat of the car and waved to me several times, crying. Then they left. I waved back. I looked at her letter and kept it in my underwear pocket, where I hid my money.

CHAPTER 30

ISTANBUL

I went inside the room to see how Fawad was doing. I told him everything about Sahar.

Fawad and I became very good friends, and we promised to help each other as much as possible. It was very late at night when the smuggler brought an old milk tanker, which had been converted to transport people because they said it would not attract police attention, which meant they could travel more easily on the main highways during daylight. It did not look big enough for so many people, but they told us that we had to get in. I was the first person who got in. I took enough spaces for Fawad and myself. He came after a short while. We were sitting down toward the front. There was not space enough for everyone to sit down. Smugglers pushed in about ten more people and kicked them. Eventually we were all in. Then they closed the door. The first couple of hours, people kept quiet. Later on, they started to fight and make a noise because there wasn't space enough to sit comfortably. There was a very bad smell, and some people had stomach trouble, some were crying, and swearing at the smugglers, asking Allah to save us. There was a small door in the roof above our heads for the air. After about fifteen hours, the smugglers dropped in some bottles of water and grapes. Sixty people all jumped at the same time to grab them. People pushed and fought just to get some water. Eventually everyone got some. Later people urinated in the bottles.

About thirteen hours later, the truck pulled over. Smugglers opened the door and told us to get out. That was the first time people did not make any quick movements. None of us could move properly, but eventually we all got out. We again went into a large room. There were many other rooms. It was like a hostel. We were all angry because the smugglers had kept us inside the truck much longer than we expected. I went to wash my face.

About an hour later, smugglers brought plenty of food for us. We were all hungry. There was a selection of food, including boiled potatoes, eggs, onions, minis (mayonnaise), meat, and bread. I went to see if there were any bathrooms, and I took a shower. There was something good about the smuggler's Istanbul hideout for everyone. There was plenty food, water, and good bathrooms, etc. There was no specific time for eating. We could have food anytime we wanted. One night, before people lay down to sleep, the smuggler said, "We will be here for quite while because getting across to Greece is not easy. We have to go by sea to get there. We can't take more than twenty people at one time. This week we are expecting some more people to come from Iran. We will divide you into groups, and then we'll go to Greece one group at a time." And then he left the room.

Everyone wanted to be in the first group, including me. Fawad and I washed our clothes by hand, and other people did the same thing. We were told to be ready to leave Istanbul sometime soon.

It was about 2:00 a.m. when Fawad woke me up, and said, "Get up, Ali, there something going on." When I opened my eyes, I heard people shouting outside the room. Other people were getting up for the same reason. I got up and walked toward the door. There were people outside, but I couldn't recognize them because it was not light enough out there. I came back to Fawad, and I told him what I saw. About twenty minutes later, we heard gunshots several times. There was a dispute going on between the smugglers. They killed each other. A short while later, the police arrived. They turned the lights on and said, "Oh . . . oh." I did not understand what they said about us because they spoke Turkish.

They brought three buses and told us all to get in. I remembered every time the smuggler brought a truck for us, people had started pushing each other to get quickly into the truck, but no one wanted to go in the bus now. Police hit people and forced them to get in. We were all clutching our sad bundles of possessions. Then they took us to a police station.

The railings across the front of the courtyard were made of fancy mental, and on top were very sharp spikes, while a high wall surrounding the rest of the complex. The station itself was a collection of various buildings, but taking them all together, the whole place was not big enough to house all of us refugees, so they told us to sit down in a big central compound. They made us sit in lines of three. It was still fairly dark and cold, and the ground felt as though it was freezing. I was sitting in the last line with

Fawad. There were three police officers guarding us. They were patrolling inside the yard around the gates. Other policemen came and went just to see how many of us there were. They laughed and joked with each other and smoked together and talked about us in Turkish. I had heard very bad stories about the Turkish police and their methods of deportation. I heard they keep people starving and then beat them up. They believe in teaching people a lesson, so that they never will come back again. There was a saying about Turkish police oppression.

"If you have come to Turkey illegally, like a lion, we will make you go back to your country like a lamb."

When I was in Iran, some people who had been deported from Turkey said a lot of bad things about Turkish police. I tried to think how to run away. The police officers were busy talking to each other. I looked around the yard. There was a one-storey building on the back right side corner of the yard. It was about two and half meters high. I thought I could manage to get up there and make a run for it.

"Fawad, I am going to escape now. I don't want to be deported. I had once a very bad experience in Iran when they deported me to Afghanistan. I am going to run right now. Do you want come with me or not?" I said quickly.

"How we can do that?" he said.

I showed him the way. "We can get ourselves on top of that roof, and then we will keep running."

"I am very afraid to do that."

"What are you afraid of?"

"Police."

"They're going to beat us up and deport us, whether we try to escape or not. There is a chance to run away from this trouble, are you coming with me or not? I am asking you for the last time."

"Let's go," he said.

"Follow me, don't stand up or make a noise."

I took only my orange T-shirt and tied it around my hand. I gave a red one to Fawad.

"We are going to leave everything here, if you have any money in your bundle, take it right now. Have this T-shirt. We will change into it if we get in the road. They will not recognize us with different colored shirts. If anyone catches us in that corner, tell them we are just having a pee and pretend to button your trousers."

I looked at the officers; they were busy talking and facing the other way. I crawled very slowly toward the wall, and Fawad was behind me. We got there in less than half a minute. I tried to reach to the roof by myself, but I was a little too short.

I told Fawad, "You bend, and I will climb on your back. That will help me to get up there. When I'm there, I will help you up. Don't make any noise, we are almost there."

He bent a little bit. I couldn't get up at first. I told him to bend down a little more. Eventually I got up there. Then I lay down on the roof and tried to catch his hands. I pulled him several times. He was about to get up when he fell down backward and banged on the ground. Everyone saw us including the police. They ran to catch us. I pulled him with all my power. I couldn't get him up because he was too short and weak to pull himself up, and he was overweight. He was really afraid, his hands were shaking. He couldn't focus on what he was doing. Police caught him and kicked him. He shouted at me to run.

I kept running. I crossed several roofs. The whole building was surrounded by the high wall. It was about eight foot high. There was a space between the building and the wall, but there were two big dogs down in the passageway barking at me. I would have to jump over the alleyway to get to the road. There was a long distance between the roof where I was standing and the outer wall. I looked at it, the distance seemed too great. I looked behind me, someone was running toward me. The choice was to chance jumping, I might fall down and be badly bitten, or I could stay and be caught. He was getting close to me. I decided to jump. I moved backward about six feet ran forward very fast and then jumped. I passed over the gap, but I fell over the wall and crashed on to the street on my knees and hands. I got up very quickly, looked behind me. The policeman couldn't jump after me. I limped away very fast. While I was stumbling about, I checked behind me hurriedly. There were not many people or vehicles on the roads at that time in the morning. My knees and my hands hurt a lot. I didn't care about it. I wanted to go somewhere and hide myself. I picked the smaller streets and changed directions a lot around the houses. I got very tired. I did not know where to go. I heard the noise of police car's siren. Oh my god, they are going to find me now. Allah, help me please, I said to myself. I couldn't run anymore because of my legs and hands. The siren noise got closer. They were not too far away from me. "Oh, Allah, you helped me to get on the roof and to run, you helped to jump, now help me please to hide myself somewhere."

A few seconds later, as I turned a corner, I saw a mosque across the street. I ran to the door. It was open, and a lot people were inside.

CHAPTER 31

ZABI

I went to the washroom. I took a little rest there to get my breath back to normal. I looked at my stinging hands and grazed and bruised knees. I was very sore, but nothing was broken. I changed my T-shirt and washed my face. I had a mixture of feelings, nervous, afraid, and pleased to be still free. The sound of a passing police siren made me realize that I had to blend in.

I went into the chapel. There were several men sitting in a circle, reading the Koran. I was surprised at there being so many people in the mosque at that time of night, and wondered what was going on. I picked up a Koran and joined them. I needed to find out where about in the Koran they were reading. I searched for a couple of pages and could not find it. I looked at these people around me; their heads were down, and they listened. They had started reading from right to the left, moving around the circle. I was the youngest in the crowd listening very carefully. They read the Koran in a different way than the way I had learned in Afghanistan, Mazar-i-Sharif. I kept searching; eventually I found exactly where they had been reading. There was a Molla sitting in the middle of the group, correcting people's mistakes. After a short while, there was a man, who sat on my right, he had stopped for a moment, and he and the Molla looked at me. I waited for a second; I thought that someone else would continue reading. There was a silence for a few seconds. They expected me to start reading, I assumed. It was very difficult for me to read the same way as they did, but I decided to read it in my own way. I took a deep breath, and I put my both hands beside my ears, balancing my book on my knees and started very loud. I tried to read it, with my best knowledge of the Koran. I read six or seven lines. When I stopped for a few second to take a breath again, the Molla said something, which I did not understand. I thought for a moment what I should do now. "I am sorry, I can't speak Turkish," I said in my first language (Dari).

There was an old man nearby me. He said, "Are you from Afghanistan?"

"*Baly Kaka* (Yes, sir)."

The Molla said, "You are very good *Qaree* (professional reader of the Koran), may Allah preserve you."

"It is very kind of you, I was once an assistant to a Molla in Mazar-e-Sharif," I said, looking to the Molla, and then the old man translated it to him.

I read a few more lines, and then I let the next person continue. After a long while, we finished reading. The Molla said, "It is time to start *Shabbe Qader* (powerful night in Ramadan) ceremony. He stood at the front, facing to *Kiblah*, we all took our places one behind the other. People made lines one after another. I stood beside the old man, in case I needed something translated. The Molla started the ceremony. I looked at the people, they were holding the Koran above their heads; so I did the same. A few minutes after the ceremony had started, the Molla stopped, and said, "Tonight is the twenty-seventh day of Ramadan, a very powerful night. Tonight you can ask Allah for your needs, your wishes, and your health. Anything you need for life, ask Allah. Tonight, Allah will grant it."

He stopped for a short while. I took the Koran in front of me, and I said, "Oh Allah, first of all, forgive me for the time I missed my fasting. Allah, please keep me in good health and help me to get to the UK safely."

I prayed for everybody's health and a safe home for all refugees, and for Fawad to get to his destination. I thanked Allah for saving me from deportation. I wanted to talk more to Allah about my problems, but the Molla did not give enough time, he restarted the ceremony. When it was finished, he started the blessing. In the blessing, he asked Allah to give good health for the whole world, etc. After the blessing, we put back the Korans onto a shelf. Right after the ceremony, they brought amazing Turkish food. We sat down to eat it, and the old man next to me said, "Allah accept your prayer."

"Thank you, the same to you, sir. My name is Ali, I am very pleased to meet you in this country. I am exiled from my home," I said.

"I am Zabi, nice to meet you. How long have been in Istanbul?" he said.

"Not too long, a couple days."

We sat down and received some Turkish food. "How long have you been here agha Zabi?"

"A long time. Are you living close by?" he asked.

"No, I am not living here at all. I am here for few a days until I have found smugglers. I will go to England."

"Who did you come with?"

He seemed wanted to know everything about me. I decided to tell him something about myself, I thought he might help me to find a smuggler.

"I came by myself all the way to Istanbul. We were about sixty or seventy people in the smuggler's house, all ready to go to Greece. Last night, there was a dispute between the smugglers. We heard gunshots. The police arrived and took everybody to the police station. I had heard awful stories about Turkish police of their deportations. I decided to run away with one of my best friends. He was too short and could not climb up on to the roof. The police caught him. I ran all over the place looking for somewhere to hide myself, Allah helped me to find this mosque and to meet you, agha Zabi."

"You are very brave. Allah kept you away from evil."

The Molla was nearby; he welcomed me to come to the mosque every day, and bring all my friends. He thought that I was living locally and new to the area. I did not tell him anything about myself. I said to him, "OK."

Then he said to everyone, "Ten minutes left to the morning prayers."

That meant that we had to stop eating and drinking our beverages at that time in the morning, and fast until very late sunset. So we would not be able to drink even water in that period. Ten minutes later, the Molla started to Azan (call for prayer). We got in lines and made morning prayers. When we finished, people started to leave because they had prayed all night long. I sat down, my back against the wall. I was very tired.

Zabi came beside me and said, "I am going home, I have prayed all night. I am very tired. I need some sleep. Where are you going to sleep? You were awake all night and ran a lot? You must be tired, my son."

"I have nowhere to go. I will stay here. Later in the day, I will go out and find smugglers to go to Greece."

"You need a rest before you do that. I do not have a beautiful house, but I have some space to let you sleep there. I will be happy if you come to my poor house."

"Thank you very much for your kindness. I do not like to bother you. You need to go to your bed, you have prayed all night. I might disturb you. I may see later on."

"No, you are very welcome. Before you have arrived here, the Molla said, "If you help anyone in the Ramadan, especially today, Allah will help you more than a hundred thousand times. Allah gave me a chance to meet you, and you need my help. Please come with me. You have the look of my son about you, don't be shy."

I went with him. He was an old man. I did not want to upset him by refusing, and I thought he might help me to find the smugglers. His house was not too far from the mosque. On the way there, we talked about Ramadan. He took me to his guest room and said,

"This is like your room, feel free. If you need anything, let me know. You can sleep here, I will wake you up for noon prayer," and then he left. I lay down and started to think about what I should do next. I could not make any decision because I was so tired, and my knees hurt a lot. Eventually, I fell asleep.

CHAPTER 32

CALLING MY UNCLE

He woke me up about twenty minutes before noon. My body was stiff, and my knees were still hurting. I wanted to lie down all day, but I had to go because the old man was waiting for me to get up. I got ready, forcing myself, and we went to the mosque for noon prayers. After prayers, he said, "I know someone who knows some smugglers. Do you want to go there now?"

"Yes, *Kaka* Zabi."

We went to find his friend, who received us well. He phoned the smuggler, who arrived an hour later. He was a Turkish man, but he could speak a little Persian. I did not have problems talking to him.

"Where are you planning to go?" the smuggler asked.

"England," I said.

"How many people are you altogether?"

"I am alone, just by myself."

"We can't take a person to England by land. We can provide you with a passport, and then you can fly to the UK. It will cost you six thousand American dollars. If you want do that, you have to pay us 50 percent of the money first. When you get your passport, you have to pay the full amount. We can take you to the plane; you will have no worry getting to England."

"Obviously, I don't have that much money to pay you now. I have only about six hundred dollars. I need to call my uncle in the UK. I will tell him about it, he said he would send me money if I needed it," I said.

When he had left, we checked out other smugglers, they were asking almost the same price. The last one we found was a Greek. He suggested that I split up my journey and go to one country after another and make my way, first, to Greece, then on to Italy, then France, and then at last to the United Kingdom. I did not know where that was, but it turned out to be what I called "England." He said he would charge me about three thousand U.S. dollars just to go to Greece. After he had gone, I told Zabi that their prices were much more than I could afford, even if I only went to Greece.

"I am not happy about trusting these smugglers again. The last group I used were nothing more than gangsters. Besides, if I went to all those different countries, I would not know all their foreign languages. I can only just make Turkish people understand what I am saying," I told my old friend.

"Yes, it can be a problem," he agreed. "I was in Athens for a while, many years ago, and I found it easier to try to speak in English. It is the capital city, and there are all nationalities there. Everyone speaks a little bit of English, but you would get along all right. I did."

Then he checked the time and said, "I need to go to the mosque for afternoon prayer. I will see you later for the evening prayers."

"OK, Kaka, you go. Thank you very much for your help. I will definitely be at the mosque tonight. I am just going to find a public telephone office, so that I can phone the UK."

We shook hands, and then he left. I kept walking northwest. Eventually I found a phone office. I walked inside. There was a person sitting at the reception. On the left side, there were a lot of cubicles, with telephones inside them. Some of them occupied. I tried to tell the man at the desk that I wanted to call the UK. I tried three different languages (Dari, Pashto, Persian). Still he did not understand me.

"English or Turkish please," he said.

"No Turkish, English OK?" I said.

I had learned some basic English words in Afghanistan. I could not remember all of them at that moment.

"Phone England *Mama* (Uncle) OK," I said it and showed him physically, by holding my hand to the side of my ear.

"Telephone England you want?" he said and showed me by his hand.

"Yes, agha (sir)."

He took me to a cubicle. I picked up the receiver, dialed my uncle's phone number several times. I got his answering machine. He was talking in English. I did not fully understand what he said. I rang off and went out of the telephone office. The weather was nice and warm. The sun was shining. I walked toward the mosque. On the way, I passed through a beautiful park. There was a bench. I sat down. I was there for a long while, thinking about what I should do next. I could not make a decision because I was very hungry. I had not eaten for the last ten hours; nevertheless, I could not have food for another three hours because I was fasting that day. I went to the mosque and sat down for a short while, and then I started to pray.

There were too many people, more than the day before. About sunset, Zabi came.

"Ali, where have you been? My wife made some Afghani food for you. I would like to invite you for dinner," he said happily.

"It is very kind of you, kaka Zabi," I said.

I went with him. The food tasted very good because I was very hungry.

After the dinner, I told Zabi about my uncle, and how I could not get hold of him.

"I have decided to stay in Istanbul. I am a good tailor. I need to find a job. I will work hard to make some money for the journey to England. Kaka Zabi, I want to rent a bachelor flat first. Do you have any idea where we can find one?" I asked.

"We will find one easily. Don't worry, Ali agha. Allah will help you. You said you are a tailor. There are a lot of places wanting tailors, they offer good wages. Just put your trust in Allah, you will be fine," Zabi said.

We looked for two days. We found three bachelor's pads. The first one was very nice; I could not rent it because it was too expensive for me. The second was just about OK to live in for a couple of days, and when I got job, I would rent the nice one, I said myself. I rented it for a hundred and twenty-five dollars a month. The same day, I bought some basic stuff for my funny little home. I went looking for a job. After about a week, I found a tailoring company. I went in with Zabi, and we talked to the manager. He gave me two shirts. He showed me that one was a made-up sample; the other was a shirt, in pieces, ready for sewing.

"I want you to make this the same as the sample. Can you make it like that?" he inquired skeptically.

"I will try my best; just give me half an hour."

"I am not expecting you to do it that fast. You have two hours to finish it."

I followed him inside the factory. He led me to a machine and tools, and then left. I looked at the sample; it was good and very similar to the ones I made in Tehran, but not as good as those I had made for Abbas and myself, in my own workshop in Iran. I tried to make it much better than anything that had been made in that company before. I asked Allah for help, and then I started. I had finished it in about twenty-eight minutes. I checked it twice to make sure everything was OK. I went to the manager's office. He looked at his watch, "What happened, is the machine not working?" he asked angrily.

"No, everything is fine," I said, and then I handed both the shirts to him. He looked at them.

"Excellent job. Would you like to have a cup of coffee, sir?" he said.

"No, I am fine."

"Take a seat, I am going to take this to the boss. I will be back shortly."

Zabi was very happy and said, "You did a great job, Ali jan. He was really surprised."

A short while later, he came with the boss, who introduced himself, and said, "Where did you learn tailoring?"

"Iran," I said. I told him about my own my business.

He talked about the company and the facilities and said, "You are very welcome. You can start work from tomorrow."

"OK," I said.

We shook hands, and then we left.

CHAPTER 33

I GO SHOPPING

The next day, I went to work. There were about thirty sewing machines and forty workers. Most of them were female. At the lunch break, the supervisor introduced me to all the workers. There were five Afghans at that company. I decided to go very early to the workshop and stay very late because I wanted to make some money to go to England as soon as possible. The job was piecework. The first week, I made one hundred and twelve American dollars. I worked from 8:00 a.m. to 7:00 p.m. six days a week. After a short while, I made six friends, who were from my country and Turkey. One of my Turkish friends was very slow at sewing. Her machine was next to mine. She wanted to learn from me so that she could improve her work. We agreed that I would teach her sewing, and she would teach me Turkish. She was a very nice girl.

About two weeks later, the supervisor came and said, "Your uncle wants to see you. He is outside."

I was very happy for a short time; I thought my uncle Nassir had come from England to see me.

I went to out and found Zabi waiting. "Salaam, Kaka Zabi," I said and shook his hand.

"Salaam, Ali jan, I have not seen you since you got this job. I was worried about you, and the Molla asked twice about you. I told him that you have got a job, and young men are not interested in going to the mosque often. Anyway, how are you doing?"

"I am fine, I can't complain. How are you doing?" I asked.

"I am here to see you and to see how you are getting on with your job. I have found two other tailoring companies. They want clever tailors like you. I mean if you are not happy with this job, we can go there."

"Thank you. It is OK for the moment. If there are any problems, I will let know."

"I have two English books. I have brought you one of them. You may need it, and want to study sometime because you are going England one day."

He handed me the book. "Thank you," I said, and then we shook hands, and he left.

I went back to my work. I was a little behind that day with my work.

One Friday, my six co-workers were planning to go to Izmir town for the weekend to stay over, and I joined them. We all planned to meet each other in the bus terminal. We all got together and got on the bus. In the bus, I had a good talk with one of my co-workers who was a fellow countryman. He was sitting next to me. He had lived in Turkey for a number of years and was able to give me very useful information about Turkey and a little about Greece. It took us many hours to get to Izmir. When we got there, we went around to see what the town looked like, then we went to the beach. It was very nice and clean. The sea was a light blue, and the sun danced and dazzled on the waves, while the incoming breeze cooled everyone.

"There are many tourists around today. It's a wonderful place to be, the air is so fresh," said one of my friends.

"Does this sea belong to Greece?" I asked.

"Yes, half the sea belongs to Greece. If you come toward night time, when it is really dark, you can see the lights of Greece," he said.

On one side of that sea was Greece, and on our side was Turkey. We walked around for a little while. There was a fairground nearby. We played some volleyball, and then we went to the cinema to watch movies together because the weather had changed a little. We stayed over that night and returned home next day.

When I got home, I made tea for myself and sat down. I started to think about my job. I had worked there six weeks and made about seven hundred U.S. dollars. My expenses were about five hundred dollars, including rent, rates, food, and transport fees, etc. The food was very expensive in Istanbul. All my friends complained about it. I saved two hundred fifty dollars in that period by my hard work. If I worked very hard for the next four years, if I did not lose my job, I would be able to pay the smuggler to take me to England, I said myself. I have to find another job, or another way to go to the UK.

Weeks later, I returned to Izmir to check how far Greece was from there. The weather was good. There were some people boating. I looked at these people. It seemed very easy. I bought a sandwich and sat down looking toward Greece and thinking about how I could cross the sea. I looked at everything very closely. I saw someone getting out of rubber inflated boat. I was in the middle of eating my sandwich. I threw it away, and I ran toward him. "Hello," I said.

I tried to ask him how much his boat cost and how far away Greece was. I spoke a little Turkish and some English. It took me a while just to make him understand that I wanted to know how much the boat cost.

"About hundred and fifty million Turkish money, about hundred twenty dollars U.S.," he said.

Then he left. I had about three hundred dollars. I decided to buy a small boat and sail it to Greece. I thought it would be very easy to do that. Otherwise, it would take me forever to go to the UK. I went home. I made everything ready. I went to the town center to buy a boat. I walked all over, I could not find any kind of boat shop because I had problems with my Turkish language and did not know where I should look.

I walked all day long. I did not take time even for lunch. I was very busy finding a boat. The shopping malls were beginning to close. I went home. Next day, I woke up very early around 5:00 a.m. I went to the mosque for the Morning Prayer. The Molla and Zabi were surprised. After the prayer, I asked Zabi, "Where I can buy a boat?"

"A boat?" He was astonished. "What kind of boat? What do you need a boat for?" he asked. He thought for a moment, then said, "I think around the Cinema Zangee area."

I talked to him for a short while, and then I said, "I am going home to make myself ready for my work, Kaka Zabi. See you later."

I went home and made a very good breakfast. About seven o'clock, I left. I had forgotten to ask Zabi how to get to Cinema Zangee. Anyway, I would find it out, I said to myself.

I went to the bus station. I found the right one to go Cinema Zangee and got off at the right stop. There were many stores selling different kinds of boats. I started to think about what kind I should buy. I decided to buy an inflatable dingy like the one that the man had.

"The boat is just for fun and used only for very short distances," a salesperson said.

I looked at the prices. They were from eighty dollars to two hundred dollars U.S. I decided to buy a good one.

I bought a boat and a pump and two paddles. That cost me altogether about one hundred fifty dollars. I took everything home. About 5:00 p.m., I went to see Zabi. Fortunately, he was at home. "Salam, agha Zabi, I am sorry if I disturbed you. I am here to see you for the last time. I thought if I went without meeting you, you will be worried about me."

"Of course, my son," he said.

"I am here to thank you for everything. Tonight, I am going to Greece."

"Why are you standing here by the door? Come in for a cup of tea with me."

We went in, and his wife brought tea for us.

"Did your uncle send you some money?" he asked, smiling.

"No, Kaka."

"I would like to know how you are going there, if you do not mind, I just want to make sure that you'll be all right."

"I bought a little funny blue boat, and tonight I have a plan to go to Greece, because during the day time, police patrol around the sea. They might stop me. *Agha* Zabi, my uncle did not answer his phone. The company where I am working, I make four hundred and fifty dollars monthly. I cannot save 70 percent of it because I have to pay rent and the other expenses. You know how the food is expensive here. If I do not go now, in the way I am planning, I will be here forever. I just want you to pray for me please."

"I would like to tell you something as a friend or as an old man. Going to England, it is not easy, Ali jan, unless you are going legally. Either way, using a false passport is dangerous. Going with this little boat, that sounds even more dangerous. That is the worst thing you can do. I am not going to discourage you, however, I have to tell something, which is very important for you. I know you are a very young man. You have a good future waiting for you. Ali jan. You are very intelligent. I know a lot young people about your age, they are afraid to go from one city to another by themselves. You came all the way from Afghanistan by yourself. Stay here. I will help you to find another job."

"Thank you very much, Zabi agha. I have nothing to lose. I have no one in the world. I am going, or I will die in the attempt. If I died, no one would care about me or miss me. If I succeed and arrive there, I will have invented an easy way for poor people to go to England. How can people make six thousand dollars in this country or Afghanistan if they needed to save their lives? I will be OK. If I do not call you for about a week, that means I am dead. If I am alive, I will call you sooner. OK?"

"I know you have made your decision about going away. I wish you all the best. Can I ask you to do one thing for me please?"

"Go ahead, Kaka Jan."

"Don't go tonight, go tomorrow night."

"OK, just for you, agha Zabi, because you have helped me a lot."

CHAPTER 34

LIFE HAS ITS UPS AND DOWNS

After tea, we went to the mosque for the evening prayer. Zabi told the Molla about me and asked him to pray for me please. Then we went to my home. Zabi was interested to see my little funny boat.

In my small bedroom, I had stood the bed on its side against the wall. I had unpacked my boat and inflated it. It almost filled the room, I could just open the door. It was not that the boat was big, it was because the room was small. When I had first pumped it up, there were other pieces of the same material as the boat left over. One was quite a large sheet, and there was also a long flat wooden plank with small oblong holes at each end. I could not read what all these things were for because the writing in the instruction book was Turkish. So I had climbed into my boat to see how it felt. I was so happy doing this, I felt like a child. I explored some pockets that were stitched into the sides, they were for storage, I could work that out, and they had covers that zipped them closed. There were fittings, straps, which would tie the long flat board into place. I now had worked out that it was the seat. There were more straps. There was a zipper strip running all the way around the upper edge, but I did not know what that was for. I took up one of the paddles and started rowing. I would be in Greece in no time at all. There was only one thing I did not like about it, and that was the smell. It smelled strongly of chemicals and rubber. I thought my head felt dizzy. But out in the open air, well, I would not even notice it.

"Oh Allah!" Zabi almost shouted. "Ali, this boat is only for a little river. It is just for fun. Are you crazy? You are not allowed to take this boat on to the sea. If the police catch you with this boat, they will put you in prison. It is only a little thicker than plastic. This is very dangerous. With a little thistle, you could puncture this boat. It will sink. If the air escaped, you will be drowned. You are Afghan. You do not have any sea there. The sea is much bigger than you think. It looks peaceful, but it is not. I advise you not to go with this boat," he said.

"Hey! Kaka Zabi, I trust Allah. I will be OK. You know everyone is going to die one day. Rich, poor, king, or beggar. For me it doesn't matter whether it is sooner or later. I have not had a lot of fun in my life since the Taliban attacked Afghanistan. There will be a chance to have a good life in the UK, like everyone else. I am going. If I stay here and work for four years, still there is no guarantee that I will get to the UK safely. Just pray for me, Kaka Zabi," I said.

"I can't stop you going because this is your life," he said, but he made it clear that he did not agree with my decision at all. He tried in different ways to divert me from my journey. However, he did not know what bad times I had had in my life. Zabi was a very good man. He was an old man; he might never have taken a risk to do something to make his life better. I think my problem was, at the time, I wanted to get everything very fast. Something positive did come out of his visit. I got him to read the instruction book to me. He told me how to install the seat properly with the straps and about securing the paddles and what each pocket was for. The large sheet turned out to be a cover, which zipped all around the top of the boat in case it rained, and then there was something about ballast, but neither of us knew what that was.

We went back to Zabi's home that night. His wife cooked some *Mantwo* (special Afghani food). He was so sad about my journey and said, "You are adventurous. I am not going say negative things about your journey, but I will worry about you and pray for you. It is so sad when your good friend is going away and you may never see them again. I do not know what will happen to, my good friend Qaree."

He said he had heard that there would be bad weather tomorrow, and I should postpone my trip.

I thought it was another ploy to get me to stay. After the dinner, I thanked him a lot. Then I went home and packed up my boat and everything else I was taking. I put my bed in place and was ready for sleep, but the smell of rubber, or whatever it was, was still very strong.

I woke up very early for the morning prayers. I went to the mosque and prayed a lot. About 8:00 a.m., I went to the city center to have a last look around, and then went to the mosque for the noon prayer. When it finished, there was a class about how to read the Koran in a professional way. I decided to join them for about a quarter of an hour.

At about 1:00 p.m., I took my boat and my clothes, and went to Zabi's home. I handed him my house keys, and said, "I will call you in about five days if I am alive. If you have not heard from me in that period, you can return the keys to the property owner." I gave him a *Tazbah* (rosary beads) as a memento and hugged him. "Good-bye, agha Zabi."

He gave me a world map and an English dictionary. "Allah save you, young man, you are going to the sea with that boat. I am shaking here. Please call me as soon as possible. I will pray for you. Good-bye," he said worriedly.

I went to the bus station. I got on the bus with the big bag. There was a huge space behind the driver's seat. He helped me to place my bag, and I sat next to it. The journey to the coast seemed longer than ever. I thought we would never get there.

When I went to the beach, the sun was setting. The sky was bright orange. The waves of the sea reflected the fiery glow making a beautiful rosy image. The weather was a little windy. I walked around to find a good space in which to pump up my boat. I found a suitable space, but I did not inflate it yet. There were some police officers walking around. I thought they might stop me going to sea in my little funny boat. There was a shop a little distance away. I decided to go there and buy some water and biscuits. I walked around the beach until it was dark, and everyone started to leave. The white sand was blowing in a continuous thin mist along the beach, stinging my face, and getting in my eyes and hair. The wind had got up, and doors were banging, and newspapers and plastic bag were scudding along. I was impatient to get started, eager to get to Greece.

When it was completely dark, I started pumping up my boat. It took me a while to do it. I could not read the instructions about how much air to put in because they were in Turkish. I decided to put in a little more air and strapped the seat in place. Then I thought it was OK. I took my clothes off, and I put them in a thick plastic bag. I threw away my pump. I thought that might be useless and make my boat a little heavier. I walked in the water pulling the boat behind me. The water was shockingly cold, but I kept walking. I walked until the water was about waist high. I tried to get onto the boat. I could not make it the first time. Every time I threw my leg over the side of the dingy to get on, the other side would rise up and throw me into the water. I was completely submerged in an instant. The water got into my nose eyes and mouth, and I struggled to get my head above the waves. I stood up blinded and spluttering for air. I coughed up saltwater and heaved for breath. This happened time and again. Once the boat rose up and turned over on top of me. I dropped my bag several times and had to search on the bottom for it. The paddles started to float away, and I had to go after them. There were so many things going against me all at the same time, that getting myself, my few belongings, and the paddles into the dingy was a massive job. Afghanistan is a landlocked country, so I had no experience of boats, saltwater, or buoyancy. I could not even swim. I had thought that getting into the craft would have been a simple affair, but here I was splashing about and coughing my heart up. I was very nervous and afraid the police might come and take me to the police station. I realized that I must take the dingy back toward the shore into shallower water and risk being seen by someone. I would have presented a sorry sight to any observer, freezing cold, spluttering, and naked. However, even here, I had not reckoned on the waves, which one minute pulled toward the land, and the next pulled back toward the sea. It was hard to keep my balance. I wanted to leave my bag behind me but could not because it was important to me. How would I be able to go to the shops in Greece without clothes, to buy new ones? Eventually, I remembered about the storage pockets in the side of the dingy and put the bags in. At last I climbed in and sat on the seat. I was in a hurry to get away from the shore and into the darkness of the sea. I paddled very fast, but the dingy did not move forward. I paddled hard, but I kept going round in circles for a long while. I changed the way I was paddling, and I moved forward a little bit. I paddled very fast. The sea was lifting up and sinking, and eventually, I got up a little speed, more than I had expected to.

After half an hour, I took a little break and looked behind me. I was surprised; I was a long way away from the shore. I was delighted. I had been right all along, things were all going to plan, I told myself.

I had not expected the sea to go up and down so much, but me and my funny little boat, we were on our way to Greece, we'd be there in a few hours.

As I got the boat away from the shelter of the land, the sea got livelier. Where, before, the swell had kept rising and falling a little, it now increased the motion, raising the dingy much higher and then suddenly letting it fall with a stomach churning lurch. Still I was making good progress. After another hour, I stretched my arms, they were becoming stiff. I had never exercised them for so long before. I would have to take it easier. The wind had really got up now, whipping the top of the sea into white waves, which turned to spray. It was getting harder to continue paddling. It was all but useless, the water started to push me back a little bit, so I tried to paddle against whatever it was that was holding me back. It was the wind. The sea was getting rougher, and I was beginning to feel unwell. I had never been in a small boat before in all my life. I had seen them sailing, but never noticed that they went up and down. Not only was my boat rising and crashing down but also it was going sideways, backward, and forward. I could not work out how to control it, and I felt very ill. I wanted to be sick but couldn't. I was beginning to run out of energy and felt tired. I could not take a break because the wind was pushing me back.

I thought I had managed to cover half of the distance to Greece, but realized instead that I had lost my sense of direction. The sea seemed to push me one way, the wind another.

At the top of one wave, I saw lights nearby, I guessed, about a mile away, but down we went again. It couldn't be Greece yet, could it? Up we went again. I looked frantically to where I thought I had seen them. They weren't there. No, the dingy must have turned because they were far over to my left now, before they had seemed to be straight ahead. I was getting dizzy. It turned out that they were only one or two of the small local fishing boats. That's what I thought they were because the sea fell away again, and I was surrounded whichever way I looked by walls of water. I lost all sight of them. I pushed my paddle a little deeper in the water, trying to make some headway, although I didn't know which direction I should try to head for. Then I got a shock, my paddle broke. I screamed and said, "No! Oh Allah, my paddle! What should I do now? Help me! You are the only one who can." I got out the other paddle, but I knew the whole attempt at paddling was pointless.

The weather was getting much stormier now, and the condition of the sea got worse. The waves were showering me with spray. A lot of water was now in my boat. I tried to bail it out, but I had nothing to bail with. The sea was lifting the dingy up often. God. I could not get the damned dingy to do anything. It had a mind of its own. I remembered the cover sheet that was in one of the pockets and struggled against the wind to line it up with the zipper teeth on the top edge of the dingy. I got it to zip a good way around the dingy, and this helped to keep the spray out, but I was now sure that the boat determined to do the very opposite of anything I wanted it to do.

I managed to bail some water out using one of my trainers, but it was hard work. It got so rough that I had to lie down and hold onto the straps at the bottom of the dingy for dear life because I was in real danger of falling into the sea. I was beginning to panic. I did not know how to swim.

My mind whirled. I was in the grip of something beyond anything I could understand. I was very, very sick. I was exhausted but held myself tensely. I had not expected the sea to go up and down so much. The water lifted the boat again. "Oh Allah, stop this rising and falling." I was wet with sweat and seawater. My shoulders hurt a lot. I had to do something. I raised myself and tried to sit up and tried to steer this thing with the remaining paddle. I looked around. I saw lights very close that encouraged me to try to paddle toward them. It was not land. It was a ship. Thank Allah. It was coming my way. It had seen me. I waved and shouted and was so relieved. Closer it came, and closer. It was coming straight at me. It would hit my flimsy little balloon of a boat. "I am a dead man, oh Allah, help me." Down we went again. Up again. It was still coming toward me, but over to my left a little bit. Still closing. It looked very big and bright. I could see its lighted portholes. It seemed to be travelling fast. Now, it was about thirty meters away, but over to the left. No one was waving or shouting. No one had seen me. "Thanks Allah, at least it will not run me down." It would pass. So it did, foam breaking at its prow, and its bright reflection fractured by the waves. Despite all my shouting and screaming, no one noticed the terrified young man in his pathetic rubber boat. Oh what a mess I was in, I felt hopeless. To make things worse, if anything could have made things worse, with the passing of the ship, it's wake increased the violence of the waves, and I rocked helplessly in every direction. I could do nothing but cling to the bottom of the dingy in a pitiful state.

How long this went on for, I could not say. It must have been several hours, but it seemed unending. The wind blew the sea over the boat constantly. Whenever I dared to raise my head, I could see nothing. The sea was howling. I couldn't see any lights anymore. There were no stars, no moon. Nothing. I started to pray to Allah for help. I prayed desperately. And with all the pleading I could manage. I was frantic.

When I got a bit of self control back, I tried to use my hands as paddles. It was too dangerous. It did not help, and I got very tired, my shoulders, my eyes, my arm, my stomach, my ribs all hurt badly. I felt freezing cold, and my body started to hurt more and more. I lay on my back in the bottom of the dingy. I could see the sky because the cover was not fully in place. I looked upward for long time and cried for help. No one heard my voice. How could I get off this crazy dingy? But there was no way because I did not even know how to swim, I stupidly had forgotten to buy a life jacket, and I did not know how far or in what direction I had drifted. I knew then that I was going to die for sure; there was no chance to save myself. I cannot express how low I felt. I washed myself with a little of the water in my boat. I cleaned myself as much as I could. I bailed out all the water that I could. There was no chance for me to stay alive. I could hear Zabi saying, "Ali, you are crazy, you are going to kill yourself with that little funny boat." I should have listened to him. It was too late to regret anything. I would have liked the boat to be facing toward kiblah. I secured my arms to the strapping as best I could. There was nothing for it. I was resigned. I had to lay there and be horribly tossed about. Physically sick and terrified that each moment a great wave would crash over the boat and that would be it, or I would be tossed out into the raging sea, and that moment would be my last. My mind was numb. Thoughts came and went. I closed my eyes. I remembered fragments of the Koran, and disconnected thoughts came into my mind, replacing each other fitfully. "I am the worst person in the world dying this way." I pleaded to Allah to forgive me if I had not been a good slave, and for anything bad I might have done, but I did not remember.

Crying and praying, rambling, and talking to Allah, remembering my mom and Zabi, eventually in my troubled exhausted state, I passed into a kind of sleep. I was too worn out and sick to care.

CHAPTER 35

BIG SHIPS

At dawn, I woke up. When I opened my eyes, I was looking into the sky. My boat was rocking still but more gently. I stretched myself. My shoulders were stiff, and my stomach muscles were sore from all my retching. I had to untie my arm from the straps. Then I sat up. We were close beside a high rock, and on the horizon, the sun was rising out of the water. The weather was going to be very nice and warm. There were many large stones around the rock. I thanked Allah a lot. I stood up uneasily and looked around. How was I going to get to the land? The large rocks were a little distance away. I looked over the side of the boat, down into the clear water, and saw that it was not deep. I guessed about a meter or more. Getting off the boat was as difficult as getting on to it, once I rested all my weight on the side to get my leg over, it tipped up, and I fell right in. Again I got a mouthful of salty seawater, but I stood up quickly, squeezing my stinging eyes. This time I did not mind. I clung onto the boat to get out my bags and my clothes. Then I walked through the waves toward the land, carrying my bag in my arms. There was no one around when I was completely out of the sea, and I put on a green T-shirt and checked that my money was still in my under pants pocket, then I struggled into my jeans. I last saw the boat moving back and forth a little way from the shore. There were cliffs a little in land, so I headed toward them and began to climb up. When I got to the top, I sat down for a short while and looked at the view. It was very beautiful, and no one seemed to live there at all. I felt very hungry. I had some biscuits in my bag. There were many trees in land, and there seemed to be a little town a very long distance away from where I was standing. I walked down from cliff top toward it. After a long while, I found a road, and then there were some houses at the side of it. I walked faster. Later I saw someone walking toward me. He was a middle-aged man, gray hair showed under his battered straw hat, and his skin was hard and brown, while his clothes were faded but clean. When I got closer to him, I stopped for a moment and looked at my English phrase book, I wanted to ask him how I could go to Athens. He got closer, and I said in very broken English, "Sir, how do I go to the city?"

He said something unintelligible and walked away. He did not understand me. I think he said he did not speak English in Greek, or something like that. I sat down and learned some English words. I followed the road. And saw some cars. I kept walking. Eventually I got into the little town. There was a little park. I went there and found a washroom. I washed my face and put some gel on my hair. I looked in the mirror. "You look just like a resident of Greece," I said to myself. Then I went to find out how I could go to Athens. I stopped a man, "Excuse me, how I go Athens?" I said.

"Sorry, no English," he said.

I stopped another man, and I decided to ask first if he spoke English. "You English, agha (sir)?" I asked.

He looked at me for a moment. "I Greek," he said and walked away.

I asked many other people, they couldn't answer my questions. I think because I did not talk properly, or they did not understand English. I saw a beautiful girl walking toward me. I took a deep breath and stood properly. She got closer. "Excuses me, you no English?" I asked.

"Yes," she said.

"Thank you. How I go to Athens?"

"Do you mean, how can I go to Athens?" she said, smiling.

"Yes, yes," I said.

She said I could go there by boat. Then she pointed out a building and said, "Go to the tickets office, there, you can buy a ship's ticket, and then you can sail to Athens."

I half understood what she had said. "Thank you," I said, and then I walked toward the tickets shop. I went in, and there were two lady officers. One of them said something in Greek that I did not understand. "English please, I go to Athens, give me tickets," I said.

"Twenty eight Euro please," she said.

I did not have European money, so I had to go out try to exchange my currency. I found a bureau de change, but I realized that my money was in my underwear pocket. I went to a washroom and took my money out. I kept it in my jeans pocket. I had U.S. dollars and changed them to the European currency. Then I went back to the same ticket office and bought the boat ticket. I spent the rest of the day looking around and had a little sleep in a park.

The ship was scheduled to leave at 8:00 p.m. and I found it very easily because there were only two big ships there. Mine was the biggest. The time was about twenty minutes past 7:00 p.m. I found the gang plank and went up it. There were two security guards standing at the top, checking people's tickets. I showed mine and walked aboard. I went to the top deck and picked a seat beside the window and sat down. I was looking at the other ship on the other dock outside the window. The ships were very beautiful. That was my first time on a ship. About twenty minutes later, a couple came beside me. They said something in Greek. I did not take any notice because I was looking out of the window. They repeated what they had said. Eventually I turned toward them. "English please," I said.

They said something in English very fast. I do not understand it. They showed me their tickets seats number and the seat number where I was sitting. I checked, and they were the same. I did not understand what that meant. I looked at my ticket number and realized I was in the wrong place. "Excuse me," I said and stood up and walked away. I started to look for my seat number. I couldn't find it. The ship was very big and had three decks. The vessel started to leave. There was a huge crowd onboard, and they had all sat down. It was very hard to find my seat. I looked around for a short while, I wanted to ask the ship's staff, but did not bother because I did have any ID. I thought they might ask where I had come from. There was a big television in the center of one of the lounges. I walked toward it. There was a big space in front of it. I looked at the floor. It was a gray carpet and very nice and clean. I sat down and looked around me. There was no one looking at me. I lay down and used my bag for a pillow and watched television. A short while later, two teenagers came beside me and lay there. A few hours later, I needed to go to a washroom. I sat up and looked around me. About six or seven children and teenagers lay around me. Oh my god, I said to myself. I thought they could not find their seats either. I watched them carefully. Their parents sat close by and called to them. They refused to go. They lay down, their hands behind their heads and enjoyed watching television. I looked around, there were two other teenagers looking for a little spaces to lie down, so I did not go to the washroom, I was afraid someone would take my place. Where should I go then? I lay down again and dozed off for a while, when I woke up, I saw most of the people around me had fallen asleep. I decided to go quickly to the washroom. When I came back, I lay down watching television again. I was only half awake when I started to think about the night before, and said, "Oh Allah, you are an amazing person, whatever I have heard about you is all true. I must trust you more and more. I was not expecting to be alive tonight."

I thanked Allah more than ever before. I remembered Zabi. How he would be worrying about me, and promised myself to call him at the first opportunity. I was very happy and excited because I had succeeded. I remembered Zabi said, "Ali, you are going to the sea. I'm shaking over here," I laughed a little bit. Oh my god, if he hears me calling him from Athens, he will be happier than me. I started to think about tomorrow. Where I should go and what I should do? I sat up and looked at my world map for a short while, then I lay down again and fell asleep. About seven o'clock, I heard a very loud noise from the speaker. Someone was talking. I did not understand it at all. A short while later, the people started to pack their stuff. Oh, we are going to arrive in Athens soon, I said to myself. I went to the washroom, washed my face, and put some gel on my hair. Then I came back very quickly and sat in the same place. I took my English book from my bag and started to study. I picked up some very useful words and read them repeatedly. The ship docked, and the sailors opened the doors to the gangways. People started to leave. I did not go out on time. I was busy reading my book. I was on the middle deck. Then I started walking toward the door. Oh my god, there were a lot people standing in lines very patiently, not making any noise, moving forward very slowly. I thought for a short while, why aren't these people pushing each other to get out faster? I remembered my journey with the smugglers; people always pushed each other to get out faster. I stood for a little while. The line moved very slowly because there were three decks of people making a huge crowd, and there was only a little door to get through. Some of them were old or had children or bags. I thought that might cause the delay. I could not stand in the line anymore. In my country, we do not understand queuing. No one does it. People who do not push themselves forward are thought of as stupid or weak. My patience ran out. I put my bag under my arm and held it properly. I asked Allah for help, and then I started to push people. I pushed very hard. I stood on somebody's feet while I was pushing them. They were very angry and shouted at me. I did not take any notice of that because I did not understand what they said. When I got down from second deck to the first, people heard the others shouting at me, they gave way easily for me to get out. I got out in a minute.

CHAPTER 36

ATHENS

I went out from the docks very quickly. I was very hungry and hadn't eaten since I left Istanbul. I decided to feed myself first. I couldn't focus to do anything whatsoever. Outside the docks, there were many taxis waiting to take people away. I did not bother with one because I knew that it would cost me a lot of money. I asked people how I could go to the city center. I had learned some English words well which were very helpful because Greek people speak broken English. Some of them spoke as I did. I decided to study my English phrase book whenever I had a little time. I found out that the city center was a long distance from where I was. I had two options, to take a bus or a train to get there. I would take a bus because I had never traveled by train before. I thought that would be difficult for the first time.

While I was looking for the bus, I found a little grocery shop and went in but did not buy anything because there was nothing that I liked to eat. There was not a bus that went directly to the city center. The driver told me I had to take his bus and change buses on the way and get another one, or I could walk for about twenty minutes to get there. I walked to the north.

On the way, I found a fruit shop and I bought some bananas and a bottle of milk. I kept walking and encountered a park. I sat down on the grass. I ate my bananas with the milk and started to think where I should go now. I counted my money, there was only a little left. I decided to keep it only for food. I looked at the map. England was very far from Athens. I decided to rent a little room and find a job, stay for a short while until I found out about how to go to the UK. There was a lot going on in my mind, but I decided to think. I thought for a long time. Eventually I remembered the first time when my parents and I went to Mazar-e-Sharif City. Mom and I went from door to doors and asking if they had some space for rent. If they had had some space available, we would have gone in and looked at the house if it was good and big enough for us, and then Father would come to see it. Then they would decide to take it, leave it, or go and to find another one. There was no home real estate at that time in Mazar-e-Sharif City. There was no such thing as computers or Internet.

If I go and knock on people's doors, that might be another stupid thing to do. I was thinking a lot about rental. I remembered about Iran. The first house I had rented by myself in Tehran. Abbas and I went to a real estate office. They had found a lot of house for me to choose from. I had chosen one and paid the first and last month. Then I received the keys and moved in. The second time, Yasmine, my fiancée, helped me to find the workshop. I had rented it in the same way. I remembered about how I rented in a little funny room in Turkey. Zabi had known lot of property owners. I did not have any problems to find one. I decided to call Mr. Zabi and tell him that I was alive and had arrived in Athens. There was a little grocery store close to that park. I went in. I asked how to make a phone call to Turkey. He gave me a phone card and said, "You can find a public telephone on the street. Then put a quarter in and dial the card number and then dial the number you wish to call." I think he said something like that. I did not understand him very well. I took the phone card and went to find a public phone, which was easy. I tried several times. I could not get through because the machine talked in Greek, and the system was different too. I was busy trying to figure out what was wrong. A girl passed by. I stopped her and asked for help. She showed me very quickly. I watched carefully what she was doing. I realized I was dialing the wrong country code. I thanked her a lot and said, "You English good." I meant, you speak very good English. She waved and said bye and walked away. I heard the phone ringing. Zabi's wife answered. She only spoke a little Dari. My Turkish was not good enough to tell her what I wanted to say. I just understood a little. She said he was in the mosque. I told her I would call him later in a mixture of Turkish English and Dari. She did not understand me very well. Then I hung up. I will try later, I said to myself. There was a bench, and I sat down. I thought for a moment about Greek people and decided to ask only young people and only girls anything I needed to know about my journey because the young people seemed to speak English better than older Greeks. I chose girls because they were attractive and more helpful than men. If you asked men, if they did not understand you first time, they walked away or gave the wrong information. Women always tried their best to help, and it was fun trying to talk to them. I enjoyed it.

I called Zabi's number again. The dialing tone was ringing, and then he picked the receiver up, and I heard his lovely old voice saying "hello" in Turkish.

"Salam, *Kaka* Zabi, this Ali. I am calling you from Athens," I said proudly in Dari.

"Oh thank Allah you are alive!" he said warmly. "Athens, so soon! You are a hero! I will tell all our friends that Ali is the world hero! How are you doing?"

"I am fine, thank you very much. What about you? I called you earlier and heard that you were in the mosque. Did you pray for me? I know you did. If you had not, I would have drowned."

"I am so excited, Ali jan. You do not know how much you have made me happy tonight. I cannot express my delight. Allah makes you happy a million times. How did you get on with the sea?"

"Hey! Kaka Jan, what should I say, I did what I needed to do. *Agha* Zabi, you lived here for a while, do you know how I can find a room here? I want to rent a room and stay here for a short while. I cannot go to UK right now because I am short of money. I have only money for food."

"Do you want some money?" he asked.

"No, Kaka Jan. Thank you very much, if I run out, I will let you know. I will be OK for a little while."

"I think there is a big *Kalessa* around the Victoria Park area. I do not know exactly where, but I am sure if you ask anyone, you will find it easily. The people there give food to the homeless and refugees. If you go there, you will find a lot of Afghan people and many other nationalities. Ask them, they will help you."

"Thank you very much, Kaka Jan. Pray for me all the time. I will keep in touch with you."

"OK, Ali Jan, that is a good deal."

"Bye, Kaka Jan."

"Bye," he said.

It was about sunset. I started to ask people how to get to the kalessa. I did not know what it was, and asked many girls if they knew anything about the big kalessa. I kept walking north, south, west, east. I asked many people, old, young, men, and women. Nobody had any idea what a kalessa was. It was completely dark, and still had no idea what it was or where it was. I was very tired and hungry and started to worry about where I should sleep that night.

I bought another phone card to call Zabi. "Salam Kaka, sorry to bother you again, I have asked a lot people. They don't know anything about a big kalessa."

"Oh my god. I am so sorry. I forget to tell you about it. We call it kalessa, they call it church, like our *Massjet,* and they call mosque."

"OK, that's why people do not understand what is kalessa. OK. agha Zabi, I have to go now and find it because it is getting late here. Thank you for that." Then we hung up.

I saw a man coming toward me and stopped him and said, "Excuse me, I want go big church around the Victoria Park. How I am going?"

"I think it is closed by now," he said.

CHAPTER 37

VICTORIA PARK

The time was about 10:00 p.m. I checked all around the big church but could not find anyone. There were many benches in Victoria Park, so I sat down for a short while and thought about where I should stay for the night. I had two options, one was go to a hotel, the other was to sleep in the park. I decided to go and find a hotel, just to ask how much it would cost me for one night. I started to ask people where I could find a hotel. Eventually I found one. It was too expensive for me. The money I had was not enough to rent a room for even half a night. I was disappointed and worried. I had never ever slept on the streets before. I walked toward the big church, thinking about my life. It had always been ups and downs. I had been so happy and excited the night before on the big ship, now I was depressed. Where was I going to find a place to sleep on the street? On the way, I saw some abandoned furniture, it was two sofas, chairs, TV, etc. They were in the corner of the street. I walked toward them. There was nobody in the street. Everything was as quiet as a mouse. I pulled the good sofa under the streetlights and cleaned it as much as possible. I sat down on it and pulled my book out and studied very hard. I finished a quarter of the book. I got tired and lay on my back, looking at sky. It was deep blue with some small clouds. I looked at my world map while I was lying on my back, thinking about my future. I fell asleep. A short while later, the garbage collector woke me up and said something in Greek I did not understand. "What you want?" I asked angrily.

"No sleep here, no good. Go home, bad boy," he said hurriedly.

I put my book in my bag and walked away. I went to Victoria Park and lay down on the grass on my back using my bag for a pillow. The grass was a little bit wet, and I was not comfortable at all. I sat up and looked around and saw a couple of benches close by. I lay down on one of them. It was made of metal. I began to feel very cold, and I sat up. I was very tired and wanted to sleep somewhere but could not find anywhere. I needed to find something to put on the cold metal bench, anything to make it a bit more comfortable. The drug addicts in Tehran used some empty cardboard boxes and made them like a mattress. I needed something like that to put on the bench, so I looked around the garbage area. I found a little dirty carpet and two boxes. I picked them up and went back to the park and placed it on the bench, and lay down on my right side. The benches were not very wide, but I managed to fall asleep for a short while. I was not comfortable on my right side, turned over automatically, and fell down on the ground and banged my face on the concrete. That hurt me a lot. I got up and lay down on the bench again, trying to ignore the pain because I was half-asleep.

I got up very early in the morning and needed to use a washroom. I took my bag and went to find a coffee shop. In the washroom, I washed my hands and face. Looking in the mirror, "Oh my god," I said. My forehead had swelled up a little. I brushed my teeth, wet my hair, and put some gel on. I had a towel in my bag. I took it and dried my face, and used some deodorant and perfume. Then went out and ordered a cup of coffee with some cookies for breakfast. After the breakfast, I walked to the city center. It was very old and very beautiful. It was also noisy and busy.

I bought a slice of pizza for my lunch. I was hungry enough to eat another two slices, but did not buy them because I was short of money. Then I went to the park, prayed there, and asked Allah for help. I was sitting in front of the big church.

The Greek people brought food for everyone. I saw a lot of refugees and homeless people, who came there to get some food for their dinner. I was the first person in the line. There was a lot of good and healthy food to choose from. I selected some and sat on the ground and ate it. I was ravenously hungry, and the food was wholesome and delicious. I went back and stood in the line three times. There was plenty for everyone. A short while later, they brought fruit and sweets. I didn't get in the line anymore because I had eaten enough for a long while.

I looked at some of the people to find someone from Afghanistan. There were many nationalities. I picked three people in my mind, whom I thought might be from Afghanistan. I asked them, the first one was from Iraq, the second one from Iran, the third was from Afghanistan.

"Salam agha, my name is Ali. I am from Afghanistan. How are you today?" I asked.

He seemed very worried and depressed. "I am fine, Ali. My name is Samah. When did you come to Athens? You look fresh and new."

We sat down on the bench. "I came yesterday. What about you?" I asked.

"Two weeks," he said.

"Where are you living?" was my next question.

"There is an Afghan man, who has been living here for twenty years. His name is Amin. He has a big house and has made it like an Afghani hotel. A lot of Afghan refugees are living there. He charges each person a hundred and twenty Euro a month. I am living there. If anyone wants work, he will find them a job and charges sixty Euro commission for finding you work."

"Wow, he does a good job for Afghan people," I said.

"He is a very nice man. If someone doesn't have any money, he helps them out."

"What are the other refugees like, the ones who live there?" I asked.

"They are a mixture. One or two Pashtoon, Hazaras, Usbeks, some don't even know where they come from. Ghazni, Helmand, Mazar. All of us are glad to be out of Afghanistan. Some of them have had bad times because of the fighting. Most of them have no families left. When I first found Amin's hotel, there were some rough men there, some were drinkers and smokers, drugs I mean. They used to cause fights sometimes, so Amin kicked them out. He doesn't want trouble with the police. That's the last thing he wants. Most of the guys are OK, but half of them don't know how to look after themselves. Typical Afghans, if there isn't a woman around to do everything for them, they're useless. They are docile enough but can't look after themselves. Tell you what, come and have a look, see what you think. OK? No harm in that, is there?"

"I am a bit short of money. It disappears fast, like snow in spring. I spent a lot on my boat," I said.

"Boat? You have a boat?" he asked, greatly interested. "A big boat?"

"No. I don't have it anymore."

He was disappointed. I told him a little bit about my journey.

"I spent six thousand dollars, and it took me four months to get here," he said.

"You must be a very rich man. I mean you spent six thousand dollars for your journey," I said, surprised.

"Oh, Ali Jan, I am glad that you are an Afghan man. I don't have trouble explaining it to you because you know about the Taliban, how they attacked Afghanistan. I worked seven years in Iran, six days a week, as a construction worker to save money to come here and save my life. I was very careful with my money," he said sadly. He complained about Iran. He had been beaten up a lot by the Iranian police and civilians.

"Hey, Samah Jan. What you have said about the Taliban and the Iranians is all true. But now we are in Athens, try to forget about your past and think about a new life in the west."

"I am hoping one day the Taliban will attack Iran in the same way as they did Afghanistan. Then Iranians will become refugees and lose their happiness. Then they will know what we have had in Afghanistan. We left to save our lives; western people know it very well. There are a lot people here from Iran, claiming to be gay refugees because they cannot claim to have been persecuted in their own country. It is safe there, and there is no trouble. They are here just to drink alcohol and have sex with prostitutes. They are not here to save their lives. Some of these stupid Iranians are claiming to be Afghan refugees to get their papers faster. Some of them have been caught because they do not have enough information about Afghanistan. Sometimes we have problems with immigration because we lived in Iran for long time and have now got Persian accents."

"Samah Jan, I have eaten a lot, let's go for a walk, and you can tell me something about Greek rules."

I told him about the ship, when I pushed people to get out. He started to laugh and said,

"Don't worry about that. I have done worse things than that. One day I went shopping and wanted to buy some clothes. There was a beautiful shop, nice and very clean, in the mall. I looked at it; they were selling very nice clothes. I looked at the ground, it was shining, and then I looked at my shoes. They were two years old and a little dirty. I took them off and walked in. I purchased some clothes. When I went out, my shoes were missing. I asked the cashiers. They fell about laughing at me. I was embarrassed and got out very quickly. I walked all the way home without shoes because I did have enough money to buy a new pair. I think the salesperson threw them in the garbage because I took them off right in front of the door."

We both laughed a lot as he took me toward Amin's Afghani hotel.

CHAPTER 38

AMIN'S AFGHANI HOTEL, ATHENS

The hotel had three floors. Each floor had a very large bedroom for about twenty people, with bathrooms, a kitchen, and a small living room with a TV. I picked a bed next to Samah's bed on the third floor. About 8:00 p.m., Mr. Amin came to the hotel and said, "Salam to everyone, I hope everyone is fine, and no more complaints tonight, please."

"I brought a friend here. He wants to be a guest for a long while," Samah said.

I was sitting in the living room watching television with the other people. I stood up and walked toward him and said, "Salam, agha Amin, my name is Ali, nice to meet you." We shook hands.

"Welcome, Ali, to my Afghani hotel in Athens City. When did you come here?" he asked.

"Yesterday," I said.

He pulled a little notebook from his pocket and wrote something in Greek. "Do you have money to pay your first month?" he asked.

"How much is it?"

"A hundred and twenty Euros."

I handed him twenty Euros and said, "Take this please, and I will pay you some more this month."

"Are you expecting some money from somewhere else?" he asked in a businesslike way.

"No, I will work here, and then I pay you as soon as possible."

"What do you do?"

"I am a tailor. I heard there is a demand for them," I answered.

"Sometimes. I know some companies, they might need tailors. I know some other jobs are available for anyone, who is a hard worker. Let me

232

know if you are interested in a different job. I will take you there, when you are ready."

"What kind of job is that?" I asked

"Collecting oranges."

"I will try the tailoring companies first. If I can't find one, I will do any kind of job that is available."

"In that case, I will make a couple of phone calls. Tomorrow be ready about 10:00 a.m. I will take you to some tailoring companies. Wait here in the hotel for me. Don't go out because I do not have time to look for you."

"OK, I will be here, for sure," I said.

Then he went away to talk to someone else. After a short while, I took a shower and shaved and was nice and clean.

Next day, Samah and I boiled some eggs for the breakfast. About half past ten, Amin showed up. We went out from the hotel. He had a list of tailoring companies. He picked one randomly, and we went there.

He asked in Greek if they needed a tailor. The manager said, "We need only profession tailors."

Amin interpreted the conversation. He looked at me and said, "What should I tell him?"

"I want to make a sample. If it is not good, tell him, don't hire me."

"Where did you work before?" the manager asked.

"I worked in Iran and Turkey, if you want to know about me. You call them and ask about me. I will be happy if you do that," I said proudly, looking at manager.

"Our system is different than Turkey, I think. We work in a big group. One person makes sleeves, the other pockets, and so on. I am going to call the supervisor; he will give you some samples to make. By the way, we are a very big company, and we have eight supervisors and about sixty workers. I need to know what language you speak because our supervisors are different nationalities, I want to get someone who you can talk to directly.

"I can speak Dari, Pashto, Persian, and little English, and Turkish."

He called a supervisor; he was from Pakistan, Peshawar City. His second language was Pashto. His accent was a little different from the way I had learned in Afghanistan, but I did not have much of a problem understanding him. He gave me two zips and one pocket to sew.

"Are we going back to the hotel proudly or will you make me embarrassed?" Amin asked.

"Agha Amin, I never try to embarrass people. I trust Allah, we will go proudly," I said hopingly.

"Many people told me that they were tailors when we went to the company to make a sample, some of them couldn't make it."

"Don't worry, I'm not lying. There is no point saying things that are untrue and wasting our time," I said, and then I followed the supervisor to the workplace. He let me use a sewing machine. I changed the thread and cleaned the machine. I checked the machine over, and found it was dry. It seemed nobody had used it for a long while, and I asked the supervisor for some oil. While I was cleaning the machine, I said silently, "Oh Allah, help me please. I don't want to embarrass Amin, let it be a great job."

It did not take me too long to finish it. I returned it to the supervisor. He liked it very much and said, "Follow me." We went to the manager's office. He handed the work I had done to him, and then he left. The manager looked at it and pulled a tape measure from his desk.

"Are you lion or fox?" Amin whispered.

"Lion, I hope to Allah," I whispered back.

"Perfect, you can come tomorrow about 8:00 a.m. and work with the same supervisor," he said, and Amin translated to me and then we shook hands and we left.

Next day, I woke up very early for morning prayers. After prayers, I studied my English phrase book.

"You are a very active person; I have not seen anyone wake up for the morning prayers and study since I came to this hotel. It seems you grew up with a good family," Samah said, surprised.

I shook my head, "Allah never said that if you grow up in a bad family, you can't pray to him and you can study this English book too. It is very easy. If you want to, I will help you."

I went to my work very early because I had to take three different buses, and did not want to be late on my first day. I got the wrong bus once, but I had plenty of time. Eventually, I arrived, and I was on time. The company was huge. There were six lines of machines; each line had twelve sewing machines, facing to the west. The machinists could not see or talk with each other while they worked because they were sitting in lines. The supervisor let me use sewing machine number 55. He brought twenty jackets, just to stitch the fronts to the backs, by joining the shoulders both sides, on the left and right. He showed me how to do it, once. I did not like him showing me how to do it. I could not stop him because that was the policy of the company, all supervisors must show the worker for the first time, like a little training.

There was a little bell on the right side of machine, he said, "Push it if you need any help, and if you want go to washroom," and then he left.

I finished my job very quickly and pressed the bell to call the supervisor. He came very quickly and checked it twice because I had finished it very fast.

"It is very nice, and you have finished it very quickly. Where did you work before?" he asked surprised.

"Iran and Turkey," I said.

"I don't know anything about Iran, but in Turkey they do piecework, you have to work your ass off to make some money. This factory is very different from anywhere else. If you work hard or not, you will get the same pay as everyone else. Everyone has to work at the same speed because it starts from the bottom line, and finishes at the top of line. You have to watch your speed."

He brought some more jobs to do, and then he left. I decided to work like everyone else, but a little faster. My wage was three Euros an hour. I worked forty to fifty hours a week. In about a two-week period, I paid Amin a hundred and sixty Euros for my bed and his commission for finding me the job.

CHAPTER 39

RAHIM

Following the other machinists in my group was very boring for me. They did not work as fast as I did. The company did not pay me enough, but I could not complain because I was afraid if I opened my mouth, they might fire me. I read my English phrase book on the bus while I was traveling to work and returning home and after the morning prayers. It was very useful. I read it through four times, and still I was interested to read it again. I worked five days a week from Monday to Friday. I wanted to make some money and move away from the Afghani hotel and rent a little bachelor flat, but I had no alternative because the money I made was not enough to rent somewhere else. I was not comfortable there because people smoked cigarettes and came in very late at night. They also made some funny loud noises in the bedroom during the night. Some people worked different shifts. They had to wake up about 4:00 a.m. to get ready for their job. I could not complain about anyone because when I woke up to get ready for my job at about 6:30 a.m., there were some people still sleeping. My alarm clock woke them up sometimes.

I thought about working at the weekends, with Samah, picking oranges, to make money faster so that I could leave Greece. I thought if I rented a bachelor flat and I had to buy a bed, sofa, TV, fridge, and some dishes, it would have cost a lot of money.

One night I cooked some food, *Qabily blow* (rice and chicken legs) for Samah and his three friends and myself because I wanted to know how I could work with their company. I did not like to pay Amin commission just for finding me a job for the weekend. I had asked my boss to give some more overtime, and I had even asked if they needed cleaning help over the weekend. They told me that I was working full time, and that I had about five to ten hours overtime every week, and there was no chance of getting a job over the weekend.

On one Friday, I left my job a little bit early. "Are you going to take your girlfriend out for dinner?" the supervisor asked, smiling. "No, I am going to have my own party tonight," I said and then left.

On the way, I got off the bus and bought some chicken legs, rice, and some fruits, and two bottles of Coke, and then went home. The kitchen needed a good clean, and I gave the floor a good scrubbing with disinfectant. I didn't take long, and with the hot weather, it dried quickly. Next was the cooking. I washed the rice and covered it with water. I made the chicken legs into nice kebabs, and then I cooked the rice. I made everything ready for the dinner. There was a lot of dishes left unwashed all over the kitchen, people ate their food and left the dishes dirty. I went to it and washed all the dishes hurriedly, and I wrote some notes and stuck them on the fridge doors and above the kitchen sink.

> *Dear residents of the Afghani hotel on the third floor,*
> *Cleanliness is part of your faith. Your health is important. Wash your dishes and clean up after yourself please, it is not someone else's job. If you don't do that, Allah will not like you. Do you want Allah to help you and save you from the Greek police? I have washed all the dishes and cleaned the kitchen. I would appreciate your co-operation.*
>
> *From your best friend,*
> *Bed number 25.*

I went to the balcony for a quick look outside just to take a little rest because washing the dishes and cleaning up had made me hot and tired. When I went to the balcony, there was a young guy about sixteen sitting alone. He seemed sad. I looked at him; his head was down, and his hands under his arms. He was praying. I listen to him carefully. He was reciting a very short part of the Koran from memory repeatedly. Eventually he stopped for a moment and looked at me.

"Salam agha," I said respectfully.

"Salam is mine."

"How are you doing? Nice weather, isn't it?" I remarked, to break the ice.

"I am fine. You have said the weather is nice, but for me it has been winter all of the four seasons."

"Why?" I asked.

"Since the Taliban cut my right hand off, my life has been all winter. I went looking for work, no one hired me because of my hand. If you cannot work and have no money, you cannot make any friends nor have any fun."

There was a slight breeze out on the balcony. Three floors below in the street were the usual noises of the traffic. Evening was coming in as the sun began to set over the city. It had been a hot day, and the cooking had made me even hotter. I had come out to take a break. I had been in a good mood contemplating the evening ahead and not expected to meet this sad young man. We began to talk, but it was as if he had not spoken to anyone for some time. It was like releasing a dam. His words flooded out.

It emerged that he had sold his house and paid the smugglers to bring him to Athens. He thought there would be a chance to get an artificial hand in the west, and he intended to work hard and have a good life like anyone else. He didn't have money to have an operation on his arm. The Greek government had refused to give him papers, and he had no money to go elsewhere. He'd been trapped in Athens for a year, trying for work and just praying to Allah, asking him for a miracle to give him his hand back or to take his life.

The smell from the oven reminded me sharply that I was supposed to be cooking chicken.

"I am sorry, I have to go to check the oven, I think I have forgotten to turn it off," I said and went to kitchen. I was thinking about him and felt very sorry. Should I invite him to dinner or not, my food might not be enough for everyone. "Oh Allah, help me to make a good decision. He is very lonely and feeling so sad, he deserves to have a dinner with us."

I reasoned that I could invite him, and I would eat a little less food myself, if there was not enough.

I went back to the balcony and said, "I am sorry I cut your story off. By the way, my name is Ali. Nice to meet you, I would like to know more about you. I am pleased to invite you for dinner tonight. I will be happy if you accept."

"Thanks for being interested. My name is Rahim, I am happy to meet you. I will join you tonight for sure," he said.

"Thank you very much," I said. I had been very affected by his story and his sad state.

Samah came in with his friends. "Salam, agha Samah, where have you been? Rahim and I cooked food for you and your friends," I said, shaking his hands and introducing Rahim to them. They greeted each other. There were not enough chairs in the kitchen for everyone. We laid a tablecloth on the floor, as is the Afghan way, because I had made it nice and clean. We put newspapers for the carpet and to sat down on it and talked for about ten minutes, and then Rahim helped me with his one hand to bring the food over. I thought there would not be enough for everyone, but there was some chicken and some rice left. We enjoyed the food, and they thanked me a lot, especially Rahim. He had not had Afghani food for a long time. He always went to the church to get food for his dinner. We had a good talk after the dinner. They all said something funny and joked a lot, and we all laughed and were happy, enjoying each other's company. We promised to be always together in a beautiful house, like brothers, and have good fun together. I made some tea; Samah washed the dishes and brought the tea for everyone. He thanked me for the dinner and the work I had done earlier that afternoon, and he read my note to everyone, twice.

"Good job," everyone said happily.

"You have made me so happy tonight," Rahim whispered.

"I think the same," I replied.

While we were drinking the tea, I asked Samah, "How is your job going?"

"It is very busy. The company needs some more people," he said.

"Is it a difficult job?" I asked.

"It all depends on you. If you want more money, you have to work hard."

"How do they pay you?"

"Every box you fill with oranges, you make a Euro. The supervisor will give a card for each box you have filled. At the end of your shift, you take all the cards to the boss' office; he will count them first and then pay you cash every night."

"I am free tomorrow. I would like to go with you, just to see how the job is, if you don't mind."

"No, not all, it's a very good idea to try different jobs. We have to be there very early in the morning because tomorrow is Saturday and a lot of people will be coming from all over the place. All the good orange trees will have been taken if we arrive late.

"What time are we supposed to go?"

"The company will be open about 6:00 a.m. We have to be there twenty minutes to six. It takes about two hours to get there. If we wake up about half past three, that should be fine."

"Isn't it too early?" I asked.

"Don't worry. We can sleep while traveling there."

It was about 11:00 p.m. We all went to bed, except Rahim, because he wasn't coming with us. He couldn't work. He needed two hands to pick oranges.

CHAPTER 40

PARTY TIME

The alarm clock rang about 3:30 a.m. several times. Eventually we all woke up and left for work. We had to walk to the train station because there was no bus at that time of night. We arrived there on time. I was very sleepy and tired. I did not like to wake up very early in the morning.

At the orange plantation, I had to register to get an employee number before I could start working. I got it very easily because I am tall, and the manager wanted workers, especially tall ones. The job was perfect for tall people but not good for short people, they were not happy because they had to climb up the trees to collect the oranges. The supervisor showed me what to do for the first two boxes, how to collect the oranges faster, and then he went to help someone else. I asked Allah for help to collect more. I started to collect as fast as possible. I filled ten boxes and gave them to the supervisor. He gave me ten little cards. I kept it in my jeans pocket. When I bent forward to move a box, my cards fell out of my pocket twice. I picked them up very quickly and looked around at the people. Everyone was busy collecting oranges. I opened my jeans and put all the cards in my underwear pocket. I had no worry about losing them because I had made very special pockets in all my underwear. I collected five more boxes, and then I decided to take a break of about fifteen minutes for lunch. I looked around to find Samah and his friends to ask if they wanted to take their break at the same time, but I couldn't find them at all because of the huge crowd. Everyone was very busy collecting the oranges. Some people needed the money and did not take any break. I took my lunch from my bag. It was some rice and the leftover chicken from the night before. I was very hungry because I did not have anything for the breakfast. I ate it very fast. The food gave me a little energy to work faster. I filled some more boxes.

About sunset, the supervisor shouted, "Attention! Attention! Everybody! Ten more minutes, and we are going to stop. Please start finishing off."

I had two more boxes to trade with him and get cards. He gave me the cards very quickly and then walked away. I took all my cards out from my underwear and counted them three times. There were thirty-one. I stood in line for about half an hour to give them to the manager and get the money. He counted them and gave me thirty-one Euros.

"Excuse me, sir, I have a friend, one hand, can I bring here you give job please?" I said in my mixture of languages. He did not understand, and I tried to make him understand what I meant.

I meant I have a friend with one hand. If I bring him here, would you give him a job please?

Eventually, he showed me his one hand and said, "How he can work with one hand?"

He meant, how he could work if he has only one hand.

"You no worry, I am help him, please he no money."

I meant, do not worry, I will help him. Please, he does not have any money.

"OK, bring him, and he work under your numbers."

He meant, OK, you can bring him, and he can work under your name and employee number.

"Thank you very much," I said very excitedly, and then went out looking for Samah. He was waiting in the line, and then we went to the hotel.

On the way, Samah remarked, smiling, "You look very happy, I think you like the job very much, how much did you make?"

"I made thirty-one Euros. The job is physically very hard for me because I had never done this kind of job before. Tailoring is very easy; you just sit down behind the machine and sew. That is about it. If I am happy today, it is because there is a reason," I answered.

"Did you meet a beautiful girl?" Samah asked and winked.

"No, not at all," I said.

"What's going on then?"

"I spoke to the manager about Rahim. Tomorrow I will bring him with us."

"How?" he asked, surprised.

"The manager said he can work with me, under my employee number."

"He will be very happy to hear that."

"I hope so," I said.

I was very tired and dozed for a short while in the train. We all went directly home. I made some food for myself very quickly. Surprisingly, the kitchen was nice and clean, and there weren't any dishes left unwashed.

I should have left notices earlier. I did not know how much they would affect people, I said to myself.

I made tea and took it into the living room. While I was drinking it, Rahim came in.

"Salam, Ali agha," he said.

I stood up and walked toward him, shook his left hand with my left hand, and said, "Salam, agha Rahim. Where have you been? I have very good news for you."

He sat down beside me. I poured him a cup of tea and left it on the table in front of him.

"I had been in the church to get some food for my dinner as usual. How did you like your new job? Tell me the good news first."

"I spoke to my boss, and I told him about you, he said you can work there with me, we will help each other."

He jumped up in middle of living room and hugged me, kissing me on my cheek.

"Thank you very much a world. Allah saves you from all calamities," he said excitedly.

We boiled some eggs and potatoes, and cut some tomatoes, onions, and chilies. We made sandwiches for the next day for breakfast and lunch, and then went to bed at about 10:00 p.m.

I set the alarm clock for twenty to 4:00 a.m. I was very tired. I lay down on my back and fell asleep right away.

Next day, the clock rang several times, I did not notice it, Samah woke me. I sat down for a short while and stretched my arms. I wanted to sleep again because my muscles were sore. I went to the washroom and got ready. On the way, I saw Rahim was praying, and he was ready.

The supervisor was a very good man. He gave us very good orange trees and encouraged me to help Rahim whom I trained more than I had been trained. We worked separately for about an hour. I made about three boxes, but Rahim made less than one box. I watched him. He was short and could not reach up properly. He could not climb up the trees because he had only one hand. He tried twice, and he fell down and looked up at me meekly. I felt very sorry for him and ran over to him and helped him to get up.

"You are all right?" I asked.

"*Baly* (yeah), I am fine, I was trying to . . ." he said. I stopped him before he explained to me what had happened.

"I have a good idea. I will collect the oranges and get up the trees if I need to, and throw the oranges down on the ground. Can you pick them up and place them into boxes?"

"It will make you tired, Ali Jan."

"Don't worry about that, we are friends, we have to help each other, come on, let's get started," I said.

I threw them as fast as I could. He was quickly putting them into boxes. He was happy because he was very confident and liked the job. We took a very short break for lunch.

At the end of our shift, we counted all our cards. There were forty-two. I stood in line for about ten minutes to get into the manager's office. He counted them up and gave me fifty Euros. I counted the money twice, it was five ten Euro bills, I remembered we had forty-two; he gave me eight Euros more.

"Excuse me, I am working forty-two, you give me very much money, you mistake," I said.

I meant, I earned forty-two Euros, but you gave me more money, you must have made a mistake.

He looked and smiled, "Don't worry, I there is no mistake, I watched you too much working fast, and how you did help your friend's one hand. You good and OK," he said, and then he called the next person to come over. I think he meant. Don't worry, it was not a mistake, I watched you for a long time. You were working very fast and helped your friend one hand (Rahim) a lot. You are fine. OK.

I was very happy because he gave me extra money, and I gratefully thanked him with my hand on my heart. I went out, Rahim was waiting for me. "Hey! Rahim agha, we have done a good job, the manager gave us eight Euros as a tip," I said happily.

I hugged him and handed him twenty-five Euros. He took it and thanked me, he was clearly delighted.

We waited for Samah and his friends to finish. Then we all went home very happy. We made a very quick dinner altogether. After which we made plenty of tea for everyone and went to the living room. Rahim was very excited; he had a little cassette player in his locker and went to bring it over. He loudly played some very old Aziragee music, *Tambora*, and started to dance in the middle of the room. A short while later, people started to come in from another floors to watch his dance. Our living room became full; people came from the first and second floors. They were standing by the door and pushing each other to get a better view. I looked at them, they were about to fight with each other because there was not space enough for everyone. The stronger men stood on weaker men's feet. They began swearing at each other.

I said to Samah, "Can we take all the sofas out and place them on the balcony or in the bedroom? With everyone pushing to get in, sooner or later they are going to start fighting. Our fun will be over. You know what Afghani people are like."

"OK, let's do it," he said.

I asked Rahim to take a rest while we moved the furniture. Then I let them in and instructed them to sit down properly on the floor. They sat in a circle, and I said, "Welcome, everybody. I know you are all here to have some fun. Please stop swearing. If anyone makes trouble, we will kick them out and never let them in again."

One of them said, "Agha, we came from the first floor. We heard the music and want to join in. We have never had a party since we came to this hotel, and really miss it."

People were whispering and asking each other if anybody knew what the party was for.

"OK, my friends, everyone wants to know what the party is about. Rahim jan, you tell them please," I said.

He pulled his money from his pocket and started to sing, "I am like anyone else in the room! I can work! I've got a good job with Ali jan! I've got friends! Allah accepted my prayers! Tonight is my best night! Ha ha oo ho, ha ha oo ho."

Then people clapped for him and started to dance one after another, like a wedding party in Afghanistan. I was standing by the door, like a security guard, in case anyone started a fight. Rahim pulled my hand and asked me to dance for them. I was very happy and pleased to do it. I remembered Father and I when we went to the wedding party in Ghazni City. There, there was a group of about twelve men dancing in a circle; Afghan people call it *Afghan attan*.

We had great fun, and enjoyed ourselves. One man told us about his own wedding party. Another told us about a crazy party he had been at, and others told stories to all their friends. Some of them remembered parties from the old days in our country even better than I did. Some of the men became sad because they knew those remembered days of happiness of long ago had gone forever, along with their families and friends.

Rahim found a radio station with some wild Iranian music, and the solo dancing began again. We were about twenty people in the room, and we started to dance in a circle. We all were very happy and enjoying the party.

Amin came in and banged the door; somebody turned the music off instantly. We all sat down very quickly, our heads down. The room was as quiet as a mouse. He was walking around us and growling like a very angry dog.

CHAPTER 41

MORE ORANGES

"If somebody calls the police and complains about this hotel, and the police finds out about all of you being illegal, they will shut the hotel down and take all of us to prison. How many times should I tell all of you that you must keep the noise level down? Look, you are living here for a few months, and then you will leave and go somewhere else. I have four children and a family in Afghanistan. They all need my help. I have only this hotel to support them. If my hotel is closed, how could I support my family? I am asking all of you, please keep your noise level down. I understand all of you want to have some fun, but please be kind and consider about my business. You can have your music, but not too loud please," Amin said, and then he left the room.

Amin's speech cut no ice. When we were sure he had gone, we closed the doors and windows, just to keep the noise in, and then we turned the music on and continued our dancing. We enjoyed the party a lot, and we promised to have another one soon, and have a special dinner with the party, just to have fun, because it felt very good. We made a list of everyone wanting to participate in the party. I was chosen to organize the party, and to control the food, the noise level, and to organize things. We made rules for our party. If anyone caused any problems or did not do what I told him, we would fine him ten Euros. If he did not pay his fine on time, we would teach him a lesson.

When the party finished, the time was about 1:00 a.m. We all went to bed. When I woke up for Morning Prayer, it was Monday morning as usual. My muscles were very sore, and I could not move properly. I decided to have about ten minutes exercise just to warm the muscles up. I had some milk and naan for my breakfast, and I went to my tailoring job.

"How was your party last Friday?" the supervisor asked.

"It was fine, how was your weekend?" I asked.

"It was very good," he said, and then somebody called him, and he walked away.

After lunch I was very tired. The supervisor brought me forty-five shirts just to make pockets for them. I finished them very quickly. The time was about 3:30 p.m. I was very tired and sleepy. I pressed the bell to call the supervisor just to let him know I wanted to go home.

"OK," he agreed. "But tomorrow, stay a little longer for overtime," he added.

"OK. If I wake up alive tomorrow," I said and then left. On the way, I bought some pizza for my dinner, and then I went home. I met Rahim in front of the hotel. "Salam, agha Rahim," I said and shook his hand with my left hand, and then we went into the living room. He brought some tea for me, and I turned the TV on. He sat opposite me with his back to the set. We started to talk. "Why have you come home early today?" he asked.

"I was tired and sleepy."

"When are we going to the oranges company again?"

"I am working from Monday to Friday with my tailoring job. I will be free Saturday and Sunday. We will go there then together. OK, agha Rahim?"

"Ali jan, I was thinking about myself, I have been here about a year, I couldn't find any job. This is a very good opportunity for me to work with you and save some money and then go to England with you. Last night I prayed and cried to Allah, just asking him to make all your wishes come true, and mine also. I woke up very early this morning just to ask Samah and his friend if they would allow me to work with them. They gave a lot of excuses but did not want me with them." He stopped. He looked very serious. "Can we work seven days with the oranges company?"

"I am sorry, I have to work with the tailoring company because it is very easy, and a nice and clean job, and also it's my career. I am very good at it, and it helps me a lot. I can find a job easily anywhere in the world. I will work with you on the weekends."

"Ali jan, please, you are the only person who treats me well, and you are my only friend. There is no chance of me getting papers to stay in Greece or get an artificial hand. Allah helped me to meet you. I cannot reward your help, but Allah will reward you a million times. You don't have to give me half of the money because I am disabled," he pleaded desperately. He was getting upset. "Ali, I will be your best friend. If you take me to the work seven days, I will pray for you for the whole my life. Oh, there is nothing I can give you. I am begging you. Help me please! I will never forget your help," he implored. I was very deeply moved by his words and the desperation in his voice.

He started to cry and talked to Allah, "Oh, Allah, why you took my hand away from me? Wasn't I a good slave for you? Did I commit a lot of sins?"

He turned his face to me and said, "Do you think I am a bad man? Am I a sinner? Why doesn't Allah want to answer me?"

I was thinking how to answer him and silently asked Allah to help me. I started to consider the situation. I needed help myself to go to UK, how could I help him? The orange-picking job was physically hard for me, and doing his part made it harder. He needed help, but why me? Oh, Allah, what should I do with him? He needs someone to take care of him.

He had stopped talking, and his eyes were close. I thought he might have fallen asleep or been praying. I stretched out on the sofa and closed my eyes, trying to think. I was about to doze off, when I heard something bang on the floor. When I opened my eyes, Rahim wasn't sitting on the sofa opposite, he had fallen down and banged his head on the floor. I sat up very quickly and went to help him. He was out cold and looked very pale. I thought he was dead. I tried patting his face, calling his name. I did not know what to do. I ran out on to the stairway and called for help. Below, four men were just arriving from their work. I could not talk properly because I was shocked and afraid. I could only shout, "Rahim! Rahim in the living room. Help me."

"What's happened?" they asked as they hurried up the stairs.

"Go, go in there please," I said.

They rushed to the living room and found him unconscious. They told me to bring some water. I ran to the kitchen room and picked a big dish and filled it up, and then ran back to the living room. I threw it all over Rahim. "Get up! Get up! I am sorry, Rahim," I said frantically. "I will take you to work seven days. Get up! Please."

I shook him hard, but one guy stopped me. Eventually he regained consciousness. I helped him up off the floor and to sit down on the couch. We gave him some water. He drank it and said he felt a little better.

"You all right?" I asked.

"Yes," he said.

"Don't worry, Rahim agha, everything will be OK."

I started to try and dry the living room. I could smell my pizza, which I had put in the oven to warm up. I left him sitting and went and brought the food in and shared it with him.

"What happened, Rahim agha?" I asked.

"I don't know, I thought I was going to die."

I thought it best to sit quietly for a few minutes. The color began to come back into his face, although he had a bump on his forehead. I asked him if it had happened to him before, and he said, "No."

"Do you need a doctor?" I asked.

But again he answered, "No. I feel a lot better now."

"You gave me such a shock."

"I am sorry, Ali jan. Very sorry." He stood up and went and dried his clothes.

He came back sheepishly and sat down, he did look a lot better.

"Right," I said, "Let's get ready for tomorrow."

"Tomorrow? What about tomorrow? What are we to get ready for?" His eyes were checking over my face.

"I told you I will take you to pick ORANGES tomorrow."

"Do you mean it?" he asked quietly and seriously in disbelief.

I stood up and went toward the kitchen. "Yes, I told you. We are going together. Now let's get our stuff ready, and I am going to bed early tonight, so come on."

He gave out a yell and jumped up and was following me and slapping my back and laughing. Then he was thanking me and chattering and laughing almost all at the same time.

When he had calmed down, we made some sandwiches for the next day and went to bed very early.

I had decided to quit my tailoring job and help Rahim because I didn't want something to happen to the poor guy. I was not sure if I was doing the right thing, but I had told him we were going together, and Allah only knows what would have happened if I told him I had changed my mind.

CHAPTER 42

TEAM WORK

Next day I woke up with the first ring of my alarm clock. I looked around the room, everyone was sleeping. I stretched my arms very quickly. I felt very relaxed and had slept well. I woke Rahim and then left him to get ready. We got ready very fast. I looked over at Samah and his friends, they were sleeping. I wanted to wake them up, but I was not sure if they were going to work or taking the day off.

"Let's go, don't worry about them because they did not help me at all," Rahim said.

"Why you no come with 'one hand' yesterday?" the manager asked.

I think he meant, why didn't you come with Rahim yesterday?

"I am very tired yesterday, excuse me too much," I said.

I meant, I was very tired yesterday, I am so sorry.

"OK, I am understand," then he looked at Rahim and said, "How is you, one hand?"

Rahim looked at me and asked what the manager had asked him.

"He is no English please, say Greek with him," I said.

I meant, he cannot speak English, can you say that in Greek please?

Rahim spoke a little Greek, and eventually answered for himself, and then we went to start the work.

Working with Rahim the first couple days was difficult for me, but when my muscles got used to it, I was OK. We earned every day one or two Euros more than the day before. We became very close friends. He was a very respectful guy and couldn't do enough for me. It was a little embarrassing the way he tried to show his appreciation all of the time.

On a special Eid-e-Ghorban, which happened to be one Friday, we planned to have our dinner party night. We had been talking about it since the first party we had had. The night before, Rahim and I wrote down a list of names of everybody who was staying on our floor. We were thirteen people altogether. We went around and collected three Euros from each person, including ourselves. I counted them, there was thirty-nine Euros. Next day, Rahim, Samah, and I left our work two hours early and went shopping for the food. Back at the hotel, we started to cook it and made everything ready. About 6:00 p.m., the other guys started to come home from their work. We made tea for them as they arrived. They were very tired.

"Today, Rahim, Samah, and I have prepared food and made everything for the party. It will be cooked and ready to eat in about an hour, but we need to clean the place up a bit first. We would like to ask everyone join us for about half an hour just cleaning everywhere on our floor," I said.

They could smell the food cooking, and everyone agreed and went eagerly to work because they knew the sooner we finished cleaning, the sooner the party would begin. They were like kids. We all took a hand cleaning, and after about forty-five minutes, we had finished mopping and sweeping. Some were cleaning bathrooms, others the windows and doors, and under the beds. Even the TV got a polish, so did the fridge and the cooker. They seemed to enjoy doing it. Then we took ten minutes break. All the guys went to get ready. They were laughing and teasing each other.

We put a *Dastarkhan* (tablecloth) on the floor. *Shorwa*, a typical Afghan dinner, was in the oven and nearly ready. (It is made of meat, potatoes, onions, tomatoes, chick peas, and beans.) And we had fresh naan bread baking, especially for the party.

By seven thirty, everybody was back and sitting expectantly in the living room, washed and changed, and some of them had even combed their hair, which was very unusual.

The tantalizing spicy smells wafted through our floor and out onto the balcony, when we brought the food in from the kitchen. There was plenty for everyone, so much that we could not eat it all. There was some food left for the next day for our lunch. Everyone enjoyed it. After the dinner, they thanked us a lot. Two of my roommates brought tea for everyone.

While we were drinking, it we began talking and some of the men said they wished we could have our Afghan food more often. Some of them were getting homesick for dishes from their homeland and talked about their favorite meal. They suggested having a good dinner once a month. Then someone thought it would be great if we had it once a week. Then an older man suggested every night. Everyone laughed at him because every night in that "hotel," on our floor, there was chaos. The fact is some of the boys did not have good dinners at all because they couldn't cook properly. Everyone arrived home hungry at the same time from work, and they argued a lot and swore at each other because there were not enough dishes or space in the oven for them all to cook different foods at the same time. Sometimes men ate someone else's food. This caused bad feelings, which was why everyone only considered themselves. This was why the place got into such a mess, why no one cleaned anything. I had been unhappy about how dirty the place was for some time, but this party was the first time we had all sat down together. This was the first time we all really talked about it.

The talk turned to discussing how we could make things better for ourselves, and one guy asked Samah, Rahim, and me what we thought. I said I had not been thinking about things myself, but that things would only improve if everyone agreed to do some work on the place, we would all have to work together. And so the talk went on, and they began to agree. The thought that we could have a good dinner together every night was powerfully attractive. They agreed that they felt better with the place being cleaner. One guy said he was sick of living like a pig, and others said the same. Slowly we got to making a plan. We took everything into account. Most of the guys couldn't take a day off because we all need the money to leave Greece.

An older man said, "We will be together for a few months, and then everybody will go away. While we are living in this hotel and working very hard, we might as well enjoy it and make it as good as we can." The others agreed, but they started looking toward me and my two friends to organize things.

I had an idea to resolve this problem. It was decided that we should make a rota and divide the company into three groups, four people in each, and they would take it in turns for each group to cook the food and wash the dishes and make tea for everyone every three days. We were thirteen people at that time. I was voted organizer. My job would be choosing who did what, making sure the food and everything else was OK. I had to make sure that people did their jobs properly and collected the money from everyone. I said I would give it a try.

Once a week, we would have a major cleanup.

"I think it is a great idea," Samah said.

"Not many people here know how to run anything," one of older men said, and I was expecting some trouble from him, but he continued, "I am agree with everything that has been proposed, but only if Ali is organizer. This party tonight was his idea, and he knows what he is doing."

We all complimented each other about our ideas, and they agreed for me to supervise them. I collected the money right away while they were enthusiastic about the plan. I was quite proud and pleased to be voted organizer, and I was pleased that they had enjoyed the food, but this was not the first time I had done something that had ended up giving me more work than I had expected.

Now it was time to start our party, and Rahim brought his cassette player and played some traditional Afghani music. I was the first person to start dancing, the other people clapped for me. Then everyone danced one by one. While the party was going on, I found time to go on the balcony and write a list of who should do what and when.

Everyone was very happy and enjoyed the party. It went on until late. People who have very little in their lives always seem able to get a lot of pleasure from simple things. Our pleasure had come from eating good plain food and chai (tea).

Next day, after work, I went shopping with the first group and helped them to cook enough food for everyone. I showed each group what to do, twice. We had decent dinners every night and began to enjoy being together. We had a big party sometimes on the weekends. At the beginning of our plan, I had to work more than anybody else. After a short while, my job turned out to be very easy because each group had learned their jobs well, even better than I had expected.

One day, we just began to eat our dinner, and I was sitting in the middle of the crowd, like a Molla, we were enjoying our food, when Amin came in.

"Salam to everyone," he said surprised. He was looking around the place at how very clean it all was. I asked my friend to move a little to the left just to make a little space for him to sit down beside me.

"Amin agha, have you lost anything on this floor?" I asked casually.

"No," he said.

"You are looking around, like you have lost something, come and sit beside me and join us for dinner for the first time," I said proudly.

He sat beside me, and I shared my food with him. He looked at each of us.

"I am puzzled. In the past, each time I came here, there was always something going on, people complaining and arguing. Swearing, everywhere dirty dishes left unwashed. But today everyone is grinning. The hotel is nice and clean, I have had this hotel about seven years, a thousand people have come and gone. I have never seen people behaving like today," he said, looking around.

"This is just the beginning. You have to come again and see us next week," one guy said.

"Amin agha, we love you very much and think you are a wonderful person," teased another.

"We all decided to try to get on with each other and keep your hotel nice and clean. Can you do us a favor please? Give us a new carpet in this room," Samah put in.

"And bring a brand-new washing machine, that one doesn't work, then we will all be very happy, and Allah too," Rahim said.

"I thought it was too good to be true. I was waiting for the complaints," Amin answered, but he was smiling as he said it. "I am surprised that you are looking after the place. I will do as you ask tomorrow, before you come from your work," he added.

"Thank you very much, Amin agha, we'll love you more," I said.

A short while later, he left and then we closed the doors and windows, to keep the noise down, and started to dance. Next day, Amin brought a very beautiful washing machine and carpets and a very big television.

CHAPTER 43

CHANGING DIRECTION

It was about 9:00 p.m., a few days later, we were drinking tea. Amin came in. With him he had brought everyone from the first and second floors to our floor. We were all surprised, looking at the crowd, wondering why he had brought them.

Amin brought everybody, just to see how good we had been doing on the third floor.

"I am proud of everyone who is resident on the third floor. I brought these people to learn your management."

They checked our kitchen room, bedroom, balcony, and living room. They found our floor was nice and clean. Then everyone went to the second floor to compare how they had been doing. Oh my God, it was so dirty, and dishes had been left unwashed, etc. Exactly like our floor before I came to the hotel. Then we went to the first floor, it was worse than the second. Amin gave us a free dinner and asked us to teach the residents of the first and second floors how to do the same as we were doing.

After the dinner, we all went to the second floor because they had a big living room. Amin asked me to talk about our rules and how I supervised them. I talked for about fifteen minutes and explained everything since I began. After I finished, people asked a lot of question. They really wanted things to improve. Amin thanked me, and he started to talk.

"I hope everyone agrees to give this idea a trial. I will have a little inspection every month. Whichever floor is the cleanest, they will have a 3 percent discount for their rent. It is up to you how you are going to keep the place clean, and challenge your neighbors."

Our neighbors cleaned their floor just for a few days. They had only dinner once, and then they could not keep it up. They wanted to get the

3 percent discount, but because they did not have a good management, they never got it. Our floor was the best and always had the discount every month. Amin offered even 5 percent discount for the floor which was the most clean and nice. Our neighbors tried to clean their floor, but they could not do it as good as us. They always argued between themselves. I had become very popular with my roommates because we got the discount every month and had wholesome, cheap dinners every night, which we always enjoyed.

One day Rahim and I came back very early from our work because the weather was bad. The season was changing, and we didn't know how much longer the job would last. I went to the tailoring company because they owed me some wages. I collected them, and the manager asked me to return to their factory, but I refused, I suppose, partly because of Rahim. I felt I had become responsible for him.

On the way home, I went to a travel office and asked them how we could go to England. We had two options. One was by air, the other by ships, first, going to Italy, then France and then the UK. I got all the information about how to get there. They gave me some colorful brochures. I told the travel agent that we did not want to consider going by air (because I had heard that we must have passports to take the plane and pass all kinds of security checks.). I found out how to go to Italy by ship. We would have to go via the Ionian Sea.

I went home; Rahim was dozing in the living room. I woke him and said, "Rahim *lala* (brother), get up. I have been out to get my money from the company I used work for. On the way back, I went to the travel information center and asked about how we could go to the UK. I would like to leave Athens tomorrow. What about you?" I asked, giving him the travel books.

"Tomorrow? Tomorrow? That's sudden. You are very impulsive. Have you made a plan yet?"

"I have always been impulsive. I'm often told to stop and think. That isn't my way. I think the orange-picking job is nearly finished, and I have been in Athens long enough. We have saved money, so I have decided I would like to go," I reasoned.

"So would I then. I will go with you anytime you want. You are my boss; just tell me what to do."

"Rahim *agha*, we are friends, the very best of friends, so please don't call me boss. The reason I am saying tomorrow is because the weather is getting colder, so we should move on. We have enough money to travel on. Do you have a jacket?"

"No, but Ali jan, I don't have enough money to go with you," he said fearfully." I haven't had a chance to earn as much as you."

"I have some money," I said. "I will spend it. When we finish our money, we'll stop our journey and work wherever we are, and make some more money and then continue our journey."

"We don't have passports or papers, that means we cannot ask anyone anything. How much money we will need to get to the UK?" he asked seriously.

"All my life I have never had the right papers nor a passport most of the time, but I'm here. I trust Allah. We'll be fine. I can always earn money. Tomorrow we will buy a jacket for you, and then we will go to Italy. Agreed?"

"OK," he said, laughing. "You're crazy, so I'll be crazy too."

I bought some fruits for that night for everyone. After the dinner, I told my roommates, "I have good news and bad news. The good news is tomorrow, Rahim and I are going to the UK. The bad news is I will miss you very much. It has been great to have been with you and have had parties, especially since we have been eating dinner together. I wish all of you the best. Please keep the peace and our rules, and pass them on to newcomers."

They were all very sad about our journey. They pleaded with me to stay with them a little longer. After an hour of talking about my journey, they were content to let us go. Everyone was very sad, except me, I was very happy, because I had saved some money and had had great times in Greece, met new people, helped Rahim and others, and made good rules for our roommates, and got 5 percent discount for everyone. We all promised to keep in touch and help each other as much as possible. (I have been in touch with some of them since I left Greece, and even today, we are sending and receiving e-mails, and have telephone conversations sometimes.)

Next day, Rahim and I went to the town center to buy a jacket.

CHAPTER 44

ONE MORE NIGHT

We spent half a day and could not find a cheap jacket for Rahim. They were all too expensive, so we decided to go to the church and get one. We waited three hours for the church to open. Eventually, they brought the food and opened the doors. We had to wait until they were serving people. When they finished, we went inside. There were a lot of jackets to choose from. He picked one very quickly, and then we went home to get everything ready. By that time, our roommates were arriving from their work. They pleaded with us to stay there one more night. I thought for a short while and asked Rahim. We decided to stay that night because we were not sure if we would ever get a chance to meet again. I liked them very much, we had had great friendship. We all had the same problems, and our goals were the same. After the dinner, Samah went to the first and second floors just to let them know we were back for one night, and asked them if they wanted to join us for tea for the last time. They all came over, and we had a good talk. Some of my roommates were really sad.

I woke up very early in the morning and woke Rahim, and went to take a shower. I was nice and clean. I stood up facing to *Kiblah* and prayed to Allah a lot, and pleaded to him to help me to arrive at my destination quickly and safely with Rahim. All of my friends took the day off, and even some of my friends from the first and second floors did the same. The time came to leave. We were hugging each other and shaking hands. Some of my roommates cried when I hugged them, and we said good-bye to each other.

I was very happy. You might know what it is like when you say good-bye to good friends whom you will never see again. I would miss all my roommates.

My face was wet with tears as I hugged everyone again and said, "I love all of you and will miss you. When I met you, I was so happy and thanked Allah because I had found my countrymen. I never expected to become so attached to all of you."

We all walked to the train station. They carried our bags and prayed a lot for our safety. I bought two tickets for Patra City, although I had no idea where it was. The travel agent had told me that that was where the ships to Italy went from. We had to wait twenty minutes for our train to arrive. The guys bought a lot of cold drink and biscuits for us. We hugged each other one more time, and then the train came, and we got on. We all waved like mad as it pulled out of the station. "Good-bye, Athens."

CHAPTER 45

SMUGGLERS AGAIN

We arrived at Patra, which is a large seaport on a wide inlet. When we were off the train, I noticed that the air was much fresher than in Athens. There was a wind blowing in from the sea. We asked people where we should go to buy tickets to get to Italy, me trying out my English, and Rahim trying out his Greek. It took us an hour to find out. We stood in the line for twenty minutes. Eventually we got a chance to talk with the salespersons. The first thing the girl asked was "Can I have looked at your passports please?"

"Sorry, we don't have passports," Rahim answered in Greek. Then she asked us for any kind of identification. We told her that we had left our wallets at home and would go and get them. We were afraid that if we told her the truth, that we had no IDs at all, we would get into trouble. We went out and headed in the general direction of the sea. We walked for about fifteen minutes to the north, looking for someone who was from the Middle East, to ask if they knew any smugglers. On a kind of promenade, we saw people sitting about and strolling around. We looked carefully. Some people were sitting in the sun, facing the sea, and others were in the shade of the trees and awnings. There was a man sitting on a little funny bench, facing away from the sea, looking at the passersby. We walked slowly and looked at him casually. He looked like he came from one of our country's neighbors, like Iran or Pakistan or Iraq. We walked toward him.

"I think he is from Iran," I said to Rahim. He was about six feet tall, green eyes, very long black hair, and skinny. He pulled a cigarette from his pocket and put it in his mouth and lit it. We went up to him and said,

"Salam agha."

He looked at me and said, "Salam."

"Are you from Iran?" I asked in Persian.

"No, I am from Iraq, but I lived Iran for a long time," he said.

"How are you doing?" I asked.

"Fine."

"My name is Ali, nice to meet you."

"My name is Khosrow. Good to see you," he said.

We shook hands. "You are speaking perfect Persian," I said.

"Are you from Iran?" he asked.

"No, we are from Afghanistan," Rahim said.

"I pulled three orange juices and some biscuits from my bag. I gave him a juice and some biscuits, and the same to Rahim. He took it without saying anything. It looked to me that he was homeless and very hungry. He finished his juice and ate all the biscuits very fast.

"Do you want some more? I think you like orange juices and biscuits," I said.

"Yes, I have not eaten anything since I woke this morning."

I gave him some more.

"Agha, we want to go Italy. We went to buy tickets; but they asked us for our passports and ID. We don't have anything with us right now. Do you know any smuggler by any chance?"

"I know a lot of smugglers; they charge different amounts of money. Tell me how much money you want to spend and how you want to go there, by air or by sea?"

"Whatever is the cheapest? We don't have a lot of money."

"I know the smugglers charge a lot of money, and take two to three weeks to get passports for you."

He looked at me and said, "You look a smart man. You gave me some orange juice and biscuits, because of that I will help you. Do you want go Italy tonight and spend only a little money?"

"How?" I asked.

"If you give me four hundreds Euros, I will show you how you can go tonight, and it is very cheap for two people."

"You have to explain about how we can go there. I can't give money if don't know how I am going."

"OK, I know a lot of trucks that go every night to Italy. If you give me money, I will take you to the fence, and you can hide yourself under the truck for about twenty minutes, and then the truck will go into the ship. I can't tell you more than this unless you give me your money. Once I get the money, I will tell you what to do when you get there."

"Look, agha Khosrow, we worked very hard collecting oranges one by one. They paid us a Euro for each box we filled. Four hundred Euros is lot of money for us. Could you please give us some discount?" I asked.

Rahim pointed to his hand and said, "Please give us some discount."

"If you go to smugglers, they will charge you two thousand Euros for each person. Four hundred Euros is nothing compared to them. I have sent a lot people this way. They all got there. Because you are good people and shared your food with me, I can give fifty Euros discount."

"No, agha, that is still too much for us. We can't afford it. We came from Turkey, it only cost about a hundred thirty U.S. dollars."

"How did you do that?" he asked, surprised.

"Look, you are asking for three hundred and fifty Euros just to show us the way to get under a truck. It only cost one hundred and thirty dollars to travel to Greece from Turkey."

He laughed and said, "Good price, if I were in Turkey, I would have given you five hundred U.S. dollars. Do you know how much money I spent to get here two years ago? I spent one thousand and nine hundred U.S. dollars. I was very lucky because the smuggler was a friend of my friend."

"Look, we have not gone around and asked other people how much they are charging. You are the first person we asked. Anyway we'll give you two hundreds Euros because you are nice person. OK?"

"No."

"Let's go," I said to Rahim. We walked away from him. He called us, "Wait."

He walked toward us and said, "Three hundred Euros."

"Two hundred fifty Euros," Rahim said.

"You should not have said that," I whispered to Rahim."No, we are not going to give you more than a hundred fifty Euros. Never mind, we'll go by ourselves," I said.

Eventually he said, "OK, two hundred Euros because I need some money. I swear to Allah if I did not need your money, I would never let you have it so cheap."

I gave him fifty Euros and told him I would pay him once we got to the trucks.

"OK, I will tell you something important before I take you to the fence. When we get there, we have to be very quick. I will show you how to hold yourself under the truck. Tonight about 6:00 p.m., trucks will start to go into the ship. There will be security checks here and in Italy. If you pass the security from our side, you will be going to Italy. When you arrive there, don't get out right away at the port, stay under the truck, and for a short while, and then when the truck stops somewhere at a red light or at the gas station, run away. One more time, you have to be very quick when you are inside the fence, and no loud talking, OK?" he said.

We walked about a kilometer to get to the fence.

The fence was like a wall. It was made of metal. He had bent the metal a little. We could only get through by pushing each other. We were short of time. We paid him, and then we got under the truck very quickly. I tied up my bag and Rahim's bag first, and then we hid ourselves by holding on with our hands. A very short while later, "Ali, Ali jan, I am falling down please, I am going to die, the truck will run over me," Rahim said.

Oh my god. I went to help him. He was shaking and wet with sweat and very afraid. He could not hold himself by one hand. I checked under the truck to see if I could find somewhere else for him. There were many places to hold ourselves, but he could not hold himself at all because he had only one hand and was very afraid.

"Rahim, you have to hold yourself somewhere please, we don't have any alternative to go to UK. We don't have money for the fare."

He started to cry and said, "I can't do it with one hand. I am afraid. I might die if I can't hold on while the truck is running."

"Oh Allah, help me, what should I do with him? If you don't have a heart like lion, you can't go to UK. Wait here, let me think what I can do. Can you go back to the hotel?"

He pleaded with me to help him and said, "I don't have anybody, please help me. I have only one hand."

I felt so sad for him, and I went out from under the truck. I looked around very quickly, there was nobody around.

"Don't make any noise. I will help you to get on to the roof of trailer."

He wanted to say something. I did not let him, "Hurry up," I said.

There was a little space between truck and trailer. We stood on top of a tank; I helped him to climb up.

We got up there very slowly. Somebody saw us. A short while later, we were surrounded by the police. They shouted at us to get down.

CHAPTER 46

POLICE STATION

The police shouted at us to get down several times. Eventually we did. I wanted to run away, but because Rahim was weak, I couldn't leave him. The police arrested us and searched us. They couldn't find anything. The police checked all over the truck and found everything was in order.

"They thought we were stealing from the truck," I said to Rahim.

Rahim asked me to forgive him.

I said, "Forget about it. It was our *qesmat* (destiny). Whatever happens to us, happens. Think about what we should do next."

They took us to the police station. On the way, I said, "Rahim Jan, don't talk. I will deal with them. If they ask you anything, just show them your arm, OK?"

"OK," Rahim said.

The police wanted to know why we were there. I didn't tell the truth. Police searched us again. And found the little money Rahim had. They never found my money.

They asked why I had no money with me and where I was going without it. I told them I had left my wallet in the Athens Hotel, and I was there with my friends. We just wanted to play around the fence. The weather was nice and warm. We just went on the top of trailer to lie down and enjoy the weather. We thought there would be a good view to look around. They didn't understand very well what I had said. I don't think they believed any of it.

They took us to another police station. On the way, I told Rahim to cry loud and show his hand to the detective and pretend that he was dumb. He agreed to do what I told him.

The detective asked us how old we were. Since I found out there was no interpreter available, I decided to be careful about which questions I answered, never to tell them the truth. I knew if I told them I had come from Turkey, they would send me back there. They had no evidence to show we committed a crime. I think they nearly believed my little funny story. They put us into a room. Rahim and I prayed a lot to Allah. A few hours later, a very good-looking woman said, "You are free, go back to Athens and carry a piece of ID with you all the time. We don't know who you are or where you come from. Don't go again to the fence. If you want to lie down, go somewhere else. Trucks are dangerous, you might have fallen down. Because we don't have any evidence that you committed a crime, you can go away!" She spoke very good English.

We went out. We were very hungry and started to look to find some food. We searched for a while and could not find anything because it was very late at night. We were very tired and went to find the fence and get on the truck again. It took us a long while to find it. There were no trucks at all. We thought probably they have all gone to Italy. The sky was cloudy, and the weather was a little cold and windy. We thought about going back to the hotel in Athens and coming back in a week's time because we did not have a lot of money left. We would have to find somewhere to sleep. We found a park and sat down on the bench and talked about what we should do next. We would have to sleep in the park. Next day, we would go to the fence, pick a truck randomly, and get on the top very quickly and hope to Allah we would pass the security check and get to Italy. We had some biscuits left in Rahim's bag and ate them and then went to find some boxes, but there was nothing around. We slept on the grass. We tried our best to sleep, but the weather was cold and windy, and we were hungry and couldn't sleep at all. We put on all our clothes; still we were not warm enough. It was so cold. We started to walk around to help us to get little warmer. Very early in the morning, we found a church and sat down in a sheltered corner, where it was a little warmer out of the wind. We spent the rest of the night pathetically dozing and waking. In the morning just after sunrise, we went to a coffee shop, washed our faces, and got cleaned up. I order a coffee for myself and tea for Rahim and some cookies for our breakfast.

After mid-day, we went to the fence. We looked around carefully and saw somebody was around a truck. We thought that would be a driver just parking his truck. A short while later, he went off, and someone else came. We kept watching. Eventually we got a chance to go inside. We chose a truck very quickly. I helped Rahim to climb up, and I gave him our bags. I got on the top very quickly. We put our bags for pillows and lay down and closed our eyes. We did not talk very loud. We started to pray to Allah. The sun was shining, and the weather was just about OK, not warm and not cold. After a long while, we heard somebody come to our truck. He turned the engine on and drove away. We were lying in middle of the trailer. The roof was blue plastic and very slippery when the truck was turning left and right. We hardly managed to hold ourselves on. Fortunately the truck was not going too fast. We were very afraid; if the truck was to get up speed, we would fall off. Eventually, the truck stopped in front of the ship. Rahim started shaking, and he was afraid. I was praying to Allah. We heard somebody shouting. I thought they were shouting to their partner or someone else. They shouted again, and their voice was very close to us. We did not take a notice. They started to shout in English. I understood a few words. They were saying, "Get off, get off." I moved my head up a little, and I opened my eyes and looked over the side. There were four policemen trying to climb up on the roof. I sat up very quickly and looked up; there were cameras just above our heads. Our truck stopped by the door of the ship. I looked at Rahim, his eyes were still closed, and he was shaking, and saying very slowly, "Oh Allah, help us and blind the police, that they can't see us."

"Agha Rahim, get up," I said.

He got up very quickly and wanted to say something, but when he saw the police, his face turned red, and he couldn't say anything at all. We got down. They searched us. One of the police officers recognized us and said, "You again," and he said something to his partner in Greek. They did not ask us anything. They took us to the police station and kept us one night and then took us to another police station. After noonday, they brought an interpreter. They asked our names and DOB and so on. They never asked us what the problem in our country was, or why we came to Greece. I gave them wrong information. I asked the interpreter, "Agha, what will they do with us?"

"They might take you to the refugee camp or deport you back to Turkey. It all depends on what you tell them."

I made up a similar story, like the first one. I told them, "We have family and friends in Athens, we lost our money, and we wanted to go back there. Rahim does not have enough money to buy tickets for us. Then we thought the best way we can go back to Athens was to get on a truck to go there. Forgive us if we made trouble for you. I promise you'll never find us around the fence anymore."

They asked me the addresses in Athens of our family and friends. As I knew a lot of place, I told them one. They wrote it down. They believed my little story. Two hours later, they gave us two tickets and told us to go back to Athens. We took the tickets and went away.

"Thanks Allah they let us go. Always act as if you are dumb if the police catch us, otherwise, if we are in different rooms, I will say something, and you say will something else. They will find out we are lying. Good man," I said.

"I hope we won't be talking to any more police, they might deport us."

We found a park, and we sat down on the bench and thought about what we should do next.

"We don't have too much time. I have a good idea. We need to buy a carpet knife and some tape, and then we'll go to the fence and get on the roof of the truck. Then we'll make a good cut in the plastic roof. We'll go inside, and I will tape it back. Then we'll hide ourselves somewhere inside. It will be safe, nice, and warm for us," I said.

"OK, Ali Jan, but how do you know if you can cut through the roof?" Rahim asked.

"We used to make sledges out of that Perspex plastic on the farm when I was a boy. If the knife is sharp, it will be easy. Don't worry, Rahim Jan," I said.

"If anyone else were in your position, he would have left me long ago. Thank you very much for taking care of me," Rahim said and hugged me.

We bought a knife and tape and some potato fries, water, and biscuits.

Then we went to the fence again. Rahim was very afraid and shaking, "What happens if they catch us again? They will send us to Turkey or put us in prison."

"Rahim agha, going to the UK with no passport and a very little money is not easy. We are Afghan. We are like lions. We have had a lot of bad times in our lives. We do not give up. Greek police are like foxes, lions are never afraid of foxes. The good thing about them is they don't beat people. They gave us a little food and treated us fairly. What are you afraid of, bad boy? Allah will help us. You know if we were in Iran, and their police found us doing something illegal, they would cut our heads off, then you would have something to worry about. Let's hurry up."

I looked around. There were more trucks, but nobody was there. We got on top of the truck very quickly. It was very easy because we were getting used to it. I pulled the knife from my bag. I made a little hole and then a cut and pushed Rahim in and then threw our bags in. I looked around, still nobody was around. I got in very fast and asked Rahim to hold the plastic up while I fixed it back in place with tape. We were on the top of a lot of large boxes, the truck was full of them. I opened one of them. Inside were shirts. I wondered if I had made some of them. It seemed strange. We managed to push them to one side, and made a little room in the case for Rahim in the corner. He sat down there, and I put boxes on top of him and said, "Rahim jan, don't make any noise. We'll pass the security check."

Then I hid myself. The boxes were very light. I managed to move very fast. After a short while, I started to sweat. I could not take my jacket off because I was sitting in a very tight position. An hour later, the driver turned the truck on and started to drive away. I started to pray to Allah. A short while later, the truck stopped for security check. "Oh Allah, help us," I said.

CHAPTER 47

ROME

The truck stopped for about five minutes, and then it went inside the ship. A short while later, the ship started to sail. Half an hour later, I chanced coming out and stretched my arms. I helped Rahim to get out. He was wet and shaking with nerves.

"Rahim, we passed one side security check. Let's have some food," I said.

I put all the boxes together and made two beds. We lay down, and we were very happy. We talked in whispers for a while. Inside the truck was nice and warm. We both dozed off because we had not been getting much sleep lately. I was dreaming about some girls when Rahim woke me up and said, "Ali, Ali, get up, I need to use the washroom."

"You woke me up for that. I was dreaming of something sweet. Can you hold it for a short while?"

"No, I can't. I am leaking."

"Oh my God. Do it somewhere."

"How and where?" he asked.

I sat up and took the shirts out from the boxes and said, "Go there and sit down in the box, and do it inside a plastic bag. Make sure you don't fart loudly. When you finish, leave everything there and put the shirts back in the case quickly before the smells get out. I will close my eyes while you are doing it."

He went there, and I closed my eyes. I dozed off again. Rahim woke me up again and said, "I can't sleep."

I sat up and said, "What is wrong?"

He pulled out a pack of cards and asked me to play. It took a long time to play cards because he had difficulty picking his cards up and, of course, he couldn't shuffle them. After about ten minutes, I said, "Rahim, we need sleep because we don't know what will happen next. Do you remember last night? We did not sleep at all. Let's try to sleep."

"OK, Ali jan," he said.

I dozed off again and slept for I don't know how long. I was woken by the sound of men opening and shutting the cab doors and guessed it was the drivers. I woke Rahim. We put back everything in order. Rahim went to his little box room, and I put the boxes neatly on the top his box. He started complaining that he was too hot and could not breathe.

"Rahim, stop it please. I will get you out once we pass the security check."

I hid myself very quickly, but there had been no need because it was a few hours later when the driver drove the truck off the ship. I was listening very carefully to the truck noise. About ten minutes later, it stopped for security check. Oh my God, I was very worried and praying to Allah to help us. I heard what I assumed was the police open the trailer doors, and saw the flash of their lights sweeping over the inside. I held my fingers between my teeth and was saying "Oh, Allah, help us please" repeatedly.

The doors slammed shut, and I heard them being locked. I took a deep breath in and thanked Allah a lot.

The truck went out from the ship yard. About two hours later, it seemed to be driving at a moderate speed, changing direction, and turning corners. I got myself out of my hiding place and pushed all the boxes aside to get to Rahim. We sat on a box for a little while and thought about how we could get out onto the road. We didn't know where the truck was heading. It had increased in speed and going in a straight line. I climbed to the roof and took a little of the tape off just enough to get my head out. Outside it was dark and very windy. We were on a highway. The truck was being driven very fast.

"We can't do anything right now because there is no stopping on the highway. We'll have to wait until the truck stops at a gas station."

We ate some food and got ready for the truck to stop. Eventually it pulled over. We waited for few minutes in case the driver might be around. I got out very quickly and helped Rahim. I looked around, it was very dark outside. We threw our bags on the ground, and I jumped down and helped Rahim to get down. We grabbed our bags and ran away. We kept running for a while, never looking behind us, not even to see if someone was chasing us. We were wet and out of breath. "I can't run anymore, Ali jan," Rahim said, and stopped, panting hard.

We had no idea where we were. I only knew we were on a highway. We looked around and saw the lights a long distance away and decided to walk toward them. Vehicles passed by very fast. The weather was a little cold and windy. Rahim was very tired; I carried his bag for him. His face was as red as blood. I pulled out a bottle of water and gave him to drink. I checked our bags to see if there was any food left. He had finished everything while I was sleeping. There was only half a bottle of water. We walked a little faster. We were very tired and hungry. In the last twenty-six hours, I had only had a bottle of water and some biscuits. We took about ten minutes break, and then continued walking. We did not have a watch to check what time it was, but dawn was breaking, so we took a rest for morning prayers. We did not have water to clean ourselves. We sat down on the side of the road and hoped we were facing *Kiblah*. We prayed and thanked Allah, and cried to him for help. After a short while, Rahim started to sing in a strong light voice, surprisingly melodious.

> *"Hay heart, why you want too much money!*
> *All your money you had saved in your life, you take a Kafan*
>   *(winding-sheet shroud) with you!*
> *You are not sure if you can take it with you or not!*
> *Allaho la-e-la ha allala!*
> *In this world, why are you so proud or conceited!*
> *If you became a king of the world!*
> *You'll die and turn to soil! Oh ho flower!*
> *Oh ho flower, alone flower!*
> *Oh ho life, alone life! In this world, nobody is without sorrow!*
> *If there is, he is someone who is not human, that is the devil!"*

"Wow! It is a very beautiful poem, sing more please," I said as we stood up.

I liked his singing, because when he was singing he walked faster. He sang repeatedly.

The sun started to shine. Rahim eventually stopped singing. When we got close to the town, I asked people where the train station was. We kept asking and asking people. Eventually we found it. I asked the time. It was about 9:00 a.m. We went to the washroom and washed our faces and put some gel on our hair. Then I took some money out, and I bought two tickets for Rome. We were two or three hours away from Rome. We waited for about half an hour and then got on the train. A few minutes later, I dozed off and Rahim too, we were exhausted.

A beautiful lady woke me up and said something in Italian, which I did not understand. "Excuse me, no Italy, you speak English please?"

"We have arrived Rome, Rome," she said.

"Oh ho, thank you very much," I said, and then I woke Rahim. We got off the train, stepping into a massive station. Everything was movement and noise. Loud speakers were announcing arrivals and destinations, the whole place was full of people, all with luggage. Food kiosks were serving coffee and all kinds of food. Destination boards clattered. Wonderful colored trains were coming in. Others were going out. We headed out from the station to find somewhere to get something to eat. We found a pizza shop. I order some chicken with fries. "Rahim, welcome to Rome," I said, smiling.

"We need to find out how we can go to Paris," I said while I eating some chicken. The food was nice, cheap and delicious. I bought some more fries and kept them in our bags in case we needed them later on. We came out of the busy café and then got ourselves lost. We had to ask a lot of people how we could catch a train to Paris. We were directed to the station. At a ticket desk, I asked how much the tickets to Paris would cost. They cost about a hundred thirty-five Euros each. We went to the washroom to count our money. We had about two hundred and ten Euros altogether.

"We can't buy two tickets," I said to Rahim.

We went out from the washroom and sat on a bench in the waiting area, thinking what we should do next. "Rahim jan, I have a very great idea. I will buy a ticket, and then we can get on to the train with one ticket. If the ticket collector comes over to ask for tickets, you must be asleep and don't wake up even if I call you or shake you. The ticket collector will eventually go away. This is the only way we can get there. Otherwise, if we stay here, we'll finish the money just buying food. We'll hope to Allah we will get there."

"What should we do if we get in trouble?" Rahim asked.

"Trust me, Allah will be with us. I will deal with everything; I won't let you have sorrow."

I bought the ticket. It was timed for 6:00 p.m.; the time was about 2:00 p.m. We went for another walk to see what Rome looked like. The weather was nice and warm. Like all cities, it was full of traffic and people. There were cafes with smart tables and busy waiters. Long streets, old buildings, big churches, squares with fountains, ruins, and lots of stairs, but we began to lose direction and returned to the station.

CHAPTER 48

ROME TO PARIS

The train station was very beautiful. There were a lot of shops inside it. We chose one of the clothes shops and went in. There were many nice shirts. I wanted to buy one for myself, another for Rahim, but I did not have enough money, so we walked out. We got tired and went to sit down in the waiting room until our train came. The station was very big. There were about fifteen platforms. I checked my ticket to find out which one we needed for our train. I could not understand it very well because it was written in Italian. I asked people how we could find our train. They showed me. My platform number was 10 B1. There was a very big screen in the waiting room. We thought that it was a TV and wondered why it was not showing movies or something else like that. People watched it very carefully; it seemed they were looking for something. "Why are people watching this TV for?" Rahim asked.

"I don't know. I have never been here before. Maybe their TV is different than in Greece," I said.

"What stupid people they are, watching some notes repeatedly," he said.

When someone pointed out something on the screen to their friend, we laugh at them a lot. They were looking at us and wondered what we were laughing at. They seemed nervous and tired, looking at the screen all the time. We did not know what that was about, or why they were doing it. I watched it very carefully and thought there must be something going on there because people watched often. I found my train number up there on the screen and what time it would come and what time it left. Oh my god. I realized we were wrong to laugh at people. They were right to watch it because they were looking at their time when their train would come. I explained to Rahim.

"You are very smart to figure that out," Rahim said.

I stood up and showed Rahim our platform number on the screen. Fortunately we were speaking Dari. Nobody understood what we had said. Or they would have thought we were stupid.

When I met Rahim the first time and invited him to join me for dinner with my other friends, I thought he was a boring person. He did not have any money, or friends.

Since working with him, we had become the best friends and traveled together. I realized he was very funny, and I enjoyed being with him. It turned out that he was about four years older than me. He listened to what I told to him to do and respected me a lot. He was really good company. He made me laugh a lot.

About five thirty, we went to wait on our platform, and a short while later the train arrived. When it had stopped, the doors opened. It was very long. We got on and looked for our berth number. Each wagon had four beds, two on the top and the other two at the bottom. We searched for about twenty minutes but could not find our bed. Then we asked people. They were all busy looking for their beds and did not give us a good answer. We got off the train. There were some security guards. I asked them, one of them took me to my bed, and then he walked away. Our bed was on the bottom line, on the left-hand side. We sat down for a while and talked about the timetable and laughed. Our roommates came in, they were an old lady with two beautiful girls about my age. A short while later, the younger girl said something in Italian to us. We did not understand and took no notice. We thought they were talking to each other. She pointed her hand at me and said something again in Italian. "Excuse me, no Italy. English! English!" I said.

I think she wanted to say something else, but she could not for some reason. Eventually she said, "How are you?"

"We good," I said.

"I think they want to know why we are laughing a lot, or wondering why two people are sitting on one bed," I said to Rahim.

"They don't even know we are Afghan and have no passports," Rahim said, and we laughed.

I talked to her for a while about the weather and so on. Her mom, or whoever she was, had chosen to lie down on the bed above on the opposite side. Rahim pulled the cards from his bag. There was a little table in our compartment. We pulled it into the middle. There was another girl in the bed above ours. Her sister asked her to come down and sit beside her. They explained the way they play cards. It was similar to the way we played. The only difference was we called it by another name. The old lady covered her face because we were making a lot of noise. First, we started to play on the table, but because the table was too small, we had to bend to reach to it. We put the table away, and we all sat down on the floor. The first few games, we were all confused and did not follow it well. After a short while, we all learned the game and understood it well. I sat beside the younger girl and Rahim beside the other one. Rahim and I were one team, they were the other. They won the game several times because we were worried about our ticket. We kept playing; eventually the ticket collector came in and asked for our tickets. Rahim looked at me and I at him, our faces turned red. "What should I do now, shall I lie down?" Rahim said in Dari.

"Just relax, don't lose your control," I said.

I saw one of the girls pull three tickets from her bag. I looked at the ticket collector; he was standing by the door. I stood up very quickly and gave him my ticket, he marked it, and then he marked the other three and then walked away. He did not see the old lady lying down on the top bunk. He must have thought we were only four people.

"He has gone and hasn't noticed anything. Just keep playing with these girls, and thanks to Allah," I said.

Rahim and I decided to cheat because we just wanted to win. Eventually we won a game. Rahim was very happy, and then we won four more times. They were very sad and never realized that we were cheating. They started to argue with each other. Rahim and I laughed at them. "I think the older girl is telling her sister she can't play very well. They are playing good, we are cheating," I said to Rahim.

"If we won't cheat, we'll never win," Rahim said.

We played a few more games. The old lady woke up and went to the washroom. When she came back, we stopped playing. They started to eat their dinner. Rahim and I went to the washroom and washed our hands. When we came back, we had some food in our bags and ate it. A short while later, they lay down and fell asleep. We were sitting on our bed and thinking about how we could sleep in one bed.

"Rahim agha, you need to sleep in the bed. I will go to another wagon to see if there is a free bed."

"Ali jan, you paid for this bed. You are supposed to sleep here, I will go somewhere else."

"You are older than me, that means I have to respect you. Don't worry, I will find somewhere. I don't want you to get into trouble. I am glad that the ticket collector did not notice we had only one ticket."

We were very happy. Then he lay down. I went out to search the next wagons for an empty bunk. I checked all of them. They were all full of sleeping people. I sat down in the hallway for a short while. I was very sleepy and dozed off. The security guard woke me up and looked at my ticket, then he told me to go and sleep in my bunk. I asked him the time; it was about half past three. Then he walked away. I went back to our wagon, and I looked at Rahim and the other passengers who were sleeping. I looked at the floor, it was not very clean. I sat down and did not care about it being dirty because I was half asleep. I put my bag for a pillow and lay down. I had just about fallen asleep, when the old lady woke me up and told me, "No, sleep here, go to your bed."

"Excuse me, I am no sleep here," I said and went out very quickly. I was very afraid she would complain to the security guards. They would find out that I did not have a bed or passport, and that would mean trouble. I went to the washroom, it was very dirty, and then I checked the other one. They all were the same. I cleaned one of them with toilet papers and locked the door. I sat down on top of toilet lid. I wanted to lie down somewhere, but there was no space. After a short while, I dozed off. Somebody banged the door twice. I did not take any notice of that. About twenty minutes later, someone banged again and again. I was very worried about what was going on outside the door. There was a lot going on in my mind. I opened the door and looked around, but there was nobody. I shut the door and sat down again and dozed off. I heard a very loud noise, and I washed my face and went to our wagon. I saw people were getting ready. It seemed we were arriving in Paris. I woke Rahim and told him to go wash his face. He came back very quickly and said, "Where did you sleep last night? I woke up very early this morning and went to the washroom. When I came back, I looked around for you and could not find you anywhere. I wondered where you were."

I did not reply to his questions. "Did you sleep well?" I asked.

"Yes, thank you very much. Where did you sleep?"

"I slept somewhere where I have never slept before. It was only for one night."

I did not tell him the truth because I thought it might make him feel guilty. I took out my English book and studied it. About 7:00 a.m., we arrived in Paris. People started to leave the train. We stood in line to get off.

We followed the crowd and did not push people at all. Eventually we got out of the station.

"Welcome to Paris, agha Rahim," I said delightedly.

CHAPTER 49

SO NEAR AND YET SO FAR

Rahim hugged me. "We are Afghan heroes! We are good lions," he said excitedly.

"We'll get to the UK one day soon," I said proudly.

We were walking very happily, enjoying Paris. I decided to phone all my friends. First, we called Greece, and then I called Zabi in Turkey. They all were very happy when I told them we had arrived in France. We went to the coffee shop and bought some coffee, which was rich and strong. We were so excited. Then we went back to the train station and asked them how we could go to England. They asked us where about in England we were going to. I said London, that was the only city I knew the name of.

They told us we had to go to another train station and catch a train to Calais City and then take the ship to UK. I bought two trains tickets and then waited there for about twenty minutes. I checked my money. We only had about twelve Euros left. We got on the train and arrived about 3:00 p.m. somewhere near Calais. Then we had to take the bus to go to the docks. We did not have money to buy bus tickets and decided to walk there. I had two Euro coins, on the way I bought some bananas. We kept asking people the way again and again. About 6:00 p.m., we found the docks. They were very large. We sat down on the ground somewhere near a wall.

"We don't know anything about these docks. Before we get to try to get on a truck, we need to ask someone. Get up. Before it gets dark, we have to find someone from the Middle East," I said.

Then we went to look for someone who could speak our language.

We stopped people and kept asking them if they were from the Middle East. Eventually we found a man who was from my country.

He told us, "Be careful. If the truck does not go into the ship within twenty minutes, it means that truck will be going to Italy or somewhere like that. Try to get off as soon as the truck stops. This dock is very big. Good luck," he said. He was in a hurry and walked away.

We thanked him and went to see which truck we should get on. It was getting dark. We looked around the docks. There was nobody about. We picked a truck and hoped it was going to the UK. We got on the top very quickly; I took my carpet knife from my bag and made a hole in the plastic. We got in very quickly. The trailer was full of sofas. We hid ourselves very quickly. We slept there for about fifteen hours. We finished our food and water. The truck did not move. Eventually we decided to get out. We thought there might be something wrong with the truck. We got out very quickly and checked around and walked carefully under the trucks, deciding which truck we should get on. We picked one and got on very fast. We did the same trick we had done to the other truck. The trailer was full boxes. I opened one; it was all cans of beans. We put the boxes to one side and made room for ourselves, and sat down for a while, thinking a lot and praying to Allah. The truck was very cold, and we could not sleep well. Very early in the morning, the driver turned the truck on and drove it away. I made a little room for Rahim very quickly. He went in, and then I put some boxes around him and two boxes on top of him. Then I hid myself. I started to pray to Allah. Half an hour passed. The truck did not stop for a security check. I waited and prayed. Another hour passed. Nothing happened. The truck was still moving. I started to worry. "Oh, Allah, help us, we only have ten Euros, and we are we hungry and have waited a long while in this truck. If it goes the wrong way, what should we do? Oh, Allah, help please!" I said.

About another two hours passed, the truck was being driven very fast. I came out from my hiding place, and I helped Rahim to get out. He was sitting very tight and praying.

"The truck is going the wrong way because it has been a long while. It did not go to the ship, pray to Allah. I'll try to do something about it," I said.

I climbed up to the roof, took the tape off and got my head out. The sky was very cloudy, and we were on a highway.

"Stop please! Stop! Stop! You are going wrong way. Stop please," I yelled and screamed for help. Nobody heard me. I took my carpet knife out from my bag and made a very big hole on the plastic above our head. I put most of the boxes one on top another. We stood up and put our heads out and yelled as loud as we could for about ten minutes. Nobody heard us. The truck was travelling very fast. We sat inside and took in a deep breath.

"Rahim, if we cried and yelled for help until tomorrow morning, nobody would hear our voices. We are on the highway; the truck is driving very fast."

I thought hard, the only solution was to get the driver's attention. I had to try.

"You just bring some cans for me, I will do the rest," I said. Very quickly I cleared the way to the front of the trailer, and then I started to make a big hole in the end wall. When I looked through it, I saw there was a little window at the back of the driver's cab. The drivers use it when they are coupling and uncoupling the trucks.

Rahim brought some cans for me. I looked at the little window. There were two people in the cab, one was the driver. I threw a can at the window, the music in the cab must have been very loud, because they did not notice anything. I picked up three more cans, holding them in my left hand. I threw them one after another at the window, still they did not notice. I made the hole a little bigger in the plastic. Rahim and I took out some more cans from the boxes. We threw them very fast one after another. Eventually we shattered the little window and threw about four or five cans inside the cab. The driver pulled over.

They opened the trailer door. We went to get out, but they were standing by the door. One of them was holding a big knife, and the other one holding a big stick. I pulled my carpet knife out from my bag. They were both about five foot eleven tall, very fat, and aged around thirty-five. I decided to give my knife to Rahim because I have two hands and thought I could defend myself. If they attack Rahim, he might not defend himself properly with one hand. He was shaking and scared.

"What should I do with this?" he asked.

"They are going to attack us, and you're asking me what to do with the knife. Just hold it and defend yourself. Hit them if they hit you. Come on, Afghan lion. You have to show me if you are the Afghan hero! Don't get down unless I tell you," I yelled at Rahim. I picked up some cans, holding them in my hand. They shouted at us. We were shouting at them. We didn't understand each other. I looked at them. They seemed more afraid than we did. We were shouting about half an hour at each other. They were telling us to get off; we were telling them to back off. Eventually somebody else pulled over. He got out of his car and walked toward us to find out what was going on. He said something in French. We all stopped shouting and listened to him. I didn't understand what he said. He looked at the driver who was holding the big knife, he ran to his car.

"Mr., Mr. Drive killing us, please help! Help! No go home," I shouted at him, and then I started to yell and scream at the driver again. I think the Frenchman went to call the police. About ten minutes later, I heard the police car. When I looked at the road, I saw it coming toward us. I grabbed the knife from Rahim's hand and put it back in my bag. I told Rahim to hold his one hand up, and I did the same. "Rahim, Rahim, be dumb, don't say anything," I shouted at him.

The police arrived. One of them pulled his gun out and pointed it at the driver and said something in French. He dropped the knife on the ground, and his mate dropped his stick. One of the police officers handcuffed them. They looked at us, we were holding our hands up, and they gestured at us to get down. I grabbed my bag and got down, and then I helped Rahim down. They searched us and found nothing, and then took us to their car. We sat down for about five minutes. I looked at the police, they were busy investigating the driver.

I looked at Rahim; he was sitting comfortably.

"We are sitting in a police car. You are not at Afghani Hotel in Greece. Get up, we are going to run for it. Hurry up," I shouted at Rahim.

"How we are going to do that?" he asked.

"Follow me!"

I opened the door very slowly and looked at the highway traffic. I thought for a moment which way we should run. If we followed the traffic, they would catch us with their car. We had to run against the traffic, I said to myself. We had to cross the highway.

I held Rahim's hand with my left hand and with my right hand carried our bags.

"We are going to run to the other side of the highway," I said.

Rahim was shaking and afraid. I watched the road very carefully. There were cars a very long distance away. I shouted at Rahim, "Run!" We ran to the little central wall, jumped over it, and ran to the other side of the road.

The cars looked very far off from where we were but reached us very quickly, much quicker than I had expected. They braked sharply while we were crossing the road, they made loud skidding noises and sounded their horns. The police looked at us, but could not run after us because we were on the other side of the road. They shouted at us to stop. We didn't take any notice. We kept running. We ran for about ten minutes. I heard a police car siren. We stopped and looked behind us, and I saw two police cars coming behind us. I grabbed Rahim and ran, dragging him to the other side of the road again. Cars were swerving, and horns were blaring. The drivers yelled at us. We kept running. The police stopped the traffic and ran after us. I shouted at Rahim to run faster. We ran very fast. A short while later, about three more police cars appeared. We stopped for a moment, and I looked around. We were surrounded by police, and the traffic was at a standstill.

CHAPTER 50

BAD LANGUAGE

I looked around to see if we could run away, but there was no way to escape from the police. I put my hands up before they told me. One of the younger policemen searched me and threw everything out from pockets and my bags. I had nothing with me; I did not even have a wallet. He said something in French I did not understand.

"English," I said.

"Where are you from?" he asked.

"We no from, we belong to Allah. Ask Allah," I said, but I think he did not understand me.

I meant, We have no country, we belong to Allah, ask Him.

He asked me again the same question, and I told him the same answer, and then he asked Rahim, "Where you are from?"

Rahim looked at me and said, "O m om." He tried to show them that he was dumb.

"He no talk, he no tongue, ask me," I said. I meant, He is dumb, he can't talk, ask me.

"Where are you going?" he asked.

"City, city, Paris."

"Oh, city," he said.

They took us to the police station. They searched us again and then put us in a room and locked us up. There were two beds and a toilet inside the room. The floor was cement, and the lights were low. We sat down on the beds.

"Look, if they isolated us, you must cry and show them your hand, don't let them take you away from me. Otherwise I can't help. When they come, I won't talk to you. We'll have communication by hands. Don't worry if you do not understand me. I will deal with everything. OK?" I asked.

"OK, I will do what you tell me, but please don't leave me alone."

"If I am alive, I will not leave you alone. Don't worry, we will take it as it comes. We have no choice."

We lay down on our beds. A short while later, they brought food for us, and some water. I put a blanket on the floor. We sat down on it and ate the food like in Afghani hotel in Greece. A few hours later, the same police officer, who had arrived the first time on the highway while we were arguing with the truck driver, took us to another room. One of the policemen was a very nice person, smiling, trying to be very friendly, and the other one was the opposite of him. They asked me a lot about our nationality. They wanted to know who we were. But I never told them. They asked where we had come from and where we were going. I made up two names and spelled them in English for them, and I told them we were students and were going to see our friends. I think they did not believe it.

They showed us on the Internet pictures of Middle East currencies and flags and images. They were asking me which one was our country or money or flag. I didn't tell them anything. About twenty-four hours later, the same police officer took us out to a police car and drove to the Iraq embassy. An Iraqi man from the embassy said something to me in Iraqis. I did not understand 80 percent of what he was saying. I began to talk with him in a mixture of languages, a little English, Turkish, Dari, Pashto, Persian, Urdu, and a few words in Greek. He did not understand me at all. He said something in French to the police. I listened very carefully and tried to understand what he was saying about us. The only thing I understood was that he mentioned Afghanistan, Iran, Pakistan, and India. I tried to think what he meant. He might have been saying that we were from one of those countries. Oh, this Iraqi man had given the police a good idea of where we came from. I decided to think what to say if they took us to another embassy. While I was sitting in the police car, Rahim was looking at me, wanting to say something, but because I told him to play dumb, he couldn't say anything. He laughed at me sometimes when I told the police rubbish.

They took us to the Iranian legation. "Salam, agha *khoshtib* (handsome), where about in Iran are you from?" a man asked in Persian.

I understood him very well. I did not speak Dari or Persian because I knew if I had spoken these languages, he would say I am from Iran or Afghanistan.

"I don't understand what you have said, fat man. I am a student, and I am going to see my friends," I said in mixture of English, Pashto, and

Urdu. He did not understand me and said, "Agha, you look like Iranian or
Afghani, but I am surprised that you are from another country, and you
don't understand Persian. I do not understand what you have said. *Bala
bala* something like that," he said in Persian. He said something in French
to the police, and then we left.

Next, we went to the Pakistan embassy. A man from the Pakistan
legation looked at us for a little while and began to talk. "Salam, how are
you doing? You are not looking like Pakistani at all. I don't know why they
brought you here."

I began to talk again in a mixture of languages and said, "I have a lot
friends in Greece, I called them, they were happy when they heard I had
arrived Paris."

He did not understand me, and he talked with police, and then we
left.

Next, we went to the Afghan embassy. Oh my god. How I am going to
deal with one of my own countrymen. What language should I speak with
them? "Oh, Allah, help me, please" I said.

"Salam countryman," a man from the embassy said.

He moved his hand to shake mine. I ignored to do it, and he said,
"Where did you come from?"

"I am sorry, I did not understand Afghani well," I said in Persian, with
accent of Tehran.

"Look, I am forty-two years old. I can tell that you are both from
Afghanistan. Don't pretend that you are Iranian. I understand your
problem. I know if I say you are from Afghanistan, they will deport you
back there. I know what it is like there at present. I like you because you
are smart and did not tell them your nationality. I will tell them that you
are not Afghan."

"Thank you, Kaka Jan, Allah grant all your wishes," I said in Dari.

He told the police that we were not Afghani, and he had no idea where
we came from.

I thanked Allah and smiled to Rahim. The police officer was really
angry and tired of taking us from one embassy to another. He drove off
angrily, then he pulled over in front of a train station. He turned to face us
and said in broken English, "Look, you are not from Iraq, Iran, Pakistan,
Afghanistan. Where are you from?" His face was very red and he shouted
at us and said, "You speak little English. Why are you not telling us where
you come from? You told us something about the truck driver, but when
we asked you where you were from, you do not answer us. I've tried to find

out where you are from. Are you from fucking America?" he snarled. He talked to his radio for a few minutes, and then surprisingly he opened the door for us and said, "Get the fuck out of this car. Go see your fucking friends." We got out and then he drove away.

"Policemen should not swear like that." I said to Rahim.

We went into the train station. I looked around. There were some benches, and we sat on one of them. We did not talk for a while. A few minutes later, four teenagers came in. I stood up and asked them how we could go back to Calais. There was no train directly there. We had to go to Paris, and then we could take the train to go there. We were very depressed, hungry, and very worried because we did not have enough money to buy tickets for the trains, but somehow we were very happy because we had been released by the police. I thanked Rahim because he did what I told him, and he thanked me because I saved him from deportation, and then we hugged each other three times. We were very proud of each other and promised to be always together. We shook hands and swore to Allah to be like brothers. We enjoyed being together.

"Rahim Jan, if we sit here until tomorrow, nobody will take us to Calais or give us some money. We will hope to Allah everything will be OK. Let's go and take the train without tickets. We don't have anything to lose."

"OK, lion brother," he said.

A short while later, we got on the train. After about two stops, the ticket collector came toward us and asked us for tickets. I looked at Rahim and said, "Can you deal with him?"

"No, lion brother, I am like a very weak fox right now," he said.

I laughed and stood up, scratched my head. I searched my pockets and then searched my bag.

"One minutes please," I said, looking at the ticket collector.

"Rahim, stand up. Check your pockets and then your bags, just pretend you are looking for the tickets, OK?"

"We do not have any tickets, why am I looking for them, lion brother?"

"Oh Allah, you never learn anything. I just want to waste his time." And then I said in English, "Hurry up, man."

I looked at the ticket collector; he seemed he to be in a hurry. He was an old man about five foot eight, with gray hair, and wearing glasses. He said something in French very angrily, which I did not understand, I just said to him, "OK, OK, Mister."

I took Rahim's bag and started to look for the tickets. Rahim looked at the old man and started to laugh and couldn't stop.

"Excuse me, Mr. Ticket, lost. No tickets."

He looked at me, groaning like an angry dog, and said, "Get out! Get out!"

"OK, Mister, no fight OK, OK," I said, Rahim was still laughing at him. There were some other passengers in the train; they began to talk with each other about us. The train stopped, and we got off.

"What you are laughing at?" I asked.

"We did not have any tickets, and you were looking like we really had one. The old man was very angry and waiting for tickets. I laughed at him because he was looking at his watch every second."

"I just wanted to take some time while the train was running. We passed two more stops since the ticket collector asked us for tickets," I said, and then we went to look at map on a wall to see how many stops were left to Paris. We checked it twice, there were about twelve stops.

"We came four stops for free," Rahim said laughing, and he mimicked the old ticket collector looking at his wrist watch. I started to laugh as well. A few minute later, we heard a train coming. It stopped at our station, and we got on very quickly.

CHAPTER 51

LONDON

After a few stops, a ticket collector asked us for tickets. Rahim showed his hand and said, "No tickets."

The ticket collector was a black man, he told us to leave to the train. When the train stopped, we got out, and there were some benches, and we sat down on one of them.

We were sad and did not talk. Another train came to our station, and we got on again. We decided not to stay in the same wagon as we entered because they could see us on the camera and find us easily. We walked toward to the end of train. We passed through two wagons and saw the ticket collector coming toward us. He caught us in the middle of a wagon. We told him the same as we had told them before. He asked us to get off. We got off the train and got onto another one. I started to think about finding another way to get to Paris. I remembered hiding myself in the washroom when we were traveling from Rome to Paris. I told Rahim to follow me when we got on the next train. We got on and went straight in a washroom together. It was very small; we hardly managed to both get in and lock the door. We waited there for a while, and then we got out and sat on the seats. The ticket collector could not find us to ask for our tickets.

Finally we arrived in Paris. We did not ask people how to get to the Calais because we remembered last time and had gone there easily. We did the same tricks all the way to Calais. Eventually about 11:00 p.m., we arrived there. We went out from the train station. The sky was very cloudy, and the weather was very windy and cold. We were very hungry and feeling cold, and were thinking what we should buy with our last ten Euros. We bought two packets of bread. It cost about four Euros and ninety cents. We were very happy with that because it was cheap and nice, and enough for two or three days if we ate them a little piece at a time. We decided to walk toward the docks and eat our bread while we were walking there. We wanted to get on the bus, but could not because we had to buy the tickets. We walked about an hour. There were claps of thunder. It seemed it would start raining. We did not take any notice because we were in a hurry to arrive at the docks and find a truck to get on.

Oh my god. A few minutes later, the sky started to rain very heavily, and there was lightning. We were running around to find a little shelter to keep out of the rain, but there weren't shops or houses nearby. We got very wet as if we had taken showers. We started to sing very loudly and asking Allah for help. We got lost, and there was nobody on the road to ask the way because of the storm. We kept walking. Eventually the rain stopped. We were very wet, and the weather was windy. We felt very cold and were shivering, and started to walk faster and got very tired and breathless. Still we could not find the docks. We took about a five-minute break and then continued walking. Eventually we found them. There were a lot of trucks. We did not know which one was going to England. I asked Allah for help. We picked one and hoped to Allah it was going to the UK. We got on very quickly and did the same trick as we had done on the other trucks. Inside, we put everything to one side just to make a little space to change our clothes. We took off our clothes and put them on top of some boxes to dry. We squeezed the rain out of them. I heard a police car siren. I did not care about it because I thought that it was going somewhere else. It was getting closer and closer. It stopped right by our truck. We were still busy drying our clothes. The driver opened the trailer door, and they got on, flashing their lights at our faces. We put our hands up. They told us to get out. They searched us and found some bread in our bags and some clothes, but nothing in our pockets. They checked the trailer and found nothing was stolen, everything was in order. It seemed the driver was sleeping in the cabin and noticed something while we were getting on. We had made some noise while moving the boxes from one side to the other. He thought we were thieves stealing his goods. I think he was afraid to check the trailer over by himself. They took us to the local police station and asked us what we were doing there. I showed them our wet clothes and told them we just got into the truck to get out of the rain. They asked us our names, DOB, and where we lived and what was our first language. I made up two names and DOB, and about the addresses, I told them I didn't know exactly, and I said, "Somewhere around Calais. We are students."

I told them my first language was Kady. It was not a name of a language. The Pakistani people call vehicles *kady*. They did not understand half the story I told them. They tried to find an interpreter, but they never found one. They put us in a room. A short while later, they brought us plenty of food. We ate some of it and put the rest in our bags, just in case we needed some later.

Next day, they took us to the reception. I thought they would take us somewhere else for further interviews. "You are free. You can go out," one of the police officers said, smiling.

I was surprised and could not believe it, "Are you joking with us?" I asked.

"No joke here in police station," he said, and then he opened the door for us to go. I shook his hand and said, "Thank you too much. You very good man."

"Merci," he said, and then we walked away. We thanked Allah for that night because we had had some good food and nice warm beds.

We went back to the dock to find a truck to get on. We walked inside the dock looking for a truck without fear of anyone. We liked French police because they never beat us and gave us some food, beds, and released us without any punishment. We got on a truck again and again. The police caught us and took us to the police station, gave us some food, and kept us for one or two days. We gave them false names each time, and then we went back to the docks and got on another truck.

We were about a month in Calais, getting on and off trucks. Eventually we got on the right truck; and the police didn't catch us. It went onto a ship. We were excited. The ship started to sail. A few hours later, the ship docked. We hid ourselves very quickly and thought there would be another security check in the UK, but there wasn't. About two hours later, I came out of my hiding place and helped Rahim to get out. We made ourselves ready and waited for the truck to pull over. Eventually it stopped. I got out from the trailer and jumped down. The driver was around and started to yell and scream at us. I did not take any notice. I helped Rahim, and then we ran away into a residential area. We heard the police cars coming. There was a public telephone on the sidewalk. I ran in, and I told Rahim to stay outside and act like he was waiting for the telephone. I picked up the receiver and held it on my ear. The police cars pulled over close by.

"How long have you been waiting here?" one the police officers asked Rahim in English.

Rahim was shaking and asked me, "Loin brother, what is he saying?"

I replaced the receiver and came out from the telephone box. "Excuse me, what you said?" I asked the police.

"Do you have any ID with you?"

"One moment please," I said, and then I started to search my pockets. He received a dispatch from somebody on his radio and said, "Come with me."

We followed him to his car. He took us to the police station. There, we sat on a bench. A short while later, a lady came and said, "You came with the truck to England. That's why we brought you here. Do you understand English?"

"I am a little English."

"What language do you speak? We can get you an interpreter that can help you."

I looked at Rahim and said, "We have arrived in England. They will help us. Be comfortable and talk freely."

"We speak Dari, Persian, Pashto, Urdu, and little English," I said, looking at police officer.

I think she did not understand what language that was.

"Where are you from?"

"Afghanistan," I said.

"Oh Afghanistan," she said, and then she walked away. A few hours later, they took us to another room and locked the door. After about seventy-four hours, they took us for an interview and brought a Persian interpreter. They told us what our rights were and how much help we could receive. They took our fingerprints and then took us to a refugee camp.

The refugee camp was very big, with about a hundred refugees from different countries. It was very beautiful. There was a church, mosque, restaurant, school, games room, and a huge space for playing football, volleyball, and other games. There were beautiful bathrooms, washing machines, lockers, big televisions, and a very huge living room. The camp was like heaven for us because all the facilities were free.

Next, we went to see the doctor just for a checkup.

After about a week, they gave us two tickets and told us they had arranged two beds for us in the Adelphi Hotel at Hasting, a town beside the sea, on the south coast. One of the immigration officers said, "The place is very beautiful, it is tourist town. Enjoy yourselves while you are there. We will send you letters to let you know if we want see you. I am going to give you a list of lawyers; you can get one of them. It is free for you. When you get there, somebody will tell you everything about Britain. Do you have any questions?"

The interpreter was one of my countrymen; he translated to me everything and told me I would be a good interpreter one day because I knew many languages.

I thanked him and said, "How can we go there?"

"Our driver will take you to a train station, and then you take a train to London. Get off there and go to another station called Charing Cross and get on the train to Hasting. Get off at the last stop. Someone will be there to take you to the Adelphi Hotel. You will be OK. Don't worry."

"I think we will get lost," I said.

The immigration officer laughed and said, "You'll never get lost. You came from Afghanistan all the way by yourselves. You are a very smart young man."

A few hours later, we left there.

The driver dropped us at the train station. We got on the train and got off in London.

"Welcome to London, the capital city of the world. I can't express my delight," I said to Rahim.

"Lion brother, I am happier than I have ever been in my life. People from the Middle East spend twenty thousand or more dollars to get here. I never dreamed that I would get here one day with only one hand and no money. We are in the capital city of the world, and we are the heroes of the world. Nobody can come to London the way we came with a little money and without a passport."

BOOK 4

Ali in Hasting UK standing beside the seaside.

CHAPTER 52

BESIDE THE SEA SIDE

Rahim hugged me, and we shook hands, and then went out from the train station for a walk. We had to find the other station, the Charing Cross, to catch the Hastings train. There were some big square black taxis waiting, but they would have cost money, so we walked for about five minutes, asking directions. The traffic was congested, and there were lots of red buses with two storeys, and there were lots of people everywhere. I think many of them were tourists. There were people there from all over the world. I knew which ones were Americans because they were photographing everything, and I had seen them in Tehran and Athens doing the same. I cannot describe how wonderful I felt. It was a lovely day, and the sun was shining. We bought a street map from a comical little stand. It was not a shop, it was a sort of kiosk on wheels selling all sorts of souvenirs and presents, mugs, tea towel, statues, figures of British policemen, guardsmen, and men dressed in historic costumes, which the stallholder said were "beef-eaters," but I don't know if he was joking me. The whole stand was decorated with red, white, and blue flags. We asked directions to get to the Charing Cross, but nearly everyone we asked was not from London either. As I spoke several Eastern languages, I asked anyone I thought was from the Middle East. At last, a man from Lebanon had a small café in one of the side streets, and we went in and had some falafel and chicken, and he gave us good directions. Then we found the Charing Cross train station very easily. I discovered that I could now read the timetable boards and screens in the station, so we found the platform and the train easily. "It is waiting for us," I told Rahim. When I looked at him, he had tears running down his face, which he wiped away quickly. We got on. There were only a few people already on it. We were happy and still could not believe that we had arrived in London. The train had tables, so we sat opposite each other and began to talk, everything we saw was something to talk about. Then we reminded each other about how we had got on the trains in France without tickets, and laughed all the way to Hastings. There were some other passengers in the compartment around us looking at us. We were laughing very loud and couldn't stop. Some of them were laughing at us, and others changed their seats and went away. We arrived in Hastings about 8:00 p.m. It was dark. There was a security guard waiting for us.

"Salam," he said. We shook hands; he was a fellow countryman. We went to the hotel, and he showed us to our rooms, they were beautiful. My room number was 101, and Rahim's was 109. Then he showed us the lounge, the TV room, and the small kitchen , where we could make some food for our supper. After that, we all had tea together, and he said (in Dari),

"Welcome to the Adelphi Hotel. I am going to tell you something about it. If you need help or have any questions, you can go to our office on the ground floor. There will be an Afghan security guard on duty every day, or you can contact 'migrant help.' Don't worry; you'll learn everything as you live here. We have about one hundred refugees in this hotel. They are all different nationalities. There are about ten to fifteen people from our country. The dining room will be open three times a day, and food will be served at certain times. You must be there during the opening hours; otherwise you will miss your food. If you have an appointment with immigration, or a doctor or lawyer, you have to let us know, and we'll keep some food for you. We'll give you cards every week, you can go to the post office and get twenty pounds. That is for you to do what you like with. Everything else is free here. Tomorrow, I will help you to find a lawyer or an English school to go to if you wish. If you need some clothes, migrant line will help you." He handed us keys and said good night, and then he walked away.

We went to our rooms. I made a list of what I should do next and what I would need for myself.

Next day, I woke up very early for morning prayers, and then I went for a walk. I felt elated walking along the long promenade in the sunshine, looking out to the south across the sea. I thought I could see France on the horizon, but it might have been low gray cloud. There were some small building on the promenade, which were only for sitting down, so I sat facing the sea. I thought about my uncle and how I could find him, and I wanted to phone all my friends, but I did not have any money to buy phone cards. I decided to call them when I received my weekly money from the government. I went back to the hotel to have my breakfast. I looked around for Rahim in the kitchen, but I could not find him there. I went to his room and knocked on the door. He opened it. He was still sleepy.

"Rahim jan, get ready for breakfast, otherwise you will miss it. Did you forget what the security guard told you last night?" I said.

"I will come in about five minutes."

I waited for him, and we went down to the kitchen together. There was a lot of food to choose from. I had some milk with bread for my breakfast, and then I went to the security guard's office and asked them how I could find my uncle. They gave me the address of the migrant help, which was near the rail station. Rahim and I went to find it. We kept asking people until we got there. There was a very beautiful English girl in the reception.

"How can I help you?" she asked.

"I am a little English, OK?"

"Don't worry, we have an interpreter. Where are you from?"

"Afghanistan."

She phoned somewhere and got a Dari interpreter on the phone.

"I want to find my uncle. He is in England somewhere, and I have his telephone number, but it is not working."

I read the telephone number from my memory to him, and I said my uncle's name. He relayed it to the receptionist, and she dialed the number and found it was disconnected. I think she called the telephone company and talked to a representative for about ten minutes. She explained my situation to them. Eventually she got the new phone number for my uncle. We ran back to the hotel. There were lots of phones free to use for local calls. I chose one, dialed my uncle's number.

"Hello," he said.

"Hello," I said.

"Who is this?" he asked in English.

"This is Ali, Uncle?" I said in Dari, and then he began to talk Dari too.

"Where are you calling from?"

"A country called England, and town called Hastings, a hotel called Adelphi, room 101."

He did not believe it, he said, "Wait there, I will be there in about two hours, and here is my mobile number in case you need it."

"OK, see you later."

We went to the living room to watch TV.

"I have not seen him for a long time. I don't know what he looks like," I said to Rahim.

"When did you see him last?" he asked.

"Oh, I can't remember. I think I was about seven years old."

We watched TV for a while, and then we went to put our nice shirts on. We wore the same shirts, which I bought from the Greek tailoring company I used to work for. We went outside and waited for him in front of the hotel. He came after about two hours and went inside. We did not recognize each other.

He asked the security guard about me. They told him to wait in the living room. Three hours passed.

I wondered where he was. We went to call him again on the phone. "Where are you?" I asked.

"I've waited for you about an hour in the living room," he said.

"I was standing in front of the main door waiting for you, but I have not seen you. I'll come there in a second."

We went to the living room to see him. There were some other people sitting on a sofa. I expected a tall, big man. I looked around. He stood up. I was much taller than him. He said, "Are you Ali?"

"Is that you, Uncle?" I replied. We hugged each other, and then I introduced Rahim to him.

He was surprised. He told me the last time I had talked to him was from Iran a long time ago. That meant it was just before I started my journey. He told me that I looked like my father. We talked for a while, and then he invited us to London for little holiday. He checked with the hotel manager and asked their permission and gave his address and contact details. Then we got in his car and went.

He took us to a very beautiful Afghani restaurant for dinner. Next day, we went to a zoo and a cinema. We were there for two days at his house. He took to us to the most beautiful places in London, and then we went back to Adelphi Hotel in Hastings. About a week later, I joined English language classes at Hastings College. From 9:00 a.m. to 1:00 p.m., I was in school. After lunch, I finished my homework. Then Rahim and I, with other refugees, went to play football in a park.

Two weeks later, immigration gave Rahim a beautiful house in Birmingham City, which was about two hundred miles away. Because he had only one hand, they took more care of him than they did ordinary men. He was to have a housekeeper, an attendant care-cleaner, and some other extra help. I felt very lonely after he had left the Adelphi Hotel. He was always really good company, and I had enjoyed being with him. I learned something while traveling to the UK. One day you meet people, and one day you lose them. It might be sooner or later.

The first few days after he had gone were hard for me. Then I met new people at the school, playing football, and at the hotel. A short while later, I had made about ten good friends, Afghani, Irani, Iraqi, and a black man from Africa, whose name was unpronounceable, so I called him "One Clock." I called him this because one Saturday night I was watching a movie with my friends, one of my friends wanted to go to the washroom, but because the movie was interesting, he waited until the last moment. When the movie stopped for commercials, he ran to the washroom. One Clock had left ten seconds before he left. The washroom light wasn't working that night. One Clock was in the cubicle behind the door, trying to take his jeans off. My friend banged the door very hard. One Clock was facing the door, and it hit his head hard. His head was swelled up. Next day when I asked him what happened, he told me it had happened one clock the night before. I could not remember his name, but I remembered the incident, and after that day, I nicknamed him "One Clock."

CHAPTER 53

BACK TO BUSINESS

The food served in the hotel was mostly English food, but because I was not an English person, I didn't enjoy it. I asked several times if we could have more spicy food sometimes. A lot of people had complained, but management did not take any notice. A person from a different country prefers food that is typical of his nation. There was no way I could have my favorite food. Every day, I was free after lunch and decided to find a part-time job and make some money to buy some of my own kind of food.

I searched Hastings for a tailoring job, but I could not find one. One day after school, I went to a little town called Bexhill with one of my friends. It was twenty minutes from Hasting by train. We searched, but we could not find a tailoring company, but we found a pizza shop, which needed flyer distributors. I thought I would work there because I had no alternative. They gave me twenty-five pounds and a free dinner for a thousand flyers. So every day after school, I went straight to work, but it took me about forty minutes walking to get there.

One of the pizza drivers took me every day to an area, where I put flyers in each house. I started my work at 2:00 p.m. and finished 7:00 or 8:00 p.m. It was up to me how fast I did it. I tried my best to drop more than a thousand flyers a day, but it was a very hard job, I could not do more than a thousand.

The first week, my boss was spying on me to find out how I was working. When he found out that I was honest and punctual, he gave me three pounds more than the other people who worked as flyer men. A few days later, I found out the other flyer men threw half of their flyers in the garbage bin. I think my boss gave me three more pounds extra because I never threw any flyers away. I was happy and enjoyed working there for a while because I could not find another job.

One day I had an appointment with the immigration department somewhere in London. On the way, returning home, I went buy a telephone card. There was a table in front of a shop selling telephone cards, cigarettes, and so on. A Pakistani man was the seller. I gave him ten pounds and asked for a card. He gave one card and six pounds back. I bought the same card in Hastings fur five pounds, so I bought two more cards. He told me if I bought ten cards, he would give me one card for free. I bought twenty-five cards, and he gave me four cards for free. I went home.

After dinner, I told all my friends and other people that I had cards to sell. The shop was selling them for five pounds. I was selling them for four pounds, fifty pence. In about two hours, I had sold all of them, and still people wanted more. I went to my room and counted my money. I had made about a hundred and eight pounds, something like that. Oh my God, in two hours, I had about twenty-eight pounds. I was very happy because I worked at the pizza shop for six or seven hours and made the same money. I thought for a while I had worked for about three months there and saved about five hundred pound. I decided to quit my job and go to London next day and spend all my money buying cards.

Next day, I woke up very early for the Morning Prayer. When I finished, I went to the train station. I got to London about 9:00 a.m. I went to find the same man. It took me two hours because one time I got on the wrong train. Eventually I found him. We talked for a short while and made a good deal. I bought cards for three pounds and eighty pence. I got all the cards and counted them three times and hid them in my underwear.

I sold them in two days and told people if they needed more, they could catch me after 7:00 p.m. in my room, otherwise I would be around the hotel. I made about a hundred and twenty pounds. I was excited. There was a Turkish and Afghani restaurant nearby. I went there and had my lunch and dinner most days. I spent 50 percent of my income enjoying myself. I went to London and bought some more cards. The man told me that he had a friend, who brought him cigarettes from France, half price, because they don't pay taxes. Stores were selling the same cigarettes for five pounds, and he sold them for three pounds a packet, but only to people he knew. He told me he would sell me a box, which had ten packets of cigarettes, for only twenty pounds. I said that I had decided to buy two boxes, if he would agree that if I could not sell them, he would buy them back. He agreed with my decision.

I put them in my bag and went to home. I hid some of the cards and cigarettes in my pillow. I took four packets of cigarettes and some cards and went to the front of the hotel to sell them. I sold cigarettes for three pounds and fifty pence a packet. People were happy with me because I gave them a little discount sometimes and treated them well. I made a lot more friends and became friendly with the security guards and hotel staff. They bought cigarettes and cards sometimes from me. My business got bigger each time I went to buy some more. People started to come to my room during the evening. I got more customers if I stayed inside my room than if I went around the hotel, so I stayed in my room to study and run my business. A few months later, I had made two thousand pounds, and I finished the level one English course and passed the exam.

There was an old man from my country, who had lived in the Adelphi for about six years. The immigration department had not given him papers. He was still waiting and hoping to Allah to get them one day. He did not like going to school and was always in his room. He came to my room to buy cigarettes or telephone cards.

One day I took him to an Afghani restaurant for dinner. I told him if he could stay in my room selling my stuff, instead of sitting to his room thinking a lot and swearing about immigration not giving him papers, I would give him ten pounds and free cigarettes just for himself. He agreed and thanked me for such a good deal. I trained him for two days and told him to look through the spy glass in the door each time anyone came to buy something. "Get the money first and then give them what they want, and don't let more than one person in at a time," I said. I brought a coffee table into my room and made a display of different cigarettes and cards on it, so customers could point to whatever they wanted because he could not remember the names of them. I made it very easy for him, and gave him free cards to call his family, and brought him his favorite food sometimes from the Afghan restaurant. He was very happy and enjoyed doing the job. After the school, I put some cigarettes and telephone cards in my bag and went around the beach and the caravan sites and tourist places to sell them.

Every night I counted my money just to find out how much we had made. The old man was doing very well. I gave him five extra pounds to stay in my room all night, which meant I could go out with my friends and sleep in his room. He accepted this happily. On the weekend, I took my best friends out for dinner, and then all of us went to a night club. I enjoyed being with my friends and having fun. They liked me very much because I had a lot of money and spent some on them.

One day the manager put a letter in my mailbox. I tried to read it, but I did not understand what was written. I took it to the security guard, and he read it to me and said the manager wanted to see me regarding my business. I went to his office on the appointed time. He called one of the security guards for translation help because my English was not good.

"I have heard that something is going on in your room. Could you explain what it is and why?" the manager said, and the security guard translated.

"Nothing to cause a problem. I have complained many times about the food. I do not like it very much. Nobody took any notice. My uncle gave me a little money to spend while I am here, but it was enough for only a couple of days. I used my money to buy telephone cards and resell them here, just to make some money to buy Afghan food for myself. Since I started this job, I have not complained about the food because I go out to eat, and I help the old man who is tired of having to eat English food for the last six years."

"Food has nothing to do with what I am talking about," he said. "You are not allowed to have a shop in this hotel."

"I do not have a shop," I said defensively. "I only sell some phone cards and some packets of cigarettes, and my friends like it, I do not cause any trouble."

"You are not allowed to do it," he said.

"It is very convenient for all the refugees, nobody has complained about it. I am selling them much cheaper than anywhere else."

"I am not interested in the prices you sell as that is not the point, you must not sell anything to the refugees, do you understand?" He looked at me while the man told me what he said in my language.

"I don't just sell to the refugees, even most of the staff working here think it is a good idea."

The man told him what I said, and he seemed to be getting angry.

"What—I—am—telling—you—is—that—you—are—not—allowed—to—do—it, and you are telling me it is good and convenient."

"Look, I don't make any trouble for anyone. I am just supporting myself, and I have not taken my weekly money from the government because I don't like to depend on them. I am going to school every day, and I finished level one, and I complied with immigration rules. I have never missed my appointments. I just like to work and support myself."

He glared at me. "You must not sell anything to anyone!" he shouted.

"I will stop selling them if you give me my favorite foods, then I will eat whatever is cooked for dinner," I offered.

"You are not in this office to bargain with me!" he seemed to be trying to calm himself down.

"Do you want me to stop it and join the gangsters selling drugs, or robbing people to support myself, or fighting with your staff asking them for good food, like the other people are doing in this hotel. If you go to the kitchen one night, you will see people fighting and swearing because they don't like the food, or there was not enough of it for everyone, and so on. People are throwing the food on the floor and breaking plates and cups sometimes. I don't do any of that. I am a good boy. I stay in my room and study English."

I talked to him for about an hour; he spent most of the time with his elbows on his desk, his hands holding his head, behind him the security guard had a wide grin on his face, I did not think the manager should get as excited as that. He would make himself ill. Eventually he said "no problem," because I had a good record there.

I had a very good time for a while, and then the manager gave everyone notice to leave the hotel because there was too much violence, and the police were called every day. The residents of that area complained to their MP. They all wanted the Adelphi Hotel to be shut down.

I had only two weeks to sell all the cards and cigarettes and had to find another job and rent a house or a little apartment and so on. First of all, I sold all the cigarettes and cards a little cheaper. I had only four days left to find somewhere to live. I searched Hastings. I looked at some bachelor's flats. It was hard to stay there because there was no job. There were jobs, but not in my profession. I had only one day left. I could not make a decision about what to do. I called my uncle. He gave me lots of excuses that his house was small and there were no jobs in London. I asked him to let me stay with him just until I found a house. He was not pleased to let me stay with him; because of that, I did not like him much.

I called Rahim on the phone. I explained the situation to him. He was so excited and told me I was very welcome to come to his house. I got his address, and he told me that he would meet me in the New Street Station in the center of Birmingham upon my arrival. After I rang off, I said to myself, "I should have called earlier." I went home and packed everything. I woke up very early and went to the station to buy a ticket to London.[3]

---

[3].   While living in Hastings, England, I made many friends. The people at the Adelphi Hotel were mainly refugees like myself, and some evenings in the lounge, we traded stories about our journeys from our homelands to the UK. I have described some of my experiences in my story here, but I have left out some of the more unpleasant incidents because I have been glad to forget them, or because they would not make comfortable reading. (After all, who wants to read a catalogue of total misery?) As Abbas always said, life has its ups and its downs. What my new friends were telling me about things that had happened to them reminded me of things I had put to the back of my mind, and it made me very thankful that we had gotten to London safely. I knew well, almost firsthand, what went on, and still does go on, in some of the capital cities on the routes we took across many countries, on our journeys where unprincipled people preyed on defenseless young refugees, taking advantage of their desperation and poverty.

For example, living in Athens, Greece, refugees were not only afraid of being caught without papers by the police, but also another danger was that some people deliberately set out to take advantage of them. They offered half-starved young women and men nice, warm shelter for the night, and food and some money, but the price was sex. They knew that many of the young travelers were alone and frightened. Sometimes these predators hung around the big church in Victoria Park, Athens, because it was well known for giving out food and clothing to refugees. These people knew they would find vulnerable young people there, who were short of money and had nowhere to live, and that they were desperate enough to accept the offers of help. Even very old men and sometimes women preyed on refugees. Rahim, my best friend, had submitted to being sexually abused and had been virtually raped because he was not physically strong, had no money, couldn't work. He was deeply ashamed about what had happened to him. The same things had happened to many others. Pathetic sex acts were performed down dark alleyways just to get the price of a pizza and a coffee. When we heard such stories being related by other hotel residents, tears ran down from Rahim's eyes, and he would be awfully upset for hours.

Our journeys were very hazardous. People-smuggling was, and still is, big business. These organized gangs made good money out of the sad people in their care. Some knew their work well and treated the refugees fairly, but others were nothing better than vicious gangsters. Each refugee meant only one thing to them, money. They seemed to think of themselves as being free to do whatever they liked and were beyond any form of law. They knew their pathetic cargo, the people they were exploiting, could not complain about them whatever they did because they could not risk going to the police for fear of police brutality and corruption, and the refugee's biggest fear was repatriation to the countries they were fleeing from.

There were many incidents of people disappearing on their journey. It is fact that many people drown in the sea when crossing from Turkey to Greece. I remember Amin, the Athens hotel owner, reading out to us an article in the news paper about smugglers who overloaded a boat with refugees, and it sank, drowning everyone. Sometimes smugglers converted old petrol tankers to hold refugees, this was to avoid police attention, but if they placed too many people inside them, they died for the lack of oxygen. Family members got separated from each other during journeys because smugglers would send the men to one room and the women to another on the excuse of decency (like Sahar. the girl I met in Turkey). Many other people attempted to cross the English channel by truck, by holding themselves under the wagons, some died from falling under the vehicle's wheels. Others died attempting to jump aboard moving trains heading into the channel tunnel, which joins the UK to France.

Thousands of refugees never completed their journey. Many of them used false passports and were caught by the authorities. They spent years in prison and were then deported back to their home countries. Despite knowing of these dangers, people risked everything to try to come to the west to save their lives. No one was pleased to leave behind their families and friends, but it was better than dying from starvation or living under the Taliban's oppression.

CHAPTER 54

RAHIM COMPLETE

I arrived in Birmingham at about 4:00 p.m. and phoned Rahim. He told me to wait at the front of the station. He arrived after twenty minutes with two hands. He was wearing a blue shirt and sunglasses, and his hair was cut very nicely. I did not recognize him until he took his sunglasses off.

"Is that Rahim?" I asked in English.

"Yes, lion brother," he said. We shook hands and hugged each other twice.

We walked to the bus stop. He was putting a little weight on and looked fresh and was so excited. We talked all the way to his house. He had a very beautiful small house. A short while later, he brought tea with some sweets.

"I have a very good news, lion brother," he said.

"What is it?" I asked.

"I had a call from my lawyer this morning. His interpreter said the immigration is going to give my papers."

"Oh thanks Allah, congratulations, Rahim agha. I am very glad for you. You look very complete now, and you have a good artificial arm," I said.

"Ali jan, I remember all your help. I remember no one helped me in the world except you. You brought me here, and you gave me this wonderful life."

"No, Rahim agha, you helped me too. You made us laugh all the way from Greece to England," I said.

I told him about my business in the Adelphi Hotel. We laughed a lot. He told me what he was doing in Birmingham. He was attending English classes; he had become a full-time student. His English was a little better than mine in writing and spelling, but in speaking I was better, and he wanted to become an interpreter. I encouraged him to keep it up. I had made a lot of money from my business, and so I wanted to give a party to celebrate him getting his papers so quickly. I think he had good evidence for the immigration to show that it would be dangerous for him if he returned to Afghanistan. Whatever it was, I was so proud of myself and happy that I had helped him to get on with his life. Because of that little help, Allah made him love me like a brother, and we were the very best of friends. He wanted to give a party himself, but he did not have enough money. I organized things and spent about four hundred pounds on the party, and I bought him some presents.

He had about twelve friends, and his friends brought their friends. We were altogether about twenty people. We made plenty different kinds of kebabs, and *Qabli blow*, salads, fruits, and so on. Rahim had already told them all about me. However, he introduced them to me. His living room was too small for twenty people to sit on sofas. We took everything out and sat down on the floor, like we did in Afghani hotel in Greece. After the dinner, I went around and asked them if anyone knew of a place for rent and a tailoring company that wanted workers. There was a tailor at the party, his name was Sabur. He was working with another Afghan man in the center of Birmingham. He knew a lot of tailoring companies. I got the address of where he was working and some other tailoring companies. After the dinner, Rahim and I brought tea for everyone. About an hour later, we all started to dance. I enjoyed the party and got a good idea of where to look for a job. About 2:00 a.m., the party broke up. They all went to their homes. Rahim thanked me for everything. We talked about ten minutes and then went up to the bedroom. Rahim had only one bed. He changed the sheets and told me to sleep in it.

"No, Rahim agha, you sleep in your bed. I will sleep on the floor," I said.

"There is no way for me to sleep there. You are my lovely brother and lion; this is your bed as long as you are here. If you don't sleep there, I will be very mad. Please sleep in it," he said.

"OK, Rahim brother, thank you very much for that," I said.

I slept there; he went to sleep on the living room sofa.

Next day was Sunday. We went to the park and played football with Rahim's friends and his classmates. On Monday, first, we went to find a place for me to live because Rahim's house was too small for both of us. In about a week, I rented a bachelor's flat and bought a new mobile phone, and secondhand TV, sofas, bed, lunch table, microwave, and so on. One day Rahim and I, with some of our friends, went to the Sunday market in Birmingham city center. I looked around and found a bicycle for twenty pounds. I took a little ride, it was very nice, so I bought it. Rahim sat on the crossbar, and I rode it all the way to his home through the Sunday traffic. I dropped him off there, and then I went to my own place. I made myself ready for the next day to go to some tailoring companies, looking for a good job. I woke up very early and took shower, I was nice and smart. I put on a new T-shirt and left home. I found many companies. They all gave me application forms to fill in. I looked at one of them and tried to fill it in by myself, but I could not understand what the questions meant. I called Rahim, he said his English was not yet good enough. Then I called Sabur, the tailor I had met at the party, he said he could not do it properly either. I asked him if his boss could do it.

"Don't ask about him. He needs someone to fill his form for him as well. Hey, don't worry, we have an English friend, his name is Mr. John. He comes here sometimes and reads the boss' letters to him and drinks some Afghan chai. I think he will be coming today about 4:00 p.m. You can come here and wait for him. He is OK, he will do it for you," he said.

The small business where Sabur worked was somewhere in a shopping mall in Birmingham city center. I cycled there much quicker than I had expected. There are many old industrial canals in that city, and I was able to cycle along the tow paths from the suburbs, where I was living, right into the center of the city. The tow paths were deserted for most of the way. In the city, the canal passed close to a massive stadium building called the National Indoor Arena, and here there was a junction of canals. They are much wider at this point. This area was all new luxury apartment buildings with first-rate restaurants and bars facing on to the canals. There were brightly painted barges known as narrow boats, which had once been industrial barges but were now holiday hire boats, and some people were living in them. Following the directions Rahim had given me, we (me and my bike) left the canal and took a short road into a big tiled square where there was a beautiful concert hall and a busy main road called Broad Street. The canals I had left five minutes ago had been deserted and quiet, now I was in a typical city center full of people, cars and buses (double-deckers), and noise; there were flower gardens and fountains and shops and banks everywhere. I found the right mall and locked my bicycle outside with others. Sabur, when I found him, was very busy repairing clothes on his sewing machine; I helped him on another machine until Mr. John arrived. Sabur introduced us. "My name is Ali, nice to meet you," I said.

"I'm John," he answered, and we shook hands.

I talked to him for a little while, and Sabur asked him to fill in my form for me.

"Mr. John, I can't speak English very well, and hardly can read or write. I came from Hastings, and I am looking for a job. I've got some application forms from tailoring companies. I am hoping to work soon," I said.

"You'll be fine. You speak good English, I don't have any problem understanding you."

He filled up all the application forms and explained every single word for me. I was so happy meeting him because he was pleasant and friendly, and I did not have any communication problems, I understood him easily, and he understood me. I thanked him a lot and then went home. Next day, I went to one of the bigger tailoring companies in the suburb and asked to see the boss.

"How can I help you?" the boss said in English with a thick Indian accent. I handed him the application form. He asked me to follow him to his office. We sat on the chairs, while he read it. Looking at me, he said, "You are very young. You might have just finished high school. You don't know anything about tailoring, I think. The job is very easy if you know what to do. My company is very big. We make different types of clothing."

I said, "I have only one question. Do you need a tailor or not?"

"Yeah, of course we need."

"OK, good, let me make you some samples. You will see if I know anything about tailoring or not. If you don't like my work, I will go away," I said.

"OK, I will call the supervisor, go with her, she will give some samples."

I went with her to the workshop. The sewing machines were the same as in Greece. The machinists sat in lines one after another, exactly like in Greece. People got hourly pay. I cleaned my machine while waiting for the supervisor to bring me some work. She was a good-looking woman from India. Her English was the same as mine, but I had no problem with her because her first language was Urdu. She showed me what she wanted me to do, and then walked away. The work was very easy for me, however I asked Allah for help and worked as fast as I could. I was pressing the accelerator all the way down. It was making a bit of a noise. The other machinists were looking at me, surprised.

CHAPTER 55

Mr. John

I worked for about four hours, and then the manager called me to go to his office. I went there.

"I spoke to the supervisor about you. You are fine. You can work for us, from tomorrow. You need to bring two pieces of identification with you and your bank account information, because we'll pay your wage directly into your account," he said.

"I don't have a bank account," I said.

"You can open one easily. We can't pay cash. You must have one. You can use a family member's account while you are getting your own. Because you seem a fast tailor, I will make an exception in your case."

I went to Rahim's home, on the way I bought some chicken with fries for lunch. Rahim had two bank accounts; he gave me one of them to use until I got mine ready. The factory work was from Monday to Friday, so the next Saturday I went to the town center to open a bank account. I was thinking my English was not good enough to do that. I went to Sabur's workplace to see if Mr. John would help me because he was the only English person who I understood and who understood me. I was very lucky that day, I found him in front of the workshop where Sabur worked.

"Hello, Mr. John. How are you?" I asked.

"Hello, how did you get on with your job?" he asked.

"I got the job. Thank you very much for your help filling in that form."

"You're welcome, I like Afghans," he said.

I wanted to ask him to help me to open a bank account but was afraid to tell him. I thought he might be busy. Looking at him, I decided to ask him, to see what happened, and said.

"Excuse me, Mr. John, I want to open a bank account. Can you come with me please?"

"Of course, when do you want to go?" he asked.

"Today please."

"Now?"

"Yes, please,"

"Let's go," he said.

We went to the bank; there was a lady in customer service. I told her that I wanted an account number. "Fine," she said.

I handed my document to her, she told us to wait for a moment. We waited for a little while, and then she came back and said, "Sorry, we can't open an account for you. Your document is not enough to do that."

Mr. John pulled his glasses from his pocket and put them on. He looked at my document and said, "He can. Why can't he have one?" And then he talked to them for a short while, and she took my document to the manager. She came back and said, "OK, you can. Take a seat please; someone will be with you shortly."

I was so happy and thanked Mr. John a lot.

"You are right, you can open an account. They are wrong."

A short while later, a very beautiful English girl came over and said, "My name is Victoria, nice to meet you." We shook hands, and I said, "My name is Ali; this is Mr. John, friend of me. He is here to help me in case if I had English problem." She did not understand what I was saying, but they shook hands, and we followed her to her desk. She asked some questions, I did not understand her. Mr. John explained everything very clearly, I understood him very well. The both of them were speaking English. I did not understand that lady, but I understood Mr. John as if he was speaking like my first language.

It was uncanny. I understood what he said, and he understood me, although neither of us could speak each other's language. He did a great job answering all her questions. It took us about an hour. Eventually we finished. I thanked Mr. John a lot, and then we went and had coffee together. I like him. I got his phone number and gave him mine, and then I went home very pleased. From that day, we became good friends. I gave my account number to my boss and returned Rahim's bank card. After a month, my boss gave me a little raise.

One day, Mr. John called on my cell phone, said he had a temporary Saturday job, if I wanted it, at the company where he was working as a supervisor. I was working Monday to Friday with the tailoring company and worked Saturday and sometimes Sunday with Mr. John. There were other Afghan young men working there. After work, we used to talk together. If we had any problems with English, or we did not understand anything, if we had letters that needed explaining, or forms to fill in, Mr. John always made time for us. He was a wonderful man. We even asked him about our own very personal problems. We were teenagers who were turning into men, but had no older experienced men who we could talk to. One of our main problems was girls. We could hardly speak English; we were from a country where young men were not allowed even to talk to young women who were covered from head to foot in clothes. Here in the UK, women dressed in anything, showing as much of themselves as they wished. We, being passionate Afghans, I cannot tell you what it was like to see what we most wanted, but did not know how to go about getting. Mr. John got bombarded with questions about women. He always answered our questions straightforwardly. I would have found it embarrassing to answer some of the things he was asked. He was not. His advice was good. We trusted him. Whatever problems we had, he always kept them to himself. Among other things, I wanted to know how to get girlfriends. He looked at me and said, "You need to get a bit of muscle; girls love boys with good arms, how about going training?"

One Saturday after the work, Mr. John talked to me again about a gym and bought some supplements because I was very skinny. He encouraged me to go and work out every day after my work, and told me if I had any problems to tell him. I liked his company a lot, although we never met socially. I have traveled all over the world, but I never saw a wonderful man like him. "God accepted my prayers and helped to find Mr. John, " I said to myself.

From that day, my enjoyment began. Every weekend, I went to work with Mr. John. After work, we had a talk. I did not like going to the gym a lot, but he really encouraged me, so I went. We checked and wrote down my measurements every Saturday morning. I had really good time with my Mr. John. We went shopping, to the library and coffee shops every weekend. He helped me a lot with language, and any other problems I had. He was always happy and made me laugh a lot.

After a while working with the tailoring company, I became a quality controller. I was making pockets most of the time. One day, the supervisor brought me some very special pockets to make. I made them very easily, much nicer and cleaner than the other tailors. The customer came, checked their order and found that the pockets were made differently. They liked my job very much and told my boss that their order should be made in the same way as I had done. My boss called me to his office and gave me a raise and said, "Teach the other tailors to do the same as you do."

One of Rahim's friends got his resident papers. He gave a party and invited us. At the party, I met a businessman, who was looking for tailors, part time or full time. I talked to him about his business, and he asked me if I could work for him.

"I am working Monday to Friday with a tailoring company and Saturday with Mr. John. Sunday, I am free sometimes, if you want, I can work for you."

"OK, come this Sunday and see if you like the job," he said.

I went there and offered to make a sample for him. He said I was professional tailor, so I didn't need to make a sample. The job turned out to be very easy, and I had more fun because we were dealing with beautiful girls. Also I made good money.

Sometime after I arrived in Birmingham, my funny uncle Nassir phoned from London, saying that he wanted to meet me, and we arranged to meet. He called me on my cell phone when he arrived in Birmingham. I met him and took him to my home. He was surprised when he saw my house was so nice and clean, and everything was brand new. I told him about my job and Mr. John. He told me I was lucky to meet him.

"Ali Jan, I am here today to tell you some good news. I have a good friend, and I showed your picture to his daughter. I told them about how wonderful you are, and you came all the way from Afghanistan to England by yourself. His daughter is a very beautiful girl. I would like you to get married with her. I have heard stories about you going to nightclubs and drinking. You are not allowed to do that. I am your uncle. Your father is dead, so I am the head of the family. You have to do what I tell you. I know you are a big man now, going to the gym. I can't force you physically to do things, like in the old days when you were a little boy, but if you don't listen to me, Allah will dislike you."

"Look, you are telling me you are my uncle? And you want me to do what you tell me? Where were you when I needed you? Where were you when I was sleeping on the street with no money? Where were you when I was traveling on the train without tickets? Why did you change your phone number? Why didn't you let me to stay with you when the hotel was getting closed and I was very worried? You never helped when I needed you. Now you see I have a good job and have a lot of friends. I am young; I have had really bad times in the past. Now I am having good times and want to enjoy my life. I will get married . . . when I find a girl I love. Look, you are only a little man and have never been a good uncle. Don't do something stupid before I hate you. Go back to your home and don't think about me getting married. Let me alone to have some fun while I am young," I said.

We went out for dinner. He talked all night about marriage and said, "You have to get married soon and have some children. I am going to talk with the girl's parents."

"I won't get married to someone I don't love, someone I don't even have an idea of how she looks. Forget about the old days and people getting married without seeing each other," I said.

"We are Afghan. We must not forget our traditions, our culture, and our religion. I am the eldest in the family."

"That is not the issue. You are changing the subject. Look, I am not the little boy you knew in the old days. I am old enough to decide what is right and wrong, and remember, we are not living in the east, we are in the west."

He made me feel so sad that night. I was enjoying my life and I had three good jobs, and I worked out five nights at the gym. Saturday mornings I was with Mr. John and had good fun. My funny uncle Nassir interrupted my life and started calling me every day on the phone, saying things that made me very sad.

I worked for about fourteen months with the tailoring company and my other part-time jobs. I saved a lot of money in that period. I decided to start up my own business and spoke to my Mr. John and told him that I had had a business in Iran, and I wanted to have the same in Birmingham.

He said, "Good idea, I will help as much as I can."

Mr. John and I went to find out about how we could start a little tailoring business. He had a lot of business friends, he told me he would ask them and let me know.

Monday when I came back from my work, I checked my mail. There was a letter from the immigration department. I opened it. The immigration rejected my asylum claim and asked me to leave the United Kingdom in about a month. Otherwise they would deport me back to my country. I could not believe it.

I called my lawyer, and he said, "Don't worry; it's happening to all refugees these days. We can appeal against deportation again and again."

That night I could not sleep at all. I was so worried in case my funny uncle did something stupid like arranging a marriage for me in London. I woke up late and was two hours late for my job. I did not talk to anybody because I was so depressed. I broke three needles, one of them went through in my finger. I started to ask all my co-workers if anyone knew a people-smuggler because I was going to leave the country. Later, a close friend gave me a telephone number.

CHAPTER 56

I AM CONTRABAND AGAIN

I rang the smuggler up. He was an Iranian. He asked to see me, and he said I would tell me everything in person. He could not trust anyone talking over the phone. I got his address; it was somewhere in London.

Next day I woke up very early and went to London by coach. At about 2:00 p.m., I found the apartment building where he lived. At the main door, I buzzed his number. He told me to come to the second floor.

"Salam agha, did you find me easily?" he asked.

"I can't complain, you know what London is like," I said.

Then he brought me a glass of orange juice, and said, "OK. I don't like talking over the phone because one of my partners went jail for five years. It is a very long story. I won't take your time because you're got to back home tonight. Which country do you wish to go to?" he asked.

"Somewhere, away from my funny uncle, he is going to make me marry someone, whom I have never seen."

I told him about my problems with immigration.

"There are only three countries accepting refugees at the moment, Canada, Australia, and America. I think Canada is the best country for you."

"I don't know anything about these countries at all. Anyway, because of funny uncle, I will choose Canada," I said impulsively. "Tell me how much it is going to cost, and how long will it take. How are you going to take me there?"

"We will make a British passport for you. It will cost you about five thousand pounds for everything. If you give me some money today, and your picture, we have a man who works for the government, he will make you your passport in about a week's time. You go back to Birmingham, and

I will phone you when it is ready. Then we can make arrangements with you about when you want to leave, and then I will buy your ticket for that date. You can go to Canada in about a week if you wish."

"That sounds very fast. Look, I came from Afghanistan. I know about smugglers lying to people. I am not saying that you are the same. You look like a good man. Tell me the truth. How much time do you really need to do all that?"

"About a week, as I said. It depends on you. You have to make up your mind when you want to go, and how soon you can provide us with a passport photographs and a cash down payment. Then I can start things moving."

We talked through other details, and I made up my mind almost right away.

"I'll have to trust you! I'll give you a thousand pounds and get my picture taken today, while I am here in London," I said.

"Fine," he said. "You make up your mind very quickly. Once you give me some cash, we will get to work." I asked a few more questions, then he told me where he thought I could get a passport photo taken right away and where there was a branch of my bank. So I left quickly.

I found a branch of my bank and withdrew some money from my account. Within about three hours, I was back at his apartment.

"Here's some of the money and my pictures. I will bring the rest of your money next time I see you, if I get my passport," I said.

"There is no worry about that. We have to trust each other. Once we start making your passport, there is no going back. My friend will be taking a big risk to get it."

We shook hands on the deal, and I left.

I arrived home very late. I was so tired and went to bed right away. I had only a few days to get everything ready. The next day I called my work, and I told them I was sick and could not come for two weeks. Then I went to the barbers shop to have my hair curled because I wanted to look different at the airport than my picture in my passport. I bought some smart clothes and went home. I did not tell anybody where I was going; I thought one of them would tell my funny uncle if he came around asking for me. I was thinking about Mr. John a lot as he was the only person I really trusted. I knew he could keep a secret, so I decided to tell him about my journey. I called him on the phone and said, "Hello, Mr. John I want to see you this afternoon, is that possible please? It is very important."

"In that case, I will get away somehow. Where and what time?" he asked.

We arranged to meet. When I told him about everything, going to London and paying the smugglers, he got very alarmed. He told me that it was a crazy thing to do, and that using a false passport would land me in prison. He is half-English and half-Scottish and, like most Europeans, has never had to do anything that was illegal in his life. With me, things had been very different, the fact was if I hadn't done illegal things, if I had waited everywhere for documents, I would still have been back in Afghanistan. Asylum seekers like me had had to break all the rules to avoid being killed and to have any chance of a decent life.

He became very serious and convinced me that I should not go to Canada in this way, especially as I knew absolutely nothing about that country. I thought he was right and told him I would cancel the deal, although it might mean losing the thousand pounds I had already paid. He said if I couldn't get it back, I would have to put it down to experience, rather than risk prison and a criminal record, and he got me to agree to phone the smuggler in London and tell him I wasn't going.

After I had had a night sleep, I decided to phone the man, but I would try to get him to give me my money back. At least I would give it a try, maybe I'd get some of it. When I phoned him, he did not like my decision and said his friend, who worked for the government, had already started getting the documents and that I couldn't back out of the deal. He got very angry when I asked for my money back. He shouted down the phone that I owed him another four thousand pounds whether I went to Canada or not. I got angry too and said I would go to the police about him. He said that that would not be a good thing for me to do, and he would cause real trouble for me if I did. Then he began to reason with me, asking me why I had changed my mind, that everything would be OK, and that he had sent other people to Canada without any trouble at all. I began to change my mind again. It was another phone call from my funny uncle from London saying that he was arranging a marriage for me that made me decide to go somewhere where he could not reach me.

The smuggler called again later to say that my passport was ready, and he could book my plane tickets as soon as I wanted him to. He was very convincing and going away was what I really wanted to do. I agreed that we should go ahead.

I called Mr. John and told him I had decided to go to Canada because the smugglers refused to give me my money back even though I had said I would report him to the police, and Mr. John seemed worried. "Did you threaten him?" he asked worriedly. "You should not have done that. You do not know who you are dealing with, these men are gangsters. You have their names an address and other details, and they know that if you gave the information to the police, they would go to prison for many years. They know you are now a danger to them."

I said that I had agreed to go through with the deal, and so there would be no worries about me reporting them. Mr. John was still unhappy. Basically he thought I should not risk going, but I had definitely made up my mind, and Mr. John would have to accept it. I was thinking what to buy for him as a memento because I liked him very much. I did not have time to look around for something special. I went to Birmingham city center and bought a beautiful watch and some aftershave.

We had arranged to meet for the last time.

"Salam, Mr. John. How are you doing?" I hugged him, and then we shook hands.

"I am fine. How are you?" he asked.

"I have good news and bad news, which one would you like to hear first?"

"Bad one first," he said.

"The bad news is I am going Canada Friday evening, and I will miss you. The good news is I have not told my funny uncle where I am going. He can't oppress me anymore. If my funny uncle searches for me and asks my friends where I am, nobody knows where I going except you and Allah. I trust you a lot. I know you won't tell anyone."

"Wow! Why are you in such a hurry? Can't you wait for another week or two and think about it? Last week you told me you were going to start a business; I was expecting to talk to you about it. I spoke to someone about you. I got some advice for you."

"Mr. John, pray for me. I will be OK. I have to go before my funny uncle does something."

"How you are going?"

"I will fly to Canada. If I am lucky, I will pass the security check. If I don't, I don't know what is going to happen. I don't care about anything except getting away from my funny uncle," I said.

"This is too fast. You should think things out. It is very dangerous, you might go to prison, or get deported."

"Mr. John, I will be OK. I came from Afghanistan all the way to England without papers or money. I have nothing to lose. If I stay here, my uncle is going to get me married, or the immigration will send me back home. I better take this chance, and I trust in Allah."

I told him that I always made decisions very quickly. I could see that he was worried. He thought it was crazy. He said that I did not know who the smugglers really were, I should not have given them so much money, I had no documents, and so on. He did not agree with any of it, but after I had talked to him for a while, eventually, he said,

"OK, you will do this whatever I say. I need to know where the smugglers live, and what time you are going to his house, just in case, if something happens to you."

I gave him the address, name, and telephone number. We made some security code, for example 10-10 meant I am in smuggler house; 20-20 meant smuggler is with me but I cannot talk, and so on. Mr. John bought me a piece of beautiful airplane luggage as a memento. I handed him my present, and then I hugged him twice and said, "You are a wonderful British man. I am really proud of you. I love you very much. I do not want to leave you, but I can't live here anymore." I hugged him one more time and said, "I will never forget your help. I don't know what will happen to me, I am sure I will be fine. I will keep in touch. Thank you very much for everything."

I was crying inside, and he was really sad and said, "When you came to Birmingham, you were only a young man. Now you are more mature. In the last year and half, you have improved a lot. First, you speak good English. Second, you have built a good body and have saved a huge amount of money. You always have been good company. Friday, I will be sitting by my phone. Promise you will call me, I am your back up. If you need anything at any time, please ring me up and let me know. You are part of my family. Your Scottish name is Alister. You've got to give me an Afghan name."

I thought for a moment and said, "Your Afghan name is—Raza, yah!"

We shook hands, and then I went home.

I called Rahim and my other friends. I had bought about four thousand pounds worth of furnishing for my home. I just picked some of clothes. I gave all the stuff away for free and told them that I was going to live with funny uncle in London. We had a party that night.

Next day, I took my bag and went to London with Rahim to the smuggler's home. We sat down for a short while until his partner brought my passport. He handed it to me and said, "I have booked a ticket to Canada for tomorrow at 6:00 p.m. We must be there at four. I looked at my passport; they had just inserted my picture in someone else's passport, nothing else. It did not look convincing to me, but they said it was as good as any genuine passport. It was in the name of "Benjamin Peter Steel," born in London, he was three inches shorter than me, his eyes were blue, hair blond, and aged five years older than me. His signature was very difficult for me to copy. Nothing matched with me, and I said, "How I am going to pass security check with this English passport? This is a very English person."

"You will be fine. You are very smart. Just be comfortable with it," he said, and then he handed me some pieces of paper to practice the passport signature. I paid him some more money and told him I would pay him off, next day in front of the airport. He said, "OK."

We went out. I called Mr. John and told him how things were going, then Rahim and I went to find a hotel to stay that night.

CHAPTER 57

MY GREEK MOM IN 2004

Next day we went to the town center to see London for the last time. After the lunch, Rahim left for Birmingham. I went to the smuggler's place; he told me something about my journey. About 4:20 p.m., we arrived at the international airport in London.

"Look, we don't have too much time to stay here; also it is not good for us. If you get in trouble, don't give any information about us. We have our lawyer who can get you out very fast if you get arrested. Don't worry, be like a gentleman, and remember your name, your DOB, and your signature. OK, give me the money and go out very fast from my car."

I handed him the money and got out very quickly. Then they drove their vehicle away. I walked into the airport. Oh my God! It was massive. I did not know where to go. I had never been there before, and I had only half an hour to pass all the security checks. There were lots of security guards hanging around. I stopped one of them and said, "Excuse me, I am going to Canada. Can you tell me how I get to the plane?"

"Would you mind telling me where about in Canada you are going because it is a very big country?" he said.

"Hold on please, a good question. I never thought about that. Let me check the ticket. My parents bought it for me."

"Go ahead."

I checked. "Toronto," I said.

"Oh, Toronto. It is a very nice city. You need to get a boarding card, and then the officer will tell you what to do next."

"OK, where can I get that?" I asked.

He showed the way by his hand and said, "Have a good journey!"

"Thank you, and you have a good weekend," I said.

I stood in line, and I was after six people. I looked at the other people; the immigration officer asked them so many questions. I started to worry and said to Allah, "Oh, Allah, You helped me to get here all the way from my country to find my funny uncle. I thought he might be helpful for me. He did not help me at all with anything. You are my witness. Please help me here, I beg you."

I was after two people; most the officers looked like English people.

"If they ask me a question, they will find out I am not English and do not look like an English person. Oh, Allah, tell me what should I do?" I said to myself.

I had two cell phones; both were ringing. Both of them were the smugglers. I did not answer them. I put them off. There were about six people serving for Toronto. I looked at them very carefully. There was a lady who looked like she was from India or Pakistan. I decided to go to her desk; otherwise I would be in trouble. because I thought she would be easy to talk to. One of the English officers called out, "Next please."

It was my turn to go over. I let someone else go. I saw the Asian lady was free. I went to her desk before she called me. I look at her for a little while. She was in her late twenties, very dark skin, green eyes, a very long black hair, wearing earrings, and little red mark on the middle of her forehead, and something in her right nostril. While she was sitting behind her desk, she was typing something in a computer, and I said, "Hi, sweetie, you have very beautiful hair."

"Thank you. How can I help you, sir?" she asked with an Indian accent.

I remember my supervisor at the tailoring company where I used to work. Her accent was the same as the immigration officer while I was talking to her. I thought she must be from India.

"Can I have a boarding card please?" I asked in Hindi (Urdu), and I handed her my passport with my ticket inside before she asked me for it.

"How many bags do you have?" she asked in Hindi.

"Two," I said, watching what she was doing. I had left my ticket inside the passport. She looked at my passport very quickly and took my passport number and then handed it to me and asked me some more questions in Hindi. Eventually she gave me the boarding card and told me where to go next and gave all the directions.

"Have a good journey, handsome young man," she said and smiled.

"Thank you very much, and you have a nice day," I said, trying to sound confident.

"See you later," I said and then walked away. I walked through the barrier. I went through a metal detector doorway. Next, I was stopped by the security guard who did a body search. Then I went to find the terminal for Toronto and found it easily. There were lots of people waiting there. I stood for a short while, and then an old lady came to me and asked me to read her ticket. She was taking the same plane as I was. She was from Greece and was speaking very broken English and carrying a small but very heavy bag. I remembered some word from Greece and spoke with her and carried her bag. She was pleased, and we kept talking in Greek. I did not understand her very well. I just said "Yeah! Yeah!" to make her happy. A short while later, someone called our airplane number on the speaker very loudly. A security guard let us go in. People started to rush. "Oh, Allah, shall I help her or not?" I asked Allah.

Half of the people hurried down the passage ramp. I looked at the old lady looking at me, and she said, "Help me please, my son."

I was so worried about my passport because there were still some security checks, and most of the people had gone. I left her and ran about three or four meters. She called me, "My son, please help me, I can't carry this. I will miss the plane." She said it half in Greek and English. I stopped for a second and thought I could not pass the security checks anyway with this funny passport. I decided to help her; at least she could get on the plane. I took my bags and her bag in my right hand, with my left hand pulling her along. Everybody had gone on. The security guard shouted at us to hurry. He asked his partner on his radio to bring a wheelchair. They brought it very quickly. She sat in it. One of them pushed the chair and told me to run. We were late when we reached to the security check. They did not check our passports but let me run because we were very late. There were two girls standing by a bus's door, which was to ferry us to the plane. They checked only our tickets and told us to get on. "Good man, take care of your mom," the security guard said and then left. I talked to her for a short while, and I called her mom because I did know what her name was. People thought she was my mom.

We got on the bus very quickly, and then the driver drove away. He dropped us by the plane. We were in the middle of the crowd. I looked up at the plane; it was very nice. I was so excited and worried. I looked carefully and saw security guards standing by the doorway, checking something. My happiness turned to sadness. I began to worry more, thinking how I would pass the next security check.

I asked Allah for help and helped the old lady all the way up the stairs. The line was moving very slowly. I was praying and asking Allah for help repeatedly. When we got close to them, I heard they were asking people their seat numbers. I took a deep breath and thanked Allah. It was not a security check.

We got on the plane. My seat was three seats away from the old lady. First, I helped her to sit down, and then I went to my seat. I took my cell phone out from my pocket and turned it on to call my Mr. John. I told him I was on the plane but forgot to tell him where the plane was heading for.

Someone called out, telling passengers to fasten their seat belts and turn all electronic devices off. The plane was going to fly shortly. The staff checked that everybody had their safety belt on. A few minutes later, we started to move around the airfield. About half an hour later, they told us we could take our safety belts off and get comfortable.

I was so excited and thanked Allah a lot. I went to see how the old lady was doing. She was so tired, and her eyes were closed. I thought she might be asleep and then went back to my seat. I had a little TV in of front my seat. I put the headphone on and enjoyed watching English movies. I could not think what to do next because I had no idea what would happen next. I hoped to Allah that everything would be all right, and then I fell asleep. I was woken by a flight attendant who told me to put my safety belt on because we were landing.

She said, "We are arriving in Canada."

"Oh really, how does it look like?" I asked in what I thought was my best English.

"Is this your first time?" she asked.

"Yes," I replied.

"Welcome to Canada," she said, then she walked away.

We landed, and I began to pick out my stuff. I was so excited and hoped that Canada would be the country that I could call home. I've been here for a number of years now, but that's another story.

THE END

CPSIA information can be obtained at www.ICGtesting.com
Printed in the USA
LVOW061110031111

253252LV00001B/1/P

9 781462 896646